MUSIC-STUDY IN GERMANY

Da Capo Press Music Reprint Series

MUSIC EDITOR
BEA FRIEDLAND
Ph.D., City University of New York

MUSIC-STUDY IN GERMANY

Amy Fay

WITH A NEW INTRODUCTION BY
EDWARD O.D. DOWNES

AND A NEW INDEX BY
ROY CHERNUS

DA CAPO PRESS • NEW YORK • 1979

Library of Congress Cataloging in Publication Data

Fay, Amy, 1844-1928.
  Music-study in Germany.

  (Da Capo Press music reprint series)
  Reprint of the 1896 ed. published by Macmillan Co.,
New York.
    1. Fay, Amy, 1844-1928. 2. Pianists—Germany—
Correspondence. 3. Music—Germany. 4. Germany—
Social life and customs. I. Title.
  ML417.F286A3 1979   786.1'092'4 [B]   79-20822
  ISBN 0-306-79541-8

This Da Capo Press edition of *Music-Study in Germany*
is an unabridged republication of the edition published
in New York and London in 1896 by The Macmillan Company.
It contains an introduction by Edward O.D. Downes and an
index by Roy Chernus, both prepared specially for this edition.

Published by Da Capo Press, Inc.
A Subsidiary of Plenum Publishing Corporation
227 West 17th Street, New York, N.Y. 10011

INTRODUCTION

WHO WAS Amy Fay? What a beguiling creature she must have been! The freshness and enthusiasm of the letters she wrote home a hundred years ago from Germany enchant us today much as they did her family, her friend Henry Wadsworth Longfellow, Sir George Grove, Franz Liszt, and Vincent d'Indy, who one after another sponsored the publication of her letters in the United States (1880), Germany (1882), England (1885), and France. The letters are more than beguiling. They are a mine of information valuable to music students, teachers, musicologists, and culture historians of a crucial period just preceding and following the Franco-Prussian War.

She was a paradox. Or so she seemed. What took this young lady, born in 1844 on a Mississippi River plantation, to teeming Berlin a quarter of a century later? We meet her first in Berlin in October 1869. Amy is a little breathless, almost school-girl gushy. For she has not just glimpsed the promised land of music, she is *in* it. She is having the time of her life. And luckily for us she is writing home about it—writing about everything from the musical scene to the political scene, even to the street scene. Her keen and sensitive mind, gentle wit, and her grace with words ensnare us, so that before we quite know what has happened, we are watching real people: from Amy's landlady Frau Geheimrätin W., to Bismarck in gala uniform, and an incredible cast of musicians. Wagner, Liszt, Clara Schumann, Anton Rubinstein, Hans von Bülow, Tausig, and Joachim crowd her pages. Yet her profiles remain sharp and her portrait of Liszt in Weimar presiding over his worshipful master classes is a model of its kind.

What took little Amy from the village of Bayou Goula (population 1000 in 1960) in Louisiana sugar cane country to the rarefied circle of Liszt in Weimar? Certainly her mother, Amy's first teacher of piano and English composition, and herself a gifted amateur pianist, supplied the motivating force. Amy's father, too, contributed to her development. He was Dr. Charles Fay, an Episcopal clergyman, a scholar and linguist who ranked second in his Harvard class of 1829—a famous class that included Oliver Wendell Holmes. Dr. Fay reputedly wanted all his seven children to read, write, and converse in Greek, Latin, French, and German. Amy's maternal grandfather played a role as well. John Henry Hopkins (1792-1868) was an eminent Episcopal Bishop of Vermont, influential even in the councils of the Archbishop of Canterbury and a man of strong convictions. His proslavery stand and his controversial publications, "The Bible View of Slavery," can hardly have been popular in New England on the eve of our Civil War.

Love of music, strong drive, and initiative seem to have been persistent family traits. Amy's only brother, Charles Norman Fay, became a highly successful busi-

ness man in Chicago. There he realized a long-cherished
dream as the principal organizer of the Chicago Symphony, with Theodore Thomas as its musical founder
and first conductor. One sister, Rose Fay, was for many
years a close friend and devoted helper of Theodore
Thomas and his wife. In 1889, Mrs. Thomas died after a
long and painful illness; thirteen months later Rose became his second wife.

Amy was only four years old when her father, presum-
ably through the influence of Bishop Hopkins, trans-
ferred from Bayou Goula to a Vermont parish: Saint
Albans on the shore of Lake Champlain. After her
mother's death Amy, at the age of nineteen, went to live
with her married sister Melusine Fay Pierce in Cambridge, Massachusetts. She entered the New England
Conservatory in Boston and continued her piano studies
under the eminent pianist and composer Otto Dresel,
one of the many liberal Germans who had emigrated to
the United States during the revolution of 1848 and 1849.
Amy showed her dedication by also undertaking separate
study of Bach with John Knowles Paine. Paine, who had
just been appointed an instructor at Harvard College,
became eventually (in 1875) Harvard's first titular professor of music and an illustrious member of its faculty.
Like many of the most serious American composers, performers, and scholars of the nineteenth century, Paine
had made his pilgrimage to Germany. He once told Amy:
"There is a young man in Berlin who plays the piano like
40,000 devils. His name is Carl Tausig." At the ripe old
age of twenty-four, Tausig, said to be Liszt's favorite

pupil, opened his own conservatory or *Akademie für das höhere Klavierspiel* and Amy decided she must study there.

In October 1869 she set out from New York on her own pilgrimage that was to last over six years. It was an exciting time. A month before she sailed, Wagner's *Rheingold* had been given its first performance in Munich and the world premiere of the *Walküre* was being prepared for spring. Wagner himself had just finished the composition of *Siegfried* and was already at work on his *Götterdämmerung*. In Vienna at the other pole of German music, Brahms was midway in a great outpouring of German lieder. At the Vienna Conservatory an obscure professor of counterpoint, Anton Bruckner, was working on the second of his nine colossal controversial symphonies.

Liszt was not due back at Weimar until spring. But in the meantime Berlin was a beehive of activity. Within a few days of Amy's arrival she had heard her first concert with Joachim and Clara Schumann, followed soon by Anton Rubinstein and Tausig, choral and orchestral programs, visits to the opera and the beginning of her rigorous studies at Tausig's conservatory, beside which, she declared, her Boston studies had been "mere play." Her music studies were complicated by her early struggles with the German language. And there were necessary social and professional contacts to be made.

The Fay family was evidently well-connected. Amy had arrived in the Prussian capital with letters of introduction, the most important of which was to the United

States Minister to the Prussian Court, George Bancroft, and his wife. Bancroft, educated at German universities, became the most distinguished American historian of his day and a skilled diplomat much admired by the Germans. This was still an era of formal visits and Mrs. Bancroft immediately returned Amy's call. The young pianist, invited to the official Thanksgiving dinner at the Minister's residence, soon became a frequent and welcome guest of the Bancrofts for opera parties, concerts, theaters, and official public ceremonies; doubtless the Bancrofts helped her with further introductions.

Politically it was a fascinating time, for the many large and small independent German states (monarchies, grand duchies, duchies, free cities, etc.) were being carefully prepared by Bismarck through the *Zollverein* and the North German Confederation for the foundation of a German Empire under Prussian hegemony. Amy witnessed the outbreak of the Franco-Prussian War and recorded in her letters the turbulent events rights up to the triumphal homecoming of the German troops, led by an array of dignitaries.

Despite Miss Fay's impressive connections, wangling the proper introductions to Liszt was no easy matter. But with the combination of persistence, luck, and charm, Amy won. Her first glimpse of Liszt was in the theater at Weimar:

> Liszt is the most interesting and striking look-
> ing man imaginable. Tall and slight, with
> deep-set eyes, shaggy eyebrows, and long iron-

gray hair, which he wears parted in the middle. His mouth turns up at the corners, which gives him a most crafty and Mephisthophelean expression when he smiles, and his whole appearance and manner have a Jesuitical elegance and ease. His hands are very narrow, with long and slender fingers that look as if they had twice as many joints as other people's. They are so flexible and supple that it makes you nervous to look at them . . .

But the most extraordinary thing about Liszt is his wonderful variety of expression and play of feature. One moment his face will look dreamy, shadowy, tragic. The next he will be insinuating, amiable, ironical, sardonic; but always the same captivating grace of manner (p. 205).

Amy's first meeting with Liszt was successful and he allowed her to join his master class. Liszt had a weakness for pretty girls and he took a fancy to her. He was kind, gallant, occasionally flattering—but always extremely demanding. For five months Amy lived with an intensity that was alternately nerve-wracking and ecstatic. Yet she kept her clear-eyed gift of observation and recorded Liszt's rare moments of cruelty when she felt he was no better than a dozen other famous teachers.

If they take a fancy to you, they will do a great deal for you; if not, *nothing!* Liszt is no exception to this rule. I have seen him snub and entirely neglect young artists of the most remarkable talent and virtuosity, merely because they did not please him personally (p. 267f).

But let Amy tell her story. You will not read far before you begin to wish you had known this remarkable young woman.

Sir George Grove in his preface to the first English edition of her letters wrote, somewhat patronizingly:

> We may laugh at the writer's enthusiasm, at the readiness with which she changes her methods [She studied successively with Tausig, Kullak, Liszt, and Ludwig Deppe.] . . . But no one can laugh at her indomitable determination, and the artistic earnestness with which she makes the most of her opportunities, or the brightness and ease with which all is described (in choice American) and each successive person placed before us in his habit as he lived.

You will read of her successful debut and the enthusiastic review in Frankfort-an-der-Oder before she left Germany. During her final weeks there she was joined by her sister "Zina" (Melusine Fay Pierce), to whom most of Amy's letters were written. They returned together to the United States where Amy performed under Theodore Thomas. At this time, the long and productive association between Thomas and the Fay family began. Years later they all (Amy, Zina, Rose Fay, and eventually Thomas too) joined Charles Norman Fay in Chicago and each in his or her own way contributed richly to the musical life of their adopted city. If Amy did not aim for the barnstorming career of a traveling virtuoso, she left us a unique and invaluable documentation of German musical life, study, and pedagogy in one of their most fruitful periods. Although these letters ran through more than twenty printings in this country alone, this is the first edition to appear with an index, which will make it especially welcome to the scholar and the casual reader alike.

EDWARD DOWNES
New York City
May 1979

MUSIC–STUDY IN GERMANY

Yours very sincerely
Amy Fay

1890.

MUSIC-STUDY IN GERMANY

FROM

THE HOME CORRESPONDENCE
OF AMY FAY

EDITED BY

MRS. FAY PEIRCE
AUTHOR OF "CO-OPERATIVE HOUSEKEEPING"

"The light that never was on sea or land."
WORDSWORTH

"Pour admirer assez il faut admirer trop, et un peu d'illusion
est necessaire au bonheur."
CHERBULIEZ

EIGHTEENTH EDITION

New York
THE MACMILLAN COMPANY
LONDON: MACMILLAN & CO., LTD.
1908

Norwood Press:
Berwick & Smith, Norwood, Mass., U.S.A.

PREFACE.

In preparing for the public letters which were written only for home, I have hoped that some readers would find in them the charm of style which the writer's friends fancy them to possess; that others would think the description of her masters amid their pupils, and especially Liszt, worth preserving; while piano students would be grateful for the information that an analysis of the piano technique has been made, such as very greatly to diminish the difficulties of the instrument.

How much of Herr Deppe's piano "method" is original with himself, pianists must decide. That he has at least made an invaluable *résumé* of all or most of their secrets, my sister believes no student of the instrument who fairly and conscientiously examines into the matter will deny.

                                        M. FAY PEIRCE.

Chicago, Dec., 1880.

PREFACE

TO THE ENGLISH EDITION.

Miss Fay's little book has been so popular in her own country as to have gone through half a dozen editions, and even in German, into which it was translated soon after its first appearance, it has had much success. It is strange that it has not been already published in England, where music excites so much attention, and where works on musical subjects are beginning to form a distinct branch of literature. This is the more remarkable because it is thoroughly readable and amusing, which books on music too rarely are. The freshness and truth of the letters is not to be denied. We may laugh at the writer's enthusiasm, at the readiness with which she changes her methods and gives up all that she has already learnt at the call of each fresh teacher, at the certainty with which every new artist is announced as quite the best she ever heard, and at the glowing and confident predictions — not, alas, apparently always realised. But no one can laugh at her indomitable determination, and the artistic earnestness with which she makes the most of each of her opportunities, or the brightness and ease with which all is described (in choice American), and each successive person placed before us in his habit as he lives. Such a gift is indeed a rare and precious one. Will Miss Fay never oblige us with an equally charming and faithful

(3)

account of music and life in the States? Hitherto musical
America has been almost an unknown land to us, described
by the few who have attempted it in the most opposite
terms.   Their singers we already know well, and in this
respect America is perhaps destined to be the Italy of the
future, if only the artists will consent to learn slowly enough.
But on the subject of American players and American
orchestras, and the taste of the American amateurs, a great
deal of curiosity is felt, and we commend the subject to the
serious attention of one so thoroughly able to do it justice.

                                          GEORGE GROVE.

December, 1885.

PREFACE

TO THE GERMAN EDITION.

———

Die vorliegenden Briefe einer Amerikanerin in die Heimath, die im Original bereits in zweiter Auflage erschienen sind, werden, so hoffen wir, auch dem deutschen Leser nicht minderes Vergnügen, nicht geringere Anregung als dem amerikanischen gewähren, da sie in unmittelbarer Frische niedergeschrieben, ein lebendiges Bild von den Beziehungen der Verfasserin zu den hervorragendsten musikalischen Persönlichkeiten, wie Liszt, v. Bülow, Tausig, Joachim u. s. w. bieten.

Wir geben das Buch in wortgetreuer Uebersetzung und haben es nur um diejenigen Briefe gekürzt, die in Deutschland Allzubekanntes behandeln. Hingegen glaubten wir die Stellen dem Leser nicht vorenthalten zu dürfen, welche zwar nicht musikalischen Inhalts sind, uns aber zeigen, wie manche unserer deutschen Zu- oder Mißstände von Amerikanern beurtheilt werden.

Robert Oppenheim, Publisher.

Berlin, 1882.

CONTENTS.

IN TAUSIG'S CONSERVATORY.

WITH KULLAK.

CHAPTER VII.

CHAPTER VIII.

CHAPTER IX.

CHAPTER X.

CHAPTER XI.

CHAPTER XII.

CHAPTER XIII.

CHAPTER XIV.

CHAPTER XV.

CHAPTER XVI.

WITH LISZT.

CHAPTER XVII.

CHAPTER XVIII.

CHAPTER XIX.

CHAPTER XX.

CHAPTER XXI.

CHAPTER XXII.

CHAPTER XXIII.

WITH DEPPE.

IN TAUSIG'S CONSERVATORY.

(11)

MUSIC-STUDY IN GERMANY.

CHAPTER I.

A German Interior in Berlin. A German Party. Joachim.
Tausig's Conservatory.

BERLIN, *November* 3, 1869.

Behold me at last at No. 26 Bernburger Strasse!
where I arrived exactly two weeks from the day I left
New York. Frau W. and her daughter, Fräulein A.
W., greeted me with the greatest warmth and cordiality,
and made me feel at home immediately. The German
idea of a "large" room I find is rather peculiar, for
this one is not more than ten or eleven feet square,
and has one corner of it snipped off, so that the room
is an irregular shape. When I first entered it I thought
I could not stay in it, it seemed so small, but when
I came to examine it, so ingeniously is every inch of
space made the most of, that I have come to the conclusion that it will be very comfortable. It is not, however,
the apartment where "the last new novel will lie upon
the table, and where my daintily slippered feet will rest
upon the velvet cushion." No! rather is it the stern
abode of the Muses.

To begin then : the room is spotlessly clean and neat.
The walls are papered with a nice new paper, grey ground
with blue figures—a cheap paper, but soft and pretty. In
one corner stands my little bureau with three deep draw-
ers. Over it is a large looking-glass nicely framed. In the
other corner on the same side is a big sofa which at
night becomes a little bed. Next to the foot of the
sofa, against the wall, stands a tiny square table, with a
marble top, and a shelf underneath, on which are a
basin and a minute soap-dish and tumbler. In the
opposite corner towers a huge grey porcelain stove, which
comes up to within a few feet of the ceiling. Next is
one stiff cane-bottomed chair on four stiff legs. Then
comes the lop-sided corner of the room, where an upright
piano is to stand. Next there is a little space where
hangs the three-shelved book-case, which will contain
my *vast* library. Then comes a broad French window
with a deep window-seat. By this window is my sea-
chair—by far the most luxurious one in the house !
Then comes my bureau again, and so on *Da Capo*. In
the middle is a pretty round table, with an inlaid centre-
piece, and on it is a waiter with a large glass bottle full
of water, and a glass ; and this, with one more stiff
chair, completes the furniture of the room. My curtains are white, with a blue border, and two transparen-
cies hang in the window. My towel-rack is fastened to
the wall, and has an embroidered centre-piece. On my
bureau is a beautiful inkstand, the cover being a carved
eagle with spread wings, perched over a nest with three
eggs in it. It is quite large, and looks extremely pretty
under the looking-glass.

After I had taken off my things, Frau W. and her daughter ushered me into their parlour, which had the same look of neatness and simplicity and of extreme economy. There are no carpets on any of the floors, but they have large, though cheap, rugs. You never saw such a primitive little household as it is—that of this German lawyer's widow. We think our house at home small, but I feel as if we lived in palatial magnificence after seeing how they live here, *i. e.*, about as our dress-makers used to do in the country, and yet it is sufficiently nice and comfortable. There are two very pretty little rooms opposite mine, which are yet to be let together. If some friend of mine could only take them I should be perfectly happy.

At night my bed is made upon the sofa. (They all sleep on these sofas.) The cover consists of a feather bed and a blanket. That sounds rather formidable, but the feather bed is a light, warm covering, and looks about two inches thick. It is much more comfortable than our bed coverings in America. I tuck myself into my nest at night, and in the morning after breakfast, when I return to my room—*agramento-presto-change !* —my bed is converted into a sofa, my basin is laid on the shelf, the soap-dish and my combs and brushes are scuttled away into the drawer; the windows are open, a fresh fire crackles in my stove, and my charming little bed-room is straightway converted into an equally charming sitting-room. How does the picture please you ?

This morning Frau and Fräulein W. went with me to engage a piano, and they took me also to the conservatory. Tausig is off for six weeks, giving concerts. As I went up the stairs I heard most beautiful playing. Ehlert, Tausig's partner, who has charge of the conservatory, and teaches his pupils in his absence, examined me. After that long voyage I did not dare attempt anything difficult, so I just played one of Bach's Gavottes. He said some encouraging words, and for the present has taken me into his class. I am to begin to-morrow from one o'clock to two. It is now ten P. M., and tell C. we have had five meals to-day, so Madame P.'s statement is about correct. The cooking is on the same scale as the rest of the establishment—a little at a time, but so far very good. We know nothing at all about rolls in America. Anything so delicious as the rolls here I never ate in the way of bread. In the morning we had a cup of coffee and rolls. At eleven we lunched on a cup of bouillon and a roll. At two o'clock we had dinner, which consisted of soup and then chickens, potatoes, carrots and bread, with beer. At five we had tea, cake and toast, and at nine we had a supper of cold meat, boiled eggs, tea and bread and butter. Fräulein W. speaks English quite nicely, and is my medium of communication with her mother. I begin German lessons with her to-morrow. They both send you their compliments, and so you must return yours. They seem as kind as possible, and I think I am very fortunate in my boarding place.

Be sure to direct your letters "Care Frau Geheimräthin W." (Mrs. Councillor W.), as the German ladies are very particular about their *titles!*

BERLIN, *November* 21, 1869.

Since I wrote to you not much of interest has occurred. I am delighted with Berlin, and am enjoying
myself very much, though I am working hard. I am so
thankful that all my sewing was done before I came, for
I have not a minute to spare for it, and here it seems to
me all the dresses fit so dreadfully. It would make me
miserable to wear such looking clothes, and as I
can't speak the language, the difficulties in the way of
giving directions on the technicalities of dressmaking
would be terrific. Tell C. he is very wise to con-
tinue his German conversation lessons with Madame P.
Even the few that I took prove of immense assist-
ance to me, as I can understand almost everything
that is said to me, though I cannot answer back. He
ought to make one of his lessons about shopping and
droschkie driving, for it is very essential to know how to
ask for things, and to be able to give directions in driving. I had a very funny experience with a droschkie
the other day, but it would take too long to write it.
Frau W. cannot understand English, and she gets dreadfully impatient when Fräulein A. and I speak it, and
always says " *Deutsch* " in a sepulchral tone, so that I
have to begin and say it all over again in German with
A.'s help.

When I got fairly settled I presented myself and my
letters at the Bancrofts, the B's. and the A's., and was very
kindly and cordially received by them all. Mrs. Bancroft
and Mrs. B. have since called in return, and I have already
been to a charming reception at the house of the latter, and

2

to the grand American Thanksgiving dinner at the Hotel
de Rome, at which Mr. Bancroft presided, and made very
happy speeches both in English and German. I enjoyed both occasions extremely, and made some pleasant
acquaintances. I have also been to one German tea-
party with Frau W. and A., and there I had " the jolliest
kind of a time." There were only twelve invited, but you
would have supposed from the clatter that there were at
least a hundred. At the American dinner there was nothing like the noise of conversation that this little handful
kept up. Before supper it was rather stupid, for the men all
retired to a room by themselves, where they sat with closed
doors and played whist and smoked. It is not considered
proper for ladies to play cards except at home, and I, of
course, did not say much, for the excellent reason that I
couldn't ! At ten o'clock supper was announced, and
the gentlemen came and took us in. Herr J. was
my partner. He is a delightful man, though an elderly
one, and knows no end of things, as he has spent his
whole life in study and in travelling. He looks to me
like a man of very sensitive organization, and of very
delicate feelings. He is a tremendous republican, and a
great radical in every respect, and has an unbounded
admiration for America.

As soon as every one was seated at the table with due
form and ceremony, all began to talk as hard as they
could, and you have no idea what a noise they made, and
how it increased toward the end with the potent libations
they had. The bill of fare was rather curious. We
began with slices of hot tongue, with a sauce of chest-
nuts, and it was extremely nice, too. Then we had ven-

ison and boiled potatoes! Then we had a dessert consisting of fruit, and some delicious cake. There were several kinds of wine, and everybody drank the greatest quantity. The host and hostess kept jumping up and going round to everybody, saying: "But you drink nothing," and then they would insist upon filling up your glass. I don't dare to think how many times they filled mine, but it seemed to be etiquette to drink, and so I did as the rest. The repast ended with coffee, and then the gentlemen lit their cigars, and were in such an extremely cheerful frame of mind that they all began to sing, and I even saw two old fellows kiss each other! The venison was delicious, and nicer than any I ever ate. Herr J. was the only man in the room who could speak any English, and since then he takes a good deal of interest in me, and lends me books. Every Sunday Frau W. takes me to her sister's house to tea. I like to go because I hear so much German spoken there, and they all take a profound interest in my affairs. They know to a minute when I get a letter, and when I write one, and every incident of my daily life. It amuses them very much to see a real live wild Indian from America. I am soon going to another German party, and I look forward to it with much pleasure; not that the parties here give me the same feeling as at home, but they are amusing because they are so entirely different.

There is so much to be seen and heard in Berlin that if one has but the money there is no end to one's resources. There are the opera and the Schauspielhaus every night, and beautiful concerts every evening, too. They

say that the opera here is magnificent, and the scenery
superb, and they have a wonderful ballet-troupe. So far,
however, I have only been to one concert, and that was
a sacred concert. But Joachim played—and Oh–h, what
a tone he draws out of the violin! I could think of
nothing but Mrs. Moulton's voice, as he *sighed* out those
exquisitely pathetic notes. He played something by
Schumann which ended with a single note, and as he
drew his bow across he produced so many shades that it
was perfectly marvellous. I am going to hear him
again on Sunday night, when he plays at Clara Schumann's concert. It will be a great concert, for she
plays much. She will be assisted by Joachim, Müller,
De Ahna, and by Joachim's wife, who has a beautiful
voice and sings charmingly in the serious German
style. Joachim himself is not only the greatest vio·
linist in the world, but one of the greatest that ever
lived. De Ahna is one of the first violinists in Ger·
many, and Müller is one of the first 'cellists. In fact,
this quartette cannot be matched in Europe—so you
see what I am expecting!

Tausig has not yet returned from his concert
tour, and will not arrive before the 21st of December. I find Ehlert a splendid teacher, but very
severe, and I am mortally afraid of him. Not that he
is cross, but he exacts so much, and such a hopeless
feeling of despair takes possession of me. His first
lesson on touch taught me more than all my other
lessons put together—though, to be sure, that is not
saying much, as they were "few and far between."
At present I am weltering in a sea of troubles. The

girls in my class are three in number, and they all play so extraordinarily well that sometimes I think I can never catch up with them. I am the worst of all the scholars in Tausig's classes that I have heard, except one, and that is a young man. I know that Ehlert thinks I have talent, but, after all, talent must go to the wall before such *practice* as these people have had, for most of them have studied a long time, and have been at the piano four and five hours a day.

It is very interesting in the conservatory, for there are pupils there from all countries except France. Some of them seem to me splendid musicians. On Sunday morning (I am sorry to say) once in a month or six weeks, they have what they call a "Musical Reading." It is held in a piano-forte ware-room, and there all the scholars in the higher classes play, so I had to go. Many of the girls played magnificently, and I was amazed at the technique that they had, and at the artistic manner in which even very young girls rendered the most difficult music, and all without notes. It gave me a severe nervous headache just to hear them. But it was delightful to see them go at it. None of them had the least fear, and they laughed and chattered between the pieces, and when their turn came they marched up to the piano, sat down as bold as lions, and banged away so splendidly!

You have no idea how hard they make Cramer's Studies here. Ehlert makes me play them tremendously *forte*, and as fast as I can go. My hand gets so tired that it is ready to break, and then I say that I cannot go on. "But you *must* go on," he will say.

It is the same with the scales. It seems to me that I
play them so loud that I make the welkin ring, and
he will say, "But you play always *piano*." And with
all this rapidity he does not allow a note to be missed,
and if you happen to strike a wrong one he looks so
shocked that you feel ready to sink into the floor.
Strange to say, I enjoy the lessons in *Zusammenspiel*
(duet-playing) very much, although it is all reading
at sight. Four of us sit down at two pianos and read
duets at sight. Lesmann is a pleasant man, and he
always talks so fast that he amuses me very much.
He always counts and beats time most vigorously, and
bawls in your ear, "*Eins—zwei! Eins—zwei!*" or sometimes, "*Eins!*" only, on the first beat of every bar.
When, occasionally, we all get out, he looks at us
through his glasses, and then such a volley of words as
he hurls at us is wonderful to hear. I never can help
laughing, though I take good care not to let him see
me.

But Weitzmann, the Harmony professor, is the funniest of all. He is the dearest old man in the world, and
it is impossible for him to be cross; but he takes so
much pains and trouble to make his class understand,
and he has the most peculiar way of talking imaginable, and accents everything he says tremendously. I
go to him because Ehlert says I must, but as I know
nothing of the theory of music (and if I did, the names
are so entirely different in German that I never should
know what they are in English) it is extremely difficult for me to understand him at all. He knew I was
an American, and let me pass for one or two lessons

without asking me any questions, but finally his German love of thoroughness has got the better of him, and he is now beginning to take me in hand. At the last lesson he wrote some chords on the blackboard, and after holding forth for some time he wound up with his usual " *Verstehen Sie wohl—Ja?* (Do you understand—Yes?)" to the class, who all shouted "*Ja*," except me. I kept a discreet silence, thinking he would not notice, but he suddenly turned on me and said, " *Verstehen* Sie *wohl—Ja?*" I was as puzzled what to say as the Pharisees were when they were asked if the baptism of John were of heaven or of men. I knew that if I said "*Ja*," he might call on me for a proof, and that if I said "*Nein*," he would undertake to enlighten me, and that I should not understand him.

After an instant's consideration I concluded the latter course was the safer, and so I said, boldly, "*Nein.*" "*Kommen Sie hierher!* (Come here!)" said he, and to my horror I had to step up to the blackboard in front of this large class. He harangued me for some minutes, and then writing some notes on the bass clef, he put the chalk into my hands and told me to write. Not one word had I understood, and after staring blankly at the board I said, "*Ich verstehe nicht* (I don't understand.)" "*Nein?*" said he, and carefully went over all his explanation again. This time I managed to extract that he wished me to write the succession of chords that those bass notes indicated, and to tie what notes I could. A second time he put the chalk into my hands, and told me to write the

chords. "Heaven only knows what they are!" thinks
I to myself. In my desperation, however, I guessed
at the first one, and uttered the names of the notes in
trembling accents, expecting to have a cannon fired
off at my head. Thanks to my lucky star, it happened
to be right. I wrote it on the blackboard, and then
as my wits sharpened I found the other chords from
that one, and wrote them all down right. I drew a
long breath of relief as he released me from his
clutches, and sat down hardly believing I had done
it. I have not now the least idea what it was he made
me do, but I suppose it will come to me in the course
of the year! As he does not understand a word of
English, I cannot say anything to him unless I can say
it in German, and as he is determined to make me learn
Harmony, it would be of no use to explain that I did not
know what he was talking about, for he would begin
all over again, and go on *ad infinitum*. I have got a
book on the Theory of Music, which I am reading
with Fräulein W. She has studied with Weitzmann,
also, and when I have caught up with the class I shall
go on very easily. I quite adore Weitzmann. He has
the kindest old face imaginable, and he hammers
away so indefatigably at his pupils! The professors I
have described are all thorough and well-known musicians of Berlin, and I wonder that people could tell
us before I came away, and really seem to believe it,
"that I could learn as well in an American conservatory as in a German one." In comparison with the
drill I am now receiving, my Boston teaching was
mere play.

CHAPTER II.

Clara Schumann and Joachim. The American Minister's.
The Museum. The Conservatory. The Opera.
Tausig. Christmas.

BERLIN, *December* 12, 1869.

I heard Clara Schumann on Sunday, and on Tuesday
evening, also. She is a most wonderful artist. In the
first concert she played a quartette by Schumann, and
you can imagine how lovely it was under the treatment of Clara Schumann for the piano, Joachim for
the first violin, De Ahna for the second, and Müller
for the 'cello. It was perfect, and I was in raptures.
Madame Schumann's selection for the two concerts
was a very wide one, and gave a full exhibition of her
powers in every kind of music. The Impromptu by
Schumann, Op. 90, was exquisite. It was full of passion
and very difficult. The second of the Songs without
Words, by Mendelssohn, was the most fairy-like performance. It is one of those things that must be
tossed off with the greatest grace and smoothness, and
it requires the most beautiful and delicate technique.
She played it to perfection. The terrific Scherzo by
Chopin she did splendidly, but she kept the great
octave passages in the bass a little too subordinate, I
thought, and did not give it quite boldly enough for
my taste, though it was extremely artistic. Clara
Schumann's playing is very objective. She seems to

throw herself into the music, instead of letting the
music take possession of her.   She gives you the most
exquisite pleasure with every note she touches, and
has a wonderful conception and variety in playing, but
she seldom whirls you off your feet.

At the second concert she was even better than at
the first, if that is possible.   She seemed full of fire,
and when she played Bach, she ought to have been
crowned with diamonds !   Such *noble* playing I never
heard.   In fact you are all the time impressed with
the nobility and breadth of her style, and the com-
prehensiveness of her treatment, and oh, if you *could*
hear her *scales!*   In short, there is nothing more to
be desired in her playing, and she has every quality of
a great artist.   Many people say that Tausig is far
better, but I cannot believe it.   He may have more
technique and more power, but nothing else I am sure.
Everybody raves over his playing, and I am getting
quite impatient for his return, which is expected next
week.   I send you Madame Schumann's photograph.
which is exactly like her.   She is a large, very German-
looking woman, with dark hair and superb neck and
arms.   At the last concert she was dressed in black
velvet, low body and short sleeves, and when she
struck powerful chords, those large white arms came
down with a certain splendor.

As for Joachim, he is perfectly magnificent, and
has amazing *power*.   When he played his solo in that
second Chaconne of Bach's, you could scarcely believe
it was only one violin.   He has, like Madame Schumann, the greatest variety of tone, only on the violin

the shades can be made far more delicate than on the piano.

I thought the second movement of Schumann's Quartette perhaps as extraordinary as any part of Clara Schumann's performance. It was very rapid, very *staccato,* and *pianissimo* all the way through. Not a note escaped her fingers, and she played with so much magnetism that one could scarcely breathe until it was finished. You know nothing can be more difficult than to play staccato so very softly where there is great execution also. Both of the sonatas for violin and piano which were played by Madame Schumann and Joachim, and especially the one in A minor, by Beethoven, were divine. Both parts were equally well sustained, and they played with so much fire—as if one inspired the other. It was worth a trip across the Atlantic just to hear those two performances.

The Sing-Akademie, where all the best concerts are given, is not a very large hall, but it is beautifully proportioned, and the acoustic is perfect. The frescoes are very delicate, and on the left are boxes all along, which add much to the beauty of the hall, with their scarlet and gold flutings. Clara Schumann is a great favorite here, and there was such a rush for seats that, though we went early for our tickets, all the good parquet seats were gone, and we had to get places on the *estrade,* or place where the chorus sits— when there is one. But I found it delightful for a piano concert, for you can be as close to the performer as you like, and at the same time see the faces of the audience. I saw ever so many people that I knew, and we kept bowing away at each other.

Just think how convenient it is here with regard to public amusements, for ladies can go anywhere alone! You take a droschkie and they drive you anywhere for five groschen, which is about fifteen cents. When you get into the concert hall you go into the *garde-robe* and take off your things, and hand them over to the care of the woman who stands there, and then you walk in and sit down comfortably as you would in a parlour, and are not roasted in your hat and cloak while at the concert, and chilled when you go out, as we are in America. Their programmes, too, are not so unconscionably long as ours, and, in short, their whole method of concert-giving is more rational than with us. I always enjoy the garde-robe, for if you have acquaintances you are sure to meet them, and you have no idea how exciting it is in a foreign city to see anybody you know.

BERLIN, *December* 19, 1869.

I suppose you are muttering maledictions on my head for not writing, but I am so busy that I have no time to answer my letters, which are accumulating upon my hands at a terrible rate. This week I have been out every night but one, so that I have had to do all my practicing and German and Harmony lessons in the day-time; and these, with my daily hour and a half at the conservatory, have been as much as I could manage.

On Monday I went to a party at the Bancroft's, which I enjoyed extremely. It was a very brilliant

affair, and the toilettes were superb.   At the entrance
I was ushered in by a very fine servant dressed in livery.   A second man showed me the dressing-room,
where my bewildered sight first rested on a lot of
Chinamen in festive attire.   I could not make out for
a second what they were, and I thought to myself,
"Is it possible I have mistaken the invitation, and
this is a masquerade?"   Another glance showed me
that they were Chinese, and it turned out that Mr.
Burlingame, the Chinese Minister, was there, and these
men were part of his suite.   The ladies and gentlemen had the same dressing-room, which was a new
feature in parties to me, and as we took off our things
the servant took them and gave us a ticket for them,
as they do at the opera.   I should think there were
about a hundred persons present.   There were a great
many handsome women, and they were beautifully
dressed and much be-diamonded and pearled.   Corn-
colour seemed to be the fashion, and there were more
silks of that colour than any other.

Mr. Burlingame seemed to be a very genial, easy
man.   I was not presented to him, but stood very
near him part of the time.   He looks upon the introduction of the Chinese into our country as a great
blessing, and laughs at the idea of it being an evil.
He says that the reason railroads can't be introduced
into China is because the whole country is one vast
grave-yard, and you can't dig any depth without un-
earthing human bones, so that there would be a revolution on the part of the people if it were done now,
but it will gradually be brought about.   He travels

with a suite of forty attendants, and says he has got all his treaties here arranged to his wishes, and that Prussia has promised to follow the United States in everything that they have agreed on with China. He is going to resign his office in a year and go back to America, where he wants to get into politics again. Mr. Bancroft introduced many of the ladies to the Chinese, one of whom could speak English, and he interpreted to the others. It was very quaint to see them all make their deep bows in silence when some one was presented to them. They were in the Chinese costume—Turkish trousers, white silk coats, or blouses, and red turbans, and their hair braided down their backs in a long tail that nearly touched their heels.

On Thursday I went to Dr. A.'s to dinner. He seems to be a very influential man here, and is a great favorite with the Americans. He has a great big heart, and I suspect that is the reason of it. Mrs. A., too, is very lovely. I saw there Mr. Theodore Fay, who used to be our minister in Switzerland, and who is also an author. He is very interesting, and the most earnest Christian I ever met. He has the tenderest sympathies in the world, and in a man this is very striking. He has a high and beautiful forehead, and a certain spirituality of expression that appeals to you at once and touches you, also. At least he makes a peculiar impression on *me*. There is something entirely different about him from other men, but I don't know what it is, unless it be his deep religious feeling, which shines out unconsciously.

Last week I made my first visit to the Museum. It

is one of the great sights of Berlin, but it is so
immense that I only saw a few rooms. In fact there
are two Museums—an old and a new. I was in the new
one. It is a perfect treasure house, and the floors
alone are a study. All are inlaid with little coloured
marbles, and every one is different in pattern. One
of the most beautiful of the rooms was a large circular
dome-roofed apartment round which were placed the
statues of the gods, and in the centre stood a statue
in bronze of one of the former German kings in a
Roman suit of armour. Half way up from the floor
ran round a little gallery in which you could stand
and look down over the railing, and here were placed
on the walls Raphael's cartoons, which are fac-similes
of those in the Vatican, and are all woven in arras.
They are very wonderful, and you feel as if you could
not look at them long enough. The contrast is
impressive as you look down and see all the heathen
statues standing on the marble floor, each one like a
separate sphinx, and then look up and see all the
Christian subjects of Raphael. The statues are so
cold and white and distant, and the pictures are so
warm and bright in colour. They seem to express the
difference between the ancient and the modern relig-
ions. We went through the rooms of Greek and
Roman statues, of which there is an immense number,
and on the walls are Greek and Italian landscapes, all
done by celebrated painters.

We had to pass through these rooms rather hastily
in order to get a glimpse of the "Treppen Halle,"
which is the place where the two grand stair-cases

meet that carry you into the upper rooms of the
Museum. This is magnificent, and is all gilding and
decoration. An immense statue stands by each door,
and on the wall are six great pictures by Kaulbach,
three on each side. "The Last Judgment," of which
you've seen photographs, is one of them. I ought to
go to the Museum often to see it properly, but it is
such a long distance off that I can't get the time.
Berlin is a very large city, and the distances are as
great as they are in New York.

At the last "Reading" at the conservatory the four
best scholars played last. One of them was an American, from San Francisco, a Mr. Trenkel, but who has
German parents. He plays exquisitely, and has just
such a poetic musical conception as Dresel, but a
beautiful technique, also. He is a thorough artist, and
he looks it, too, as he is dark and pale, and very striking. I always like to see him play, for he droops his
dark eyes, and his high pale forehead is thrown back,
and stands out so well defined over his black brows.
His expression is very serious and his manner very
quiet, and he has a sort of fascination about him. He
is a particular favorite of Tausig's.

After he played, came a young lady who has been a pupil of Von Bülow for two years. She plays splendidly,
and I could have torn my hair with envy when she got
up, and Ehlert went up to her and shook her hand and
told her before the whole school that she had "*real*
talent. After her came *my* favorite, little Fräulein
Timanoff, who sat down and did still better. She
is a little Russian, only fifteen, and is still in short

dresses. She has almost white hair, it is so light, and she combs it straight back and wears it in two long braids down her back, which makes her look very childish. It is really wonderful to see her! She takes her seat with the greatest confidence, and plays with all the boldness of an artist.

Almost all the scholars in Tausig's class are studying to play in public, and I should think he would be very proud of all those that I have heard. There are many scholars in the conservatory, but he teaches only the most advanced. He only returned to Berlin on Saturday, and I have not yet seen him, though I am dying to do so, for all the Germans are wild over his playing. The girls in his class are mortally afraid of him, and when he gets angry he tells them they play " like a rhinoceros," and many other little remarks equally pleasing.

BERLIN, *January* 11, 1870.

Since my last letter I have been quite secluded, and have seen nothing of the gay world. I have been to the opera twice—once to *"Fantaska,"* a grand ballet, and the second time to *"Trovatore."* The opera house here is magnificent, and I would that I could go to it every week. It is extremely difficult to get tickets to it, as the rich Jews manage to get the monopoly of them and the opera house is crowded every night. It is the most brilliant building, and so exquisitely painted! All the heads and figures of the Muses and portraits of composers and poets which decorate it, are

3

so soft and so beautifully done.   The curtain even is
charming.   It represents the sea, and great sea mon-
sters are swimming about with nymphs and Cupids
and all sorts of things, and one lovely nymph floats in
the air with a thin gauzy veil which trails along after
her.   The scenery and dresses are superb, and I never
imagined anything to equal them.   The orchestra, too,
plays divinely.

The singing is the only thing which could be im-
proved.   The Lucca, who is the grand attraction, is a
pretty little creature, but I did not find her voice remarkable.   The Berlinese worship her, and whenever
Lucca sings there is a rush for the tickets.   Wachtel
and Niemann are the star singers among the men.
Niemann I have not heard, but Wachtel we should
not rave over in America.   I am in doubt whether
indeed the Germans know what the best singing is.
They have most wonderful choruses, but when it
comes to soloists they have none that are really great
—like Parepa and Adelaide Phillips; at least, that is
my judgment after hearing the best singers in Berlin,
though as the voice is not my "instrument," I will
not be too confident about it.   Everything else is so
far beyond what we have at home that perhaps I unconsciously expect the climax of all—the solo singing, to be proportionally finer also.

They have beautiful ballet-dancers here, though.
There is one little creature named Fräulein David,
who is a wonderful artist.   She does such steps that
it turns one's head to see her.   She is as light as down,
and so extremely graceful that when you watch her

floating about to the enchanting ballet music, it is too captivating. There were four other dancers nearly as good, who were all dressed exactly alike in white dresses trimmed with pink satin. They would come out first, and dance all together, sometimes separately and sometimes forming a figure in the middle of the stage. Then suddenly little David, who was dressed in white and blue, would bound forward. The others would immediately break up and retire to the side of the stage, and she would execute a wonderful *pas seul.* Then *she* would retire, and the others would come forward again, and so it went. It was perfectly beautiful. Finally they all danced together and did everything exactly alike, though little David could always bend lower, and take the " positions " (as we used to say at Dio Lewis's,) better than all the rest.

On Friday I am going to hear Rubinstein play. I suppose he will give a beautiful concert, as he and Bülow, Tausig and Clara Schumann are the grand celebrities now on the piano, Liszt having given up playing in public. After our lesson was over yesterday, Ehlert took his leave, and left us to wait for TAUSIG—my dear !—who was to hear us each play. He came in very late, and just before it was time to give his own lesson. He is precisely like the photograph I sent you, but is very short indeed—too short, in fact, for good looks—but he has. a remarkably vivid expression of the eyes. He came in, and, scarcely looking at us, and without taking the trouble to bow even, he turned on me and said, imperiously, " *Spielen Sie mir Etwas vor.* (Play something for

me.)" I got up and played first an *Etude*, and then he
asked for the scales, and after I had played a few he told
me I "had talent," and to come to his lessons, and I
would learn much. I went accordingly the next afternoon. There were two girls only in the class, but they
were both far advanced. I had never heard either of
them play before. The second one played a fearfully
difficult concerto by Chopin, which I once heard from
Mills. It is exquisitely beautiful, and she did it very
well. From time to time Tausig would sweep her off
the stool, and play himself, and he is indeed a perfect
wonder! If, as they say, Liszt's trill is "like the war-
ble of a bird," his is as much so. It is not surprising
that he is so celebrated, and I long to hear him in
concert, where he will do full justice to his powers.
He thrills you to the very marrow of your bones. He
is divorced from his wife, and I think it not improbable
that she could not live with him, for he looks as
haughty and despotic as Lucifer, though he has a
very winning way with him when he likes. His playing is spoken of as *sans pareil*.

I spent a very pleasant Christmas. The family had
a pretty little tree, and we all gave each other presents.
It was charming to go out in the streets the week
before. The Germans make the greatest time over
Christmas, and the streets are full of Christmas trees,
the shops are crammed with lovely things, and there
are little booths erected all along the sidewalks
filled with toys. They have special cakes and con-
fections that they prepare only at this season.

CHAPTER III.

Tausig and Rubinstein. Tausig's Pupils. The Bancrofts. A
German Radical.

BERLIN, *February* 8, 1870.

I have heard both Rubinstein and Tausig in concert
since I last wrote. They are both wonderful, but in
quite a different way. Rubinstein has the greatest
power and *abandon* in playing that you can imagine,
and is extremely exciting. I never saw a man to whom
it seemed so easy to play. It is as if he were just
sporting with the piano, and could do what he pleased
with it. Tausig, on the contrary, is extremely
restrained, and has not quite enthusiasm enough, but
he is absolutely *perfect*, and plays with the greatest
expression. He is pre-eminent in grace and delicacy
of execution, but seems to hold back his power in
a concert room, which is very singular, for when he
plays to his classes in the conservatory he seems all
passion. His conception is so very refined that sometimes it is a little too much so, while Rubinstein is
occasionally too precipitate. I have not yet decided
which I like best, but in my estimation Clara Schumann as a whole is superior to either, although she
has not their unlimited technique.

This was Tausig's programme :

1.	Sonate Op. 53.	-	-	-	-	Beethoven.
2. a.	Bourrée	-	-	-	-	Bach.
b.	Presto Scherzando,		-	-	-	Mendelssohn.
c.	Barcarole Op. 60,	-	-			
d.	Ballade Op. 47,	-	-		-	Chopin.
e.	Zwei Mazurkas Op. 59 u 33,					
f.	Aufforderung zum Tanz,		-	-		Weber.

3.	Kreisleriana Op. 16,			
	8 Phantasie Stücke,		- -	Schumann.
4. a.	Ständchen von Shakespeare			
	nach Schubert,			Liszt.
b.	Ungarische Rhapsodie,			

Tausig's octave playing is the most extraordinary I ever heard. The last great effect on his programme was in the Rhapsody by Liszt, in an octave variation. He first played it so *pianissimo* that you could only just hear it, and then he repeated the variation and gave it tremendously *forte*. It was colossal! His scales surpass Clara Schumann's, and it seems as if he played with velvet fingers, his touch is so very soft. He played the great C major Sonata by Beethoven— Moscheles' favorite, you know. His conception of it was not brilliant, as I expected it would be, but very calm and dreamy, and the first movement especially he took very *piano*. He did it most beautifully, but I was not quite satisfied with the last movement, for I expected he would make a grand climax with those passionate trills, and he did not. Chopin he plays divinely, and that little Bourrée of Bach's that I used to play, was magical. He played it like lightning, and made it perfectly bewitching.

Altogether, he is a great man. But Clara Schumann always puts herself *en rapport* with you immediately. Tausig and Rubinstein do not sway you as she does, and, therefore, I think she is the greater interpreter, although I imagine the Germans would not agree with me. Tausig has such a little hand that I wonder he has been able to acquire his immense virtuosity. He is only thirty years old, and is much younger than Rubinstein or Bülow.

The day after Tausig's concert I went, as usual, to hear him give the lesson to his best class of girls. I got there a little before the hour, and the girls were in the dressing-room waiting for the young men to be through with their lesson. They were talking about the concert. "Was it not beautiful?" said little Timanoff, to me; "I did not sleep the whole night after it!" —a touch of sentiment that quite surprised me in that small personage, and made me feel some compunctions, as I had slept soundly myself. "I have practiced five hours to-day already," she added. Just then the young men came out of the class-room and we passed into it. Tausig was standing by the piano. "Begin!" said he, to Timanoff, more shortly even than usual; "I trust you have brought me a study *this* time." He always insists upon a study in addition to the piece. Timanoff replied in the affirmative, and proceeded to open Chopin's *Etudes*. She played the great A minor "Winter Wind" study, and most magnificently, too, starting off with the greatest brilliancy and "go." I was perfectly amazed at such a feat from such a child, and expected that Tausig would

exclaim with admiration. Not so that Rhadaman-
thus.   He heard it through without comment or
correction, and when Timanoff had finished, simply
remarked very composedly, "So! Have you taken
the *next* Etude, also?" as if the great A minor were
not enough for one meal! It is eight pages long to
begin with, and there is no let-up to the difficulty all
the way ¡through.   Afterward, however, he told the
young men that he "could not have done it better"
himself.

Tausig is so hasty and impatient that to be in his
classes must be a fearful ordeal.   He will not bear the
slightest fault.   The last time I went into his class to
hear him teach he was dreadful.   Fräulein H. began,
and she has remarkable talent, and is far beyond me.
She would not play *piano* enough to suit him, and
finally he stamped his foot at her, snatched her hand
from the piano, and said : " *Will* you play *piano* or
not, for if not we will go no farther?" The second
girl sat down and played a few lines. He made her
begin over again several times, and finally came up
and took her music away and slapped it down on the
piano,—" You have been studying this for weeks and
you can't play a note of it; practice it for a month
and then you can bring it to me again," he said.

The third was Fräulein Timanoff, who is a little genius, I think.   She brought a Sonata by Schubert—the lovely one in A minor—and by the way he
behaved Tausig must have a particular feeling about
that particular Sonata.   Timanoff began running it
off in her usual nimble style, having practiced it evi-

dently every minute of the time when she was not asleep, since the last lesson. She had not proceeded far down the first page when he stopped her, and began to fuss over the expression. She began again, but this time with no better luck. A third time, but still he was dissatisfied, though he suffered her to go on a little farther. He kept stopping her every moment in the most tantalizing and exasperating manner. If it had been I, I should have cried, but Timanoff is well broken, and only flushed deeply to the very tips of her small ears. From an apple blossom she changed to a carnation. Tausig grew more and more savage, and made her skip whole pages in his impatience. "Play here!" he would say, in the most imperative tone, pointing to a half or whole page farther on. "This I cannot hear!—Go on farther!—It is too bad to be listened to!" Finally, he struck the music with the back of his hand, and exclaimed, in a despairing way, "*Kind, es liegt eine Seele darin. Weiss du nicht es liegt eine* SEELE *darin?* (Child, there's a soul in the piece. Don't you know there is a *soul* in it?)" To the little Timanoff, who has no soul, and who is not sufficiently experienced to counterfeit one, this speech evidently conveyed no particular idea. She ran on as glibly as ever till Tausig could endure no more, and shut up the music. I was much disappointed, as it was new to me, and I like to hear Timanoff's little fingers tinkle over the keys, "Seele" or no "Seele." She has a most accurate and dainty way of doing everything, and somehow, in her healthy little brain I hardly wish for *Seele!*

Last of all Fräulein L. played, and she alone suited Tausig. She is a Swede, and is the best scholar he has, but she has such frightfully ugly hands, and holds them so terribly, that when I look at her I cannot enjoy her playing. Tausig always praises her very much, and she is tremendously ambitious.

Tausig has a charming face, full of expression and very sensitive. He is extremely sharp-sighted, and has eyes in the back of his head, I believe. He is far too small and too despotic to be fascinating, however, though he has a sort of captivating way with him when he is in a good humor.

I was dreadfully sorry to hear of poor Gottschalk's death. He had a golden touch, and equal to any in the world, I think. But what a romantic way to die! —to fall senseless at his instrument, while he was playing "*La Morte.*" It was very strange. If anything more is in the papers about him you must send it to me, for the infatuation that I and 99,999 other American girls once felt for him, still lingers in my breast!

On Saturday night I went for the first time to hear the Berlin Symphony Kapelle. It is composed only of artists, and is the most splendid music imaginable. De Ahna, for instance, is one of the violinists, and he is not far behind Joachim. We have no conception of such an orchestra in America.* The Philharmonic of New York approaches it, but is still a long way off. This orchestra is so perfect, and plays with such pre-

*This was written before the full development of the Thomas Orchestra. The writer had heard it only in its infancy.

cision, that you can't realize that there are any performers at all. It is just a great wave of sound that rolls over you as smooth as glass. As the concert halls are much smaller here, the music is much louder, and every man not only plays *piano* and *forte* where it is marked, but he draws the *tone* out of his violin. They have the greatest pathos, consequently, in the soft parts, and overwhelming power in the loud. Where great expression is required the conductor almost ceases to beat time, and it seems as if the performers took it *ad libitum;* but they understand each other so well that they play like one man. It is *too* ecstatic! I observed the greatest difference in the horn playing. Instead of coming in in a monotonous sort of way as it does at home, and always with the same degree of loudness, here, when it is solo, it begins round and smooth and full, and then gently modulates until the tone seems to sigh itself out, dying away at last with a little tremolo that is perfectly melting. I never before heard such an effect. When the trumpets come in it is like the crack of doom, and you should hear the way they play the drums. I never *was* satisfied with the way they strike the drums in New York and Boston, for it always seemed as if they thought the parchment would break. Here, sometimes they give such a sharp stroke that it startles me, though, of course, it is not often. But it adds immensely to the accent, and makes your heart beat, I can tell you. They played Schubert's great symphony, and Beethoven's in B major, and I could scarcely believe my own ears at the difference between this orchestra and ours. It is as great as between —— and Tausig.

BERLIN, *March* 4, 1870.

Tausig is off to Russia to-day on a concert tour, and will not return until the 1st of May. Out of six months he has been in Berlin about two and a half! However, as I am not yet in his class it doesn't affect me much, but I should think his scholars would be provoked at such long absences. That is the worst of having such a great artist for a master. I believe we are to have no vacation in the summer though, and that he has promised to remain here from May until November without going off. Ehlert and Tausig have had a grand quarrel, and Ehlert is going to leave the conservatory in April. I am very sorry, for he is an admirable teacher, and I like him extremely.

We had another Musical Reading on Sunday, at which I played, but all the conservatory classes were there, and all the teachers, with Tausig, also, so it was a pretty hard ordeal. The girls said I turned deadly pale when I sat down to the piano, and well I might, for here you cannot play any thing that the scholars have not either played themselves or are perfectly familiar with, so they criticise you without mercy. Tausig plays so magnificently that you know beforehand that a thing can never be more than comparatively good in his eyes. Fräulein L. is the only one of his pupils that plays to suit him. I do not like her playing so much myself, because it sounds as if she had tried to imitate him exactly—which she probably does. It does not seem spontaneous, and she is an affected creature. They all think ' the world ' of her at the conservatory, and I suppose she *is* quite extraordinary ; but I prefer Fräulein Timanoff—"*die kleine Person*," as Tausig calls her—and she is, indeed, a "little person." On Sunday Fräulein L. played the first part of a Sonata by Chopin, and Tausig was quite enchanted with her performance. I thought he was going to embrace her, he jumped up so impetuously and ran over to her. He declared that it could not be better played, and said he would not hear anything else after that, and so the school was dismissed, although several had not played that expected to do so.

Tausig has one scholar who is a very singular girl—the Fräulein H. I mentioned to you before, who has studied with Bülow. She is half French and half German, and speaks both languages. She is full of talent and cannot be over eighteen, but she is the most intense character, and is a perfect child of nature. One can't help smiling at everything she does, because she goes at everything so hard and so unconsciously. When the other girls are playing she folds her arms and plays with her fingers against her sides all the time, and when her turn comes she seizes her music, jumps up, and rushes for the piano as fast as she can. She hasn't the least timidity, and on Sunday when Tausig called out her name he scarcely got the words out before she said, "*Ja*," to the great amusement of the class (for none of us answered to our names) and ran to the piano.

She sat down with the chair half crooked, and almost on the side of it, but she never stopped to arrange herself, but dashed off a prelude out of her own head, and then played her piece. When she got through she never changed countenance, but was back in her seat before you could say " Jack Robinson." She is as passionate as Tausig, and so they usually have a scene over her lesson. He is always either half amused at her or very angry, and is terribly severe with her. When he stamps his foot at her she makes up a face, and the blood rushes up into her head, and I believe she would beat him if she dared. She always plays as impetuously as she does every-thing else, and then he stops his ears and tells her she makes too much " *Spectakel* " (his favorite expression). Then she begins over again two or three times, but always in the same way. He snatches the music from the piano and tells her that is enough. Then the class bursts out laughing and she goes to her seat and cries. But she is too proud to let the other girls see her wipe her eyes, and so she sits up straight, and tries to look unconcerned, but the tears trickle down her cheeks one after the other, and drop off her chin all the rest of the hour. By the time she has had a piece for two lessons she comes to the third, and at last she has managed to tone down enough, and then she plays it splendidly. She is a savage creature. The girls tell me that one time she sat down to the piano (a concert-grand) with such violence as to push the instrument to one side, and began to play with such vehemence that she burst the sleeve out of her dress behind! She is going to be an artist, and I told her she must come to America to give concerts. She said " *Ja,*" and immediately wanted to know where I lived, so she could come and see me. I think she will make a capital concert player, for she is always excited by an audience, and she has immense power. I am a mere baby to her in strength. Perhaps when she is ten years older she will be able to restrain herself within just limits, and to put in the light and shade as Fräulein L. does.

Since I last wrote I have been to hear Rubinstein again. He is the greatest sensation player I know of, and, like Gottschalk, has all sorts of tricks of his own. His grand aim is to produce an *effect*, so it is dreadfully exciting to hear him, and at his last concert the first piece he played—a terrific composition by Schubert—gave me such a violent headache that I couldn't hear the rest of the performance with any pleasure. He has a gigantic spirit in him, and is extremely poetic and original, but for an entire concert he is too much. Give me Rubinstein for a few pieces, but Tausig for a whole evening. Rubinstein doesn't care how many notes he misses, provided he can bring out his conception and make it vivid enough. Tausig strikes *every* note with rigid exactness, and perhaps his very perfection makes him at times a little cold. Rubinstein played Schubert's Erl-König, arranged by Liszt, *gloriously*. Where the child is so frightened, his hands flew all over the piano, and absolutely made it shriek with terror. It was enough to freeze you to hear it.

Last week I went to a party at Mrs. Bancroft's in honour of Washington's birth-day, and had a lovely time, as I always do when I go there. Bismarck was

present, and wore a coat all decorated with stars and
orders. He is a splendid looking man, and is tall
and imposing. No one could be kinder than Mr.
Bancroft. He and Mrs. Bancroft live in a beautiful
house, furnished in perfect taste and full of lovely
pictures and things, and they entertain most charmingly. They seem to do their utmost for the Americans who are in Berlin, and I am very proud of our
minister. His reputation as our national historian,
together with his German culture and early German
associations, all combine to render him an admirable
representative of our country to this haughty king-
dom, and I hear that he is very popular with its self-
satisfied citizens. As for Mrs. Bancroft, one could
hardly be more elegant, or better suited to the position. Mr. Bancroft is passionately fond of music, and
knows what good music is,—which is of course an
additional title to *my* high opinion !

The other day Herr J. called for me to go and take
a walk through the Thier-Garten, and see the skating.
It was the first time I had been there, though it is not
far from us, and I was delighted with it. It is the
natural forest, with beautiful walks and drives cut
through it, and statues here and there. We went to
see the skating, and it was a lovely sight. The band
was playing, and ladies and gentlemen were skating in
time to the waltz. Many ladies skate very elegantly,
and go along with their hands in their muffs, swaying
first to one side and then to the other. It is grace
itself. Carriages and horses pranced slowly around
the edge of the pond, and at last the Prince and Prin-

cess Royal came along, drawn by two splendid black horses.

The carriage stopped and they got out to walk. "Now," said I to Herr J., "you must take off your hat"—for everybody takes off his hat to the Crown Prince. As they passed us he did take it off, but blushed up to his ears, which I thought rather odd, until he said, in a half-ashamed tone, "That is the first time in my life that I ever took off my hat to a Prince." "Well, what did you do it for?" said I. "Because you told me to," said he. He is such a red hot republican, that even such a little act of respect as this grated upon him! I only told him in fun, any way, but I was very much amused to see how he took it. He always raves over the United States, and says we are the greatest country in the world. He is a strange man, and you ought to hear his theory of religion. He sets the Bible entirely aside—like most German cultivated men. We were talking of it one night, and he said, "We won't speak of that *blockhead* Peter, stupid fisherman that he was! but we will pass on to Paul, who was a man of some education." David, he calls "that rascal David, etc." Of course, I hold to my own belief, but I can't help laughing to hear him, it sounds so ridiculous. The world never had any beginning, he says, and there is no resurrection. We live only for the benefit of the next generation, and therefore it is necessary to lead good lives. We inherit the result of our father's labours, and our children will inherit ours. So we shall go on until the human race comes to a state of perfection. "And then what?" said I. Oh—

4

then, he didn't know. Perhaps the world would explode, and go off in meteors. "We *do* know," said he, "that there are lost stars. Occasionally a star disappears and we can't tell what has become of it; and perhaps the earth will become a wandering star, or a comet. The intervals between the stars are so great as to admit of a world wandering about—and there is no police in those regions, I fancy," concluded he, with a shrug of his shoulders. "Do you really *believe* that, Herr J.?" I asked. "Oh," said he, "we won't speak about *beliefs*. Now we are *speculating!*" He is a delightful companion, and I think he is scrupulously conscientious. Though he does not profess the Christian faith, he acts up to Christian principles.

CHAPTER IV.

Opera and Oratorio in Berlin. A Typical American. Prussian Rudeness. Conservatory Changes. Easter.

BERLIN, *March* 20, 1870.

On Wednesday the Bancrofts most kindly called for me to go to the opera with them. They came in their carriage, with two horses and footmen, so it was very jolly, and we bowled rapidly through Unter den Linden (the Broadway of Berlin), in rather a different manner from the pace I usually crawl along in a droschkie. They had fine opera glasses, of course, and we took our seats just as the overture was about to begin, so that everything was charming except that instead of Lohengrin, which we had expected to hear, they had changed the opera to Faust, which I had heard the week before. Faust is, however, a fascinating opera, and it is beautifully given here, albeit the Germans stick to it that it is Gounod's Faust and not Goethe's.

Since I have come here I have a perfect passion for going to the opera, for everything is done in such superb fashion, and they have the orchestra of the Symphony Kapelle, which is so splendid that it could not be better. It is a pity the singers are not equally good, but I don't believe Germany is the land of great voices. However, the men sing finely, and the prima donnas have much talent, and *act* beautifully. The prima donna on this occasion was Mallinger, the rival of Lucca. She is espe-

(51)

cially good as Margaretta. Niemann and Waehtel are
the great men singers. Wachtel was formerly a coach-
man, but he has a lovely voice. His acting is not
remarkable, but Niemann is superb, and he sings and
acts delightfully. He is very tall and fair, with light
whiskers, and golden hair crowning a noble head, in truth
a regular Viking. When he comes out in his crimson
velvet mantle and crimson cap, with a white plume, and
begins singing these delicious love songs to Margaretta,
he is perfectly enchanting! He and Mallinger throw
themselves into the long love scene which fills the third
act, and act it magnificently. It was the first time I
ever saw a love scene well done. The fourth act is most
impressive. The curtain rises, and shows the interior of
a church. The candles are burning on the altar, and
the priests and acolytes are standing in their proper order
before it. The organ strikes up a fugue and all the
peasants come in and kneel down. Then poor Margaretta comes in for refuge, but when she kneels to pray
a voice is heard which tells her that for her there is
no refuge or hope in heaven or earth.

This scene Mallinger does so well that it is nature
itself. When the voice is heard she gives a shriek, tot-
ters for a moment, and then falls upon the floor senseless, and O, *so* naturally that one is entirely carried away
by it. The organ takes up the fugue, and the curtain
drops. The contrast between the two acts makes it all
the more effective, for in the third it is all love and
flowers and languishing music, and in the fourth one is
suddenly recalled to the sanctity and severity of the
church ; also, after the orchestra this subdued fugue on

the organ makes a very peculiar impression. In the fifth act Margaretta is in prison, and Faust and Mephistopheles come to rescue her. This is a powerful scene, for at first she hesitates, and thinks she will go with them, and then her mind wanders, and she recalls, as in a vision, the happy scenes of earlier days. They keep urging her, and try to drag her along with them, but at last she breaks free from them and cries, "To Thee, O, God, belongs my soul," and falls upon her straw pallet, and dies. Then the scene changes, and you see four angels gradually floating up to heaven, supporting her dead body, while the chorus sings :

> " Christ ist erstanden
> Aus Tod und Banden
> Frieden und Heil verkeisst
> Aller Welt er, die ihn preist."*

This ends the opera, which is very exciting throughout. I am going to read the original as soon as I know a little more German, so that I shan't have to read with a dictionary. I am just getting able to read Goethe without one, and think he is the most entrancing writer. There never could have been a man who understood women so well as he ! His female characters are perfectly captivating, but he is not very flattering to his own sex, and generally makes them, in love, (what they are) weak and vacillating.

I met a very agreeable young countryman at a dinner the other day—a Mr. P.—and a great contrast to any of Goethe's ill-regulated heroes. He was the typical Amer-

---

*Christ is risen out of bonds and death. He promises joy and blessing to all the world, which for this glorifies Him.

ican, I thought. Wide awake, bright, with a sharp eye
to business, very republican, with a hearty contempt for
titles and a great respect for women, practical and clear-
headed. When the wine was passed round he refused
it, and said he had never drunk a glass of wine or
touched tobacco in his life. I was so amused, for he
looked so young. I said to myself, " probably you are
just out of college, and are travelling before you settle
down to a profession." After a while he said something
about his wife. I was a little surprised, but still I
thought " perhaps you have only been married a few
months." A little further on he mentioned his children.
I was still more surprised, but thought he couldn't have
more than two ; but when Mrs. B. asked him how many
he had, and he said " three living and two dead," adding
very gravely, " I have been twice left childless," I could
scarcely help bursting out laughing, for I had thought
him about twenty-one, and these revelations of a wife
and numerous family seemed too preposterous !—But it
was very nice to see such a model countryman, too. It
is such men that make the American greatness.

After dinner I went with my hostess to hear Mendelssohn's Oratorio of St. Paul. It is a great work, a
little tedious as a whole, but with wonderfully beautiful
numbers interspersed through it. There are several
lovely chorales in it. I was disappointed in the performance, though, for in the first place there is no organ in
the Sing-Akademie, and I consider the effect of the
organ and the drums indispensable to an oratorio ; and
in the second, the solos all seemed to me indifferently
sung. The choruses were faultless, however. They

understand how to drill a chorus here! Next Friday I
am going to Haydn's "Jahreszeiten," which I never happened to hear in Boston.

Germany is a great place for birds and flowers. All
winter long we have quantities of saucy-looking little
sparrows here, and they have the most thievish expression when they fly down for a crumb. I sometimes
put crumbs on my window-sill, and in a short time
they are sure to see them. Then they stand on the
edge of a roof opposite, and look from side to side for
a long time, the way birds do. At last they make up
their minds, swoop down on the sill, stretch their
heads, give a bold look to see if I am about, and
then snatch a crumb and fly off with it. They never
can get over their own temerity, and always give a
chirp as they fly away with the crumb; whether it is
a note of triumph over their success, or an expression
of nervousness, I cannot decide. One cold day I
passed a tree, on every twig of which was a bird. They
were holding a political meeting, I am sure, for they
were all jabbering away to each other in the most
excited manner, and each one had his breast bulged
out, and his feathers ruffled. They were " awfully
cunning !"

On Tuesday I went out to Borsig's greenhouse. He
is an immensely rich man here, who makes a specialty
of flowers. He lives some way out of Berlin, and has
the largest conservatories here. The inside of the
portico which leads into them is all covered with ivy,
which creeps up on the inside of the walls, and covers
them completely. When we came within, the flowers

were arranged in perfect *banks* all along the length of
the greenhouse, so that you saw one continuous line
of brilliant colours, and oh—the perfume! The hya-
cinths predominated in all shades, though there were
many other flowers, and many of them new to me.
Camelias were trained, vine fashion, all over the
sides of the greenhouse, and hundreds of white and
pink blossoms were depending from them. All the
centre of the greenhouse was a bed of rich earth covered with a little delicate plant, and at intervals
planted with azalea bushes so covered with blossoms
that one could scarcely see the leaves. At one end
was a very large cage filled with brilliant birds, and
at the other was a lovely fountain of white marble—
Venus and Cupid supported on three shells. But I
was most struck by the tree ferns, which I had never
before seen. They were perfectly magnificent, and
were arranged on the highest side of the greenhouse
with many other rare plants most artistically mingled
in. After we had finished looking at the flowers we
went into a second house, where were palm trees, ferns,
cacti and all sorts of strange things growing, but all
placed with the same taste. It was a beautiful sight,
and I never had any idea of the garden of Eden before. I must try and bring home a pot of the "Violet
of the Alps." It is the most delicate little flower, and
looks as if it grew on a high, cold mountain.

BERLIN, *April* 1, 1870.

To-day is April Fool's day, and the first real month of spring is begun. I have not fooled anybody yet, but as soon as dinner is ready, I shall rush to the window and cry, " There goes the king !" Of course they will all run to see him, and then I shall get it off on the whole family at once. I shall wait until the " kleiner Hans," Frau W.'s son, comes home. I call him the " Kleinen " in derision, for in reality he is immense. I have been very much struck with the height of the people here. As a rule they are much taller than Americans, and sometimes one meets perfect giants in the streets. The Prussian men are often semi-insolent in their street manners to women, and sometimes nearly knock you off the sidewalk, from simply not choosing to see you. I suppose this arrogance is one of the benefits of their military training ! They *will* have the middle of the walk where the stone flag is laid, no matter what *you* have to step off into !

I went to hear Haydn's Jahreszeiten a few evenings since, and it is the most charming work—such a happy combination of grave and gay ! He wrote it when he was seventy years old, and it is so popular that one has great difficulty in getting a ticket for it. The *salon* was entirely filled, so that I had to take a seat in the *loge*, where the places are pretty poor, though I went early, too. The work is sung like an oratorio, in arias, recitatives and choruses, and is interspersed with charming little songs. It represents the four seasons of the year, and each part is prefaced by a little overture appropriate

to the passing of each season into the next. The recitatives are sung by Hanna and Lucas, who are lovers,
and by Simon, who is a friend of both, apparently.
The autumn is the prettiest of the four parts, for it
represents first the joy of the country people over the
harvests and over the fruits. Then comes a splendid
chorus in praise of Industry. After that follows a little
love dialogue between Hanna and Lucas, then a description of a hunt, then a dance; lastly the wine is brought,
and the whole ends with a magnificent chorus in praise
of wine. The dance is too pretty for anything, for the
whole chorus sings a waltz, and it is the gayest, most
captivating composition imaginable. The choruses here
are so splendidly drilled that they give the expression in
a very vivid manner, and produce beautiful effects. All
the parts are perfectly accurate and well balanced. But
the solo singers are, as I have remarked in former letters,
for the most part, ordinary.

I took my last lesson of Ehlert yesterday. I am very
sorry that he and Tausig have quarrelled, for he is a
splendid teacher. He has taught me a great deal, and
precisely the things that I wanted to know and could not
find out for myself. For instance, those twists and turns
of the hands that artists have, their way of striking the
chords, and many other little technicalities which one
must have a master to learn. He always seemed to take
great pleasure in teaching me, and I am most grateful to
him for his encouragement. I think Tausig behaves
very strangely to be off for such a long time. He does
not return until the first of May, and all this month we
are to be taught by one of his best scholars until he

comes back and engages another teacher. He has just given concerts at St. Petersburg, and I am told that at a single one he made six thousand rubles. They are in an immense enthusiasm there over him.

Last night I went with Mr. B. to hear Bach's Passion Music. Anything to equal that last chorus I never heard from voices. I felt as if it ought to go on forever, and could not bear to have it end. That chorale, "O Sacred Head now wounded," is taken from it, and it comes in twice; the second time with different harmonies and without accompaniment. It is the most exquisite thing; you feel as if you would like to die when you hear it. But the last chorus carries you straight up to heaven. It begins:

> "We sit down in tears
> And call to thee in the grave,
> Rest soft—rest soft."

It represents the rest of our Saviour after the stone had been rolled before the tomb, and it is *divine*. Everybody in the chorus was dressed in black, and almost every one in the audience, so you can imagine what a sombre scene it was. This is the custom here, and on Good Friday, when the celebrated "Tod Jesu" by Graun, is performed, they go in black without exception.

BERLIN, *April* 24, 1870.

I thought of you all on Easter Sunday, and wondered what sort of music you were having. I did not go to the English church, as is my wont, but to the

Dom, which is the great church here, and is where all the court goes. It is an extremely ugly church, and much like one of our old Congregational meeting-houses; but they have a superb choir of two hundred men and boys which is celebrated all over Europe. Haupt (Mr. J. K. Paine's former master) is the organist, and of course they have a very large organ. I knew, as this was Easter, that the music would be magnificent, so I made A. W. go there with me, much against her will, for she declared we should get no seat. The Germans don't trouble themselves to go to church very often, but on a feast day they turn out in crowds.

We got to the church only twenty minutes before service began, and I confess I was rather daunted as I saw the swarms of people not only going in but coming out, hopeless of getting into the church. However, I determined to push on and see what the chances were, and with great difficulty we got up stairs. There is a lobby that runs all around the church, just as in the Boston Music Hall. All the doors between the gallery and the lobby were open, and each was crammed full of people. I thought the best thing we could do would be to stand there until we got tired, and listen to the music, and then go. Finally, the sexton came along, and A. asked him if he could not give us two seats; he shrugged his shoulders and said, "Yes, if you choose to pass through the crowd." We boldly said we would, although it looked almost hopeless, and then made our way through it, followed by muttered execrations. At last the sexton unlocked a door, and gave us two excellent seats, and there was plenty of room for a dozen more people; but I don't doubt he frightened them away just as he would have done us if he could. He locked us in, and there we sat quite in comfort.

At ten the choir began to sing a psalm. They sit directly over the chancel, and a gilded frame work conceals them completely from the congregation. They have a leader who conducts them, and they sing in most perfect time and tune, entirely without accompaniment. The voices are tender and soft rather than loud, and they weave in and out most beautifully. There are a great many different parts, and the voices keep striking in from various points, which produces a delicious effect, and makes them sound like an angel choir far up in the sky. After they had finished the psalm the organ burst out with a tremendous great chord, enough to make you jump, and then played a chorale, and there were also trombones which took the melody. Then all the congregation sang the chorale, and the choir kept silence. You cannot imagine how easy it is to sing when the trombones lead, and the effect is overwhelming with the organ, especially in these grand old chorales. I could scarcely bear it, it was so very exciting.

There was a great deal of music, as it was Easter Sunday, and it was done alternately by the choir and the congregation; but generally the Dom choir only sings one psalm before the service begins, and therefore I seldom take the trouble to go there. The rest of the music is entirely congregational, and they only

have trombones on great occasions. We sat close by
the chancel, and the great wax candles flared on the
altar below us, and the Lutheran clergyman read the
German so that it sounded a good deal like Latin. I
was quite surprised to see how much like Latin German *could* sound, for it has these long, rolling words,
and it is just as pompous. Altogether it made a
strange but splendid impression. I thought if they
had only had their choir in the chancel, and in white
surplices, it would have been much more beautiful,
but perhaps the music would not have sounded so fine
as when the singers were overhead. The Berlin
churches all look as if religion was dying out here, so
old and bare and ill-cared for, and so few in number.
They are only redeemed by the great castles of organs
which they generally have ; and it is a difficult thing
to get the post of organist here. One must be an
experienced and well-known musician to do it. They
sing no chants in the service, but only chorales.

To-night is the last Royal Symphony Concert of this
season, and of course I shall go. This wonderful orchestra carries me completely away. It is too marvellous how they play ! such expression, such *élan!* I
heard them give Beethoven's Leonora Overture last
week in such a fashion as fairly electrified me. This
overture sums up the opera of Fidelio, and in one part
of it, just as the hero is going to be executed, you hear
the post-horn sound which announces his delivery.
This they play so softly that you catch it exactly as if
it came from a long distance, and you cannot believe

it comes from the orchestra. It makes you think of
"the horns of elf-land faintly blowing."

Tausig is expected back this week, and he has indeed been gone long enough. He is going to give a
lesson every Monday to the best scholars who are not
in his class, and as I stand at the head of these I hope
to have a lesson from him every week. This would
suit me better than two, as he is so dreadfully exact-
ing, and it will give me time to learn a piece well.
Then I should have my regular lesson beside from Mr.
Beringer, or whoever he appoints to take Ehlert's place.
Beringer, who is a young man about twenty-five years
old, has turned out a capital teacher, and I am
learning much with him. He plays beautifully
himself, and is a great favorite of Tausig's. He has
been with him so long that he teaches his method ex-
cellently, and gives me pieces that he has studied with
him. I believe he is to come out at the Gewandhaus,
in Leipsic, in October, and after that he will settle in
London.

CHAPTER V.

The Thier-Garten.　A Military Review.　Charlottenburg.
Tausig.　Berlin in Summer.　Potsdam and Babelsberg.

BERLIN, *June* 5, 1870.

We've had the vilest possible weather this spring, but
Berlin looks perfectly lovely now.　There are a great
many gardens attached to the houses here.　Everything is in bloom, and is laden with the scent of lilacs
and apple blossoms.　The streets are planted with lin-
dens and horse chestnut trees, and on the fashionable
street bordering on the Thier-Garten, all the houses
have little lawns in front, carpeted with the most dazzling green grass, and rising out of it are solid banks
of flowers.　The shrubs are planted according to their
height, close together, and one behind the other, and
as they are all in blossom you see these great masses of
colour.　It is like a gigantic bouquet growing up before you.

The Thier-Garten is perfectly beautiful.　It is so
charming to come upon this unfenced wood right in
the heart of an immense city, with roads and paths
cut all through it, and each over-arched with vivid
green as far as the eye can reach.　When you see the
gay equipages driving swiftly through it, and ladies
and gentlemen glancing amid the trees on horseback,
it is very romantic.

Frau W.'s brother, "Uncle S." as I call him,

announced the other day that he was going to take us to Charlottenburg. I had often been told that I must go there and see the " Mausoleum," but as you know I never ask for explanations, this did not coi, vey any particular idea to my mind, and I started out _n this excursion in my usual state of blissful ignorance. We took two droschkies for our party, and meandered slowly through the Thier-Garten and along the Charlottenburg road till we arrived at our point of destination. This was announced from afar by an absurd statue poised on one toe on the top of the castle which stands in front of the park containing the Mausoleum.

The first thing we did on alighting was to go into a little beer garden close by to take coffee. It was a perfect afternoon, and the trees and flowers were in all their June glory. We sat down around one of those delightful tables which they always have under the trees in Germany. The coffee was soon served, hot and strong, and Uncle S. took out a cigar to complete his enjoyment. Then we began to stroll. We went through a gate into the grounds surrounding the castle, and after passing through the orangery emerged into a garden, which soon spread into a beautiful park filled with magnificent trees, and with beds of flowers cut in the smooth turf for some distance along the borders of the avenues. We turned to the right (instead of to the left, which would have brought us directly to the Mausoleum) in order to see the flowers first, then the river, and then come round by the pond where the carp are kept.

5

The Germans certainly understand laying out parks to perfection. They are not *too* rigidly kept, and there is an air of nature about everything. This Charlottenburg park is a particularly fascinating one. A dense avenue borders the River Spree, which is broad at this point, and flows gloomily and silently along. The branches of the trees overhang the stream, and also lock together across the walk, forming a leafy avenue before and behind you. We met very few people, scarcely any one, in fact, and the songs of the birds were the only sounds that broke the all-pervading calm. The path finally left the river, and we came out on an open spot, where was a pretty view of the castle through a little cut in the trees. We sat down on a bench and looked about us for awhile, and then went up on the bridge which crosses the pond where the carp are kept. The Germans always feed these carp religiously, and that is a regular part of the excursion. The fish are very old, many of them, and we saw some hoary old fellows rise lazily to the surface and condescend to swallow the morsels of cake that we threw them. They were evidently accustomed to good living, and, like all swells, considered it only their due !

At last we came gradually round towards the Mausoleum. An avenue of hemlocks led to it—" Trauer-Bäume (mourning-trees)," as the Germans call them, and it was an exquisite touch of sentiment to make *this* avenue of these dark funereal evergreens. At first you see nothing, for the avenue is long, and you turn into it gay and smiling with the influence of the birds, the trees, and the flowers fresh upon you. But the drooping boughs of the sombre hemlocks soon begin to take effect, and the feeling that comes over one when about half way down it is certainly peculiar. It seems as if one were passing between a row of tall and silent *sentinels* watching over the abode of death!

Involuntarily you begin repeating from Edgar Poe's haunting poem:

> "Then I pacified Psyche and kissed her,
> And conquered her scruples and gloom,
> And banished her scruples and gloom,
> And we passed to the end of the vista
> Till we came to the door of a tomb;
> And I said, 'What is written, sweet sister,
> On the door of this legended tomb?'
> And she said, 'Ulalume, Ulalume,
> 'Tis the vault of thy lost Ulalume."

And so, too, does *your* eye become fixed upon a door at the end of *this* vista, which comes nearer and nearer until finally the Mausoleum takes form round it in the shape of a little Greek temple of polished brown marble. A small flower garden lies in front of it, and it would look inviting enough if one did not know what it was. Two officials stand ready to receive you and conduct you up the steps.

Within these walls a royal pair lie buried—King Friedrich Wilhelm III. and his beautiful wife, Luisa, who so calmly withstood the bullying of Napoleon I. and for whom the Prussians cherish such a chivalrous affection. They are entombed under the front portion of the temple, and two slabs in the pavement mark their resting places. These are lit from above by a

window in the roof filled with blue glass, which
throws a subdued and solemn light into the marble
chamber. You walk past them to the other end of
the temple, which is cruciform in shape, go up one
step between pillars, and there, in the little white
transept, lie upon two snowy marble couches the sculp-
tured forms of the dead king and queen side by side.
Though this apartment is lit by side windows of plain
glass high up on the walls, so that it is full of the
white daylight, yet the blueish light from the outer
room is reflected into it just enough to heighten the
delicacy of the marble and to bestow on everything
an unearthly aspect.

Queen Luisa was celebrated for her beauty, and
the sculptor Rauch, who knew and adored her, has
breathed it all into the stone. There she lay, as if
asleep, her head easily pressing the pillow, her feet
crossed and the outlines of her exquisite form veiled
but not concealed by the thin tissue-like drapery. It
covered even the little feet, but they seemed to define
themselves all the more daintily through the muslin.
There is no look of death about her face. She seems
more like a bonny " Queen o' the May," reclining with
closed eyes upon her flowery bed. The statue has been
criticised by some on account of this entire absence of
the " *beauté de la mort.*" There is no transfigured or
glorified look to it. It is simply that of a beautiful
woman in deep repose. But it seems to me that
this is a matter of taste, and that the artist had a perfect right to represent her as he most felt she was.
The king's statue is clothed in full uniform, and he

looks very striking, too, lying there in all the dignity of manhood and of kingship, with the drapery of his military cloak falling about him. His features are delicate and regular, and he is a fit counterpart to his lovely consort. Against the back wall an altar is elevated on some steps, and there is an endless fascination in leaning against it and gazing down on those two august forms stretched out so still before you. On either side of the statues are magnificent tall candelabra of white marble of very rich and beautiful design, and appropriate inscriptions from the German Bible run round the carved and diapered marble walls. Altogether, this garden-park, with its river, its Mausoleum, its avenue of hemlocks, and its glorious statues of the king and queen, is one of the most exquisite and ideal conceptions imaginable. As we returned it was toward sunset. The evening wind was sighing through the tall trees and the waving grasses. An indefinable influence hovered in the air. The supernatural seemed to envelop us, and instinctively we hastened a little as we retraced our steps.

When we emerged from the hemlock avenue Uncle S., I thought, seemed rather relieved, for the contemplation of a future life is not particularly sympathetic to him! After he had asked me if I did not think the Mausoleum "*sehr schön* (very beautiful)," and had ascertained that I *did* think so, he restored his equilibrium by taking out another cigar, which he lighted, and we leisurely made our way through the garden to our droschkies and drove home. It was quite dark as we were coming through the Thier Garten, and it seemed like a forest. The stars were shining through the branches overhead, and their soothing light gave the last poetic touch to a lovely day.

BERLIN, *June* 26, 1870.

Last week the Emperor of Austria was here, and they had a parade in his honour. The B.'s took me in their carriage to see it. We drove to a large plain outside the city, and there we saw a mock battle, and all the manœuvers of an army—how they advance and retreat, and how they form and deploy. There was a continual fire of musketry and artillery, and it was very exciting. The enemy was only imaginary, but the attacking party acted just as if there were one, and at last it ended with the taking by storm, which was done by the attacking party rushing on with one continued cheer, or rather yell, from one end of the lines to the other. Then they all broke up, the bands played the Russian Hymn, the King and the Emperor mounted horses and led off a great body of cavalry, and away we all clattered home—carriages and horses all together. It was a great sight, and I enjoyed it very much.

I am going to play before Tausig next Monday, and have been studying very hard. He praised me very much the last time, and said he would soon take me into his regular class; but he is such a whimsical creature that one can't rely on him much. Two of the girls have almost finished their studies with him, and soon are going to give concerts. I am playing

Scarlatti, which he is *aufully* particular with, and expect to have my head taken off. Two of his scholars are playing the same pieces that I am, and he told one of them that she played " like a nut-cracker." He is very funny sometimes. The other day one of the young men played the Pastoral Sonata to him. Tausig gave a sigh, and said, " This *should* be a garden of roses, but, as you play it, I see only potato plants." Scarlatti is charming music. He writes *en suite* like Bach, and is still more quaint and full of humour.

I find Berlin very pleasant, even in summer. Most of the better houses are made with balconies or bow windows, and around each one they will have a little frame full of earth in which is planted mignonette, nasturtiums, geraniums, etc., which trail over the edge, and as you look up from the street it seems as if the houses were festooned with flowers. On many of them woodbine is trained so that every window is set in a deep green frame. All the nice streets have pretty little front yards in which roses are planted, and I never saw anything like them. The branches are cut to one thick, straight stem, which is tied to a stick. They grow very tall, and each one is crowned with a top-knot of superb roses. Every yard looks like a little orchard of roses, and they are of every imaginable shade of colour. Every American who comes here must be struck with the want of beauty in the cities he has left at home; and it is really shameful, that when our people are so much better off, and when such immense numbers of them see this European culture every year, still they do not introduce the same

things into our country. Take Fifth Avenue or Beacon
Street, for example, and one won't see anything the
whole length of them but a little green grass and an
occasional woodbine, whereas here they would be
adorned with flowers and all sorts of contrivances to
make them beautiful.

On Thursday a little party of three, including myself, was made up to take me out to Potsdam. The
Museum, Charlottenburg and Potsdam, are, as Mr. T.
B. says, "the three sights of Berlin." I have written
you of the first two, and you shall now have the third.
Potsdam is sixteen miles from here, and it took about
as long to go there by train as it does from Boston to
Lynn. It is the royal summer residence. On arriving we bought a large quantity of cherries and
then seated ourselves in a carriage to drive through
the city to Charlottenhof. Here we got out and
walked into a superb park, filled with splendid old
trees. The first thing we saw was a beautiful little
building in the Pompeian style. This was where
Humboldt used to stay with the last king and queen
in summer. We went into it and found it the sweetest little place you can imagine. When we opened
the door, instead of a hall was a little court with a
fountain in it and two low, broad staircases (of
marble, I think) sweeping up to the main story. The
walls were delicately tinted and frescoed all round the
borders with Pompeian devices. The windows were
of some sort of thin transparent stained glass, through
which the light could penetrate easily, and were also in
the Pompeian fashion, with chariots, and horses, and

goddesses, etc. The rooms all opened into each other, but we were obliged to go through them so hastily that I could not look at them much in detail. The walls were covered with lovely pictures, and there were tables inlaid with precious marbles and all sorts of beautiful things. We saw the table and chair where the king always sat, just as he had left it, with his papers and drawings; and the queen's boudoir, with her writing materials and her sewing arrangements. From her window one looked out on a fountain at the right, and on the left was a long arcade covered with vines which led to a garden of roses.

We opened a door and passed through this arcade, and, after looking at the flowers, went on through the park until we came to another house, which was Pompeian, also, or Greek, I couldn't exactly tell which. It was built only to bathe in. The floors were all of stone, and it was as cool and fresh as could be. The bath itself was a large semi-circular place into which one went down by steps. It was large enough to swim in. Those old peoples understood pretty well how to make themselves comfortable, didn't they? There was an ancient bath-tub there, set upon a pedestal, made of some precious stone, which Humboldt had appraised at half a million of thalers. Outside was a lovely little garden, of course, and one of the prettiest things I saw was a quantity of those flowers which only grow in cool, moist places, sheltered under an awning. The awning was circular, and stretched down to the ground on three sides, so that one could only see the flowers by standing just in front. There were any

number of lady-slippers of every shade, each mottled
exquisitely with a different colour, and behind them
rose other flowers in regular gradation, and all of
brilliant tints. It seemed as if they were all nestling
under a great shaker bonnet, and they looked as coy
and bewitching as possible. I thought it was a charming idea.

After we left this place we went on until we came
to Sans Souci, which was built simply for the benefit
of the orange trees—to give them a shelter in winter.
At least, this was the pretext. It has a most dazzling
effect in the sunshine as you look at it from below.
Terrace rises above terrace, and at the top is this airy
white building rising lightly into the sky, with galleries and towers, groups of statuary, colonnades, fountains, flowers, and every device one can imagine to
make it look as much like a fairy palace as possible.
The great burly orange trees stand in rows in the gardens in large green pots. Many of them were in blossom, and cast their heavy perfume on the air. You
couldn't turn your eyes any where that *something* was
not arranged to arrest and surprise them. Here I
saw another way of training roses. Running along on
the green turf was a certain low growing variety, the
branches of which they pin to the earth with a kind
of wooden hair-pin, so that it does not show. They
thus lie perfectly flat, and the grass is *literally* " carpeted " with them. It was lovely. After we had sufficiently admired the exterior of the palace, we ascended the flights of steps which lead up the terraces,
and went into it. Outside were the long galleries

where the orange trees stand, and then we passed into
the large and noble rooms. First came the one which
is devoted to Raphael's pictures. Copies of them all
hang upon the walls. After we had gazed at them a
long time, we looked at the other apartments, all of
which were furnished in some extraordinary way, but
I glanced at them too hastily to retain any recollec-
tion of them. I only remember that one was all of
malachite and gold.

The next thing we did was to go over the palace
originally named " Sans Souci," where Frederick the
Great lived. We saw the benches—ledges rather—on
which his poor pages had to sit in the corridor, and
which were purposely made so narrow in order to prevent their falling asleep while on duty. The arm-
chair in which he died is there, and the bust of Charles
XII still stands on the floor at the foot of the statue
of Venus, where Frederick placed it in derision,
because Charles was a woman-hater. I think it was
a very small piece of malice on Frederick's part, and
in fact he had such a bad heart that none of his relics
interested me in the least.

After we had seen everything we went to a little
restaurant at the foot of Sans Souci, where we drank
beer and coffee and ate cake seated round a little table
under the trees. This fashion that the Germans have
of eating out of doors in summer is perfectly delightful, I think. I laid in a fresh stock of cherries, though
I had already eaten an immense quantity, but they
looked so nice, piled in little pyramids upon a vine
leaf, like the cannon balls at the Cambridge arsenal,

that there was no resisting them. I've thought of you
ever since the cherry season began. They are so extremely cheap here, that two groschens (about six
cents) will buy as many as two persons can eat at one
time. We drove from Sans Souci to Fingstenberg,
which is only a place to see a view of the country.
The landscape was perfectly flat, but it had the charm
of quiet cultivation. It was green with beautiful trees,
and the river wound along dotted with white sails, and
there were wind-mills turning in every direction.
After we left Fingstenberg we drove down to an inn
where we ordered dinner, and this also was served out
of doors. It was about six o'clock in the evening, and
we were all very hungry, so we enjoyed this part of
the programme very much.

When we had finished our cutlet and green peas we
got into the carriage again, and drove to Babelsberg.
This is a little retreat which belongs to the queen,
and where the royal family sometimes passes a few
weeks in summer. We walked through a noble park
where the ground swelled upward on our left and
sloped downward on our right. After following the
windings of the road for a long distance, we at last
arrived at the little castle, perched upon a hill-side
and embowered in trees. A smart looking maid
showed us through it, and I was more impressed here
than by all I had previously seen. As Balzac says,
" People who talk about a house ' being like a palace '
should see one first,"—although, as Herr J. observed,
" Babelsberg is not a palace, but is more like the home
of an English nobleman." It is just a quiet little re-

treat, but the beauty with which everything is arranged is quite indescribable. Every window is planned so that you cannot look out without having something exquisite before you. Here it will be a little mosaic of rare flowers ; there a fountain, etc. And then the bronzes, the pictures, the rare old pieces of glass and china, the thousand curious and beautiful objects of art that one must see over and over again to be able really to take in. In these castles, too, there are no end of little nooks and crannies where two or three persons, only, can sit and talk. Dainty little recesses made for enjoyment.

I walked into the grand salon and imagined an elegant assemblage of people in it, with all the means of entertainment at hand. It was a circular room, and large enough to dance the German in very comfortably. We went up stairs and through the different apartments. I went into the Princess Royal's room, and "surveyed my queenly form" in the superb mirror, and arranged my veil by her toilette glass—which I envied her, I assure you, for it shone like silver. We saw the cane of Frederick the Great, with a lion couchant on it—the one which he shook on some occasion and frightened somebody—(now you know, don't you?) Last of all we went up into the tower, and after climbing the dizzy staircase, we stood on the balconies for a long time, and looked over the splendid park about the country. Altogether, I was enchanted with Babelsberg, and nothing will suit me now but to have it for the retreat of my old age. I think I shall apply to be a servant there, for it must be a delightful situation. The royal family is only a short time there, and the servants have this exquisite habitation, which is always kept in perfect order, all the rest of the year, and have nothing to do but show visitors over it and take in half thalers!

After we left Babelsberg we took a carriage and drove to the station, where we got into the cars about half-past nine, and went back to Berlin. Herr J. had made himself extremely agreeable, and had exerted himself the whole day on our behalf. We had a most perfect time of its kind, and I enjoyed every minute of it, but came back in the worst of spirits, as I generally do. It seems so hard that one can never get together *all* the elements of perfect happiness! Here in Babelsberg everything was so lovely that one could scarcely believe that there had ever been a "Fall." It seemed as if people *must* be happy there, and yet I'm told that the queen is very unhappy. I suppose because she has such a faithless old husband.

CHAPTER VI.

The War. German Meals. Women and Men. Tausig's
Teaching. Tausig Abandons his Conservatory.
Dresden. Kullak.

BERLIN, *July* 23, 1870.

Just now the grand topic of course is this dreadful
war that has just been declared between Prussia and
France, and everybody is in the wildest state of excitement over it. It broke out so very suddenly that it
is only just one week since it has been decided upon, and
ever since, the drafting has been going on, and the
streets are filled with regiments and with droves of
horses, cannon, and all the implements of war. The
trains are going out all the time packed with soldiers,
and the railroad stations are the constant scene of
weeping women of all classes, come to see the last of
their dear ones. There is such a storm of indignation
against Napoleon that one hears nothing but curses
against him. I am entirely on the German side, and
am anxious to see the result, for between two such
great nations, and with so much at stake, it will be a
tremendous struggle.

We are promised a holiday soon, when I shall have
a let-up from practicing, and only practice three hours
a day, instead of five or six. Don't think I am making extraordinary progress because I practice so much. I
find that the strengthening and equalizing of the fingers

(79)

is a terribly slow process, and that it takes much more time to make a step forward than I expected. You may know how a thing *ought* to be played, but it is another matter to get your hands into such a training that they obey your will. Sometimes I am very much encouraged, and feel as if I should be an artist "immediately, if not sooner," and at others I fall into the blackest despair. I don't know but that S. J. was in the right of it, not to attempt anything, for it is an awful pull when you *do* once begin to study!

I wish S. could come here and spend a winter. I am sure it would be capital for her health. The Germans have a great idea that you must "*stärken* (strengthen)" yourself. So they eat every few hours. When you first arrive you feel stuffed to bursting all the time, for you naturally eat heartily at every meal, because, as we only eat three times a day in America, we are accustomed to take a good deal at once. Here they have five meals a day, and one has to learn how to take a little at a time. But it is a pretty good idea, for you are continually repairing yourself, and you never have such a strain on your system as to get hungry! The German women are plump roly-polies, as a general rule, and it is probably in consequence of this continual "strengthening." One has full opportunity to observe their condition, for they generally have their dress "*aus-geschnitten* (square neck)," as they call it, in order to save collars, and you will see them strolling along the streets with their dresses cut open in front. They are not handsome—irregular features and muddy complexions being the rule. The way they neglect their teeth is the worst. They are always complimenting Americans on what they call our "fine Grecian noses," and, in fact, since they have said so much about it, I have noticed that nearly all Americans *have* straight and reasonably proportioned noses.—One sees a great many handsome *men* on the street, however—many more than we do at home. Perhaps it is because the Prussian uniform sets them off so, and then their blonde beards and moustaches give them a *distingué* air.

From what you tell me of the shock of our respected friend —— over B.'s travelling from the West under Mr. S.'s escort, I think the "conventionalities" are taking too strong a hold in America, and it will not be many years before they are as strict there as they are here, where young people of different sexes can never see anything of each other. I regard it as a shocking system, as the Germans manage it. Young ladies and gentlemen only see each other in parties, and a young man can never call on a girl, but must always see her in the presence of the whole family. I only wonder how marriages are managed at all, for the sexes seem to live quite isolated from each other. The consequence is, the girls get a lot of rubbish in their heads, and as for the men, I know not what they think, for I have not seen any to speak of since I have been here. You can imagine that with my co-education training and ideas, I have given Fräulein W.'s moral system a succession of shocks. She has been fenced up, so to speak, her whole life, and, consequently, was dumbfounded at the bold stand I take. I cannot resist

giving her a sensation once in a while, so I come out
with .some strong expression.   Do you know, since I've
seen so much of the world I've come to the conclusion
that the New England principle of teaching daughters
to be independent and to look out for themselves from
the first, is an excellent one.   I've seen the evil of this
German system of never allowing children to think
for themselves.   It *does* make them so mawkish.   A
girl here nearly thirty years old will not know where
to buy the simplest thing, or do without her mother
any more than a baby.   The best plan is the old-
fashioned American one, viz. : Give your children a
" stern sense of duty," and then throw them on their
own resources.

BERLIN, *August* 6, 1870.

Until yesterday I have had no holiday, for I got into
Tausig's class finally, so I had to practice very hard.
He was as amiable to me as he ever can be to anybody,
but he is the most trying and exasperating master you
can possibly imagine.   It is his principle to rough you
and snub you as much as he can, even when there is
no occasion for it, and you can think yourself fortunate if he does not hold you up to the ridicule of the
whole class.   I was put into the class with Fräulein
Timanoff, who is so far advanced that Tausig told her
he would not give her lessons much longer, for that she
knew enough to graduate.   You can imagine what an
ordeal my first lesson was to me.   I brought him a
long and difficult Scherzo, by Chopin, that I had prac-

ticed carefully for a month, and knew well. Fancy how easy it was for me to play, when he stood over me and kept calling out all through it in German, " Terrible ! Shocking ! Dreadful ! O Gott ! O Gott !" I was really playing it well, too, and I kept on in spite of him, but my nerves were all rasped and excited to the highest point, and when I got through and he gave me my music, and said, " Not at all bad " (very complimentary for him), I rushed out of the room and burst out crying. He followed me immediately, and coolly said, " What are you crying for, child? Your playing was not at all bad." I told him that it was " impossible for me to help it when he talked in such a way," but he did not seem to be aware that he had said anything.

And now to show how we all have our troubles, and that blow falls upon blow—I will tell you that at our last lesson Tausig informed us that he was *not going to give another lesson to anybody*, and that the conservatory would be shut up on the first of October ! ! This is the most *awful* disappointment to me, for just as I have worked up to the point where I am prepared to profit by his lessons, he goes away ! I suppose that he has left Berlin by this time, or that he will very soon, but he wouldn't tell when or where he was going, and only said that he was going off, and did not know when he was coming back, or what would become of him. Of course he *does* know, but he does not want to be plagued with applications from scholars for private lessons. I heard that he was only going to retain two of his scholars, and that one was a princess and the other a countess.

He is a perfect rock. I went to his house to see if I could persuade him to give me private lessons. He came into the room and accosted me in his sharpest manner, with "*Nun, was ist's?* (Well, what is it ?)" I soon found that no impression was to be made on him. He only said that when he happened to be in Berlin, if I would come and play to him, he would give me his judgment. But I never should venture to do this, for as likely as not he would be in a bad humour, and send me off—he is such a difficult subject to come at. I told him I thought it was very hard after I had come all this way, and had been at so much expense only to have lessons from him, that I should have to go back without them. He said he was very sorry, but that most of his scholars came from long distances, and that he could not show any special favor to me. He asked me why I insisted upon having lessons from him, and said that Kullak or Bendel both teach as well as he does. The fact is, he is a capricious genius, entirely spoiled and unregulated, and the conservatory is a mere plaything to him. He amused himself with it for a while, and now he is tired of it, and doesn't like to be bound down to it, and so he throws it up. Money is no consideration to him.

It really seems almost as difficult to get a *great* teacher in Europe as in America. Tausig is the only celebrity who teaches, and now he has given up. He rather advised my taking lessons of Bendel, who is a resident artist here, and a pupil of Liszt's.

I suffered terribly over Tausig's going off. I heard

of it first two weeks ago, and couldn't sleep or anything. The only consolation I have is that I should have been "worn to the bone," as H. C. says, if I had kept on with him, for all his pupils except little Timanoff, who is at the age of plump fifteen, look as thin as rails. However —"the bitterness of death is past!" When one is stopped off in one direction, there is nothing for it but to turn in another. But it seems as if the more one tried to accomplish a thing, the thicker hindrances and difficulties spring up about one, like the dragon's teeth. I suppose I shall end by going to Kullak. He used to be court pianist here before Tausig and has had immense experience as a teacher. Indeed, Professor J. K. Paine recommended me to go to him in the first place, you remember. If I do, I hope I shall have a better fate than poor young N., whom, also, Professor Paine recommended to go to Kullak. He could not stand—or else *under*stand the snubbing and brow-beating they gave him in Kullak's conservatory, and from being deeply melancholy over it, he got desperate, and actually committed suicide!

Germans cannot understand blueness. They are never blue themselves, and they expect you always to preserve your equanimity, and torment you to death to know "what is the matter?" when there is nothing the matter, except that you are in a state of disgust with everything. Moods are utterly incomprehensible to them. They feel just the same every day in the year.

BERLIN, *August* 21, 1870.

I suppose that C. has described to you in full our Dresden visit, and what a lovely time we had. It was really a poetic five days, as everything was new to both of us. We were a good deal surprised at many things in Dresden. In the first place, the beauty of the city struck us very forcibly, and we both remarked how singular it was that of all the people we know who have been there no one should have spoken of it. The Brühl'sche Terrasse is the most lovely promenade imaginable. It runs along the bank of the Elbe River, which is here quite broad and handsome, and I always felt myself under a species of enchantment as soon as we had ascended the broad flight of steps that lead to it. We always took tea in the open air, and listened to a band of music playing. The Germans just live in the open air in summer, and it is perfectly fascinating. They have these gardens everywhere, filled with trees, under which are little tables and chairs and footstools; and there you can sit and have dinner or tea served up to you. At night they are all lighted up with gas.

It seemed like fairy land, as we sat there in Dresden. The evenings were soft and balmy, the very perfection of summer weather. The terrace is quite high above the river, and you look up and down it for a long distance. The city lies to the left, below you, and the towers rise so prettily—precisely as in a picture. This air of the culture of centuries lies over everything, and the soft and lazy atmosphere lulls the soul to rest.

We used to walk until we came to the Belvidere, which
is a large restaurant with a gallery up-stairs running
all round it. There was a band of music, and here we
sat and took our tea, and spent two or three hours,
always. The moonlight, the river flowing along and
spanned with beautiful bridges, the thousands of lamps
reflected in it and trembling across the water and
under the arches, the infinity of little steamers and
wherries sailing to and fro and brilliantly lighted up,
the music, and the throngs of people passing slowly
by, put one into a delicious and bewildered sort of
state, and one feels as if this world were heaven!

The day after we arrived we went, of course, to the
picture gallery, and here I was entirely taken by surprise. Nothing one reads or hears gives one the
least idea of the magnificence of the pictures there.
I never knew what a picture was before. The softness
and richness of the colouring, and their exquisite
beauty, must be seen to be understood. The Sistine
Madonna fills one with rapture. It is perfectly glorious, and one can't imagine how the mind of man could
have conceived it. One sees what a flight it was
after looking at all the other Madonnas in the Gallery,
many of which are wonderful. But this one soars above
them all. Most of the Madonnas look so stiff, or so
old, or so matronly, or so expressionless, or, at best, as
in Corregio's Adoration of the Shepherds (a magnificent picture), the rapture of the mother only is
expressed in the face. In the Sistine Madonna the
virgin looks so young and innocent—so virgin-like—
not like a middle-aged married woman. The large,

wide-open blue eyes have a dewy look in them, as if
they had wept many tears, and yet such an innocence
that it makes you think of a baby whom you have
comforted after a violent fit of crying. The majesty
of the attitude, and the perfect repose of the face,
upon which is a look of *waiting*, of ineffable expect-
ancy, are very striking. Mr. T. B. says it looked to
him as though she had been overwhelmed at the tremendous dignity that had been put upon her, and was
yet lost in the awe of it—which I think an exquisite
idea. St. Sixtus, who is kneeling on the right of the
virgin, has an expression of anxious solicitude on his
features. He is evidently interceding with her for the
congregation toward whom his right hand is out-
stretched, for this picture was intended to be placed
over an altar. The only fault to be found with the
picture, I think, is in the face of Santa Barbara, who
kneels on the left. She looks sweetly down upon the
sinners below, but with a slight self-consciousness.
The two cherubs underneath are exquisite. Their little round faces wear an exalted look, as if their eyes
fully took in the august pair to whom they are
upturned. The background of the picture—all of the
faces of angels cloudily painted—gives the finishing
touch to this astounding creation. But you must see
it to realize it.

Since my return I have finally decided to take private
lessons of Kullak. Kullak is a very celebrated teacher,
and plays splendidly himself, I am told, though he
doesn't give concerts any more. He used to be court
pianist here, and has had so much experience in teach-

ing that I hope a good deal from him, though I don't believe he will equal our little Tausig, capricious and ill-regulated though he is. Never shall I forget the *iron* way he used to stand over those girls, his hand clenched, determined to *make* them do it! No wonder they played so! They didn't dare not to. He told one of the class that "it was *in* me, and he could knock it out of me if he had chosen to keep on with me." And I know he could—and that is what distracts me!

But just think what a way to behave—to leave his conservatory so, at a day's notice, in holiday time, without even informing his teachers! He left everything to be attended to by Beringer. Many of the scholars are very poor, and have made a great effort to get here in order to learn his method. Off he went like a shot, because he suddenly got disgusted with teaching, and he hasn't told a soul where he was going, or how long he intended to remain away. He wrote to Bechstein, the great piano-maker here, "I am going away—away—away." He wouldn't condescend to say more. Mr. Beringer has been to his house to see him on business connected with the conservatory, but he was flown, and his housekeeper told Beringer that both letters and telegrams had come for Tausig, and she did not know where to send them. Did you ever hear of such a capricious creature? I was so provoked at him that after the first week I ceased to grieve over his departure. One cannot rely on these great geniuses, but I hope that, as Kullak makes a business of teaching, and not of playing, more is to be gained from him. At any rate, he will not be off on these long absences.

I am just studying my first concerto. It is Beethoven's C minor, and it is extremely beautiful. Mr. Beringer tells me that two years is too short a time to make
an artist in ; and indeed one does not know how extremely
difficult it is until one tries it. He plays splendidly himself, and is to make his *début* in the Gewandhaus in
Leipsic, this October. The best orchestra in Germany
is there. Tausig has turned out five artists from his
conservatory this summer. Time will show if any of
them become first class.

Aunt H. was right in thinking that this would be one
of the most dreadful wars that ever was, though she
needn't be anxious on my account. The Prussians are
winning everything, and are pushing on for Paris as
hard as they can go. They have just taken Chalons.
The battles have been *terrible,* and immense numbers
have been killed and wounded on both sides. They have
really fought to the death. The spirit of the two peoples seems to me entirely different. The French seem
only to be possessed by a mad thirst for glory, and man-
ifest a blood-thirstiness which is perfectly appalling.
One reads the most revolting stories in the papers about
their creeping around the battle-field after the battle is
over, and killing and robbing the wounded Prussians,
cutting out their tongues and putting out their eyes.
The Prussians are so on the alert now, however, that I
hope few such things can take place. One Prussian
writes that he was lying wounded upon the field of battle, and another man was not far off in the same help-
less condition, when an old Frenchman came up and
clove this other man's head with a hatchet. The first

screamed loudly for help, when a party of Prussians rushed up and rescued him, and overtook the old man, and shot him. We hear every day of some dreadful thing. O.'s cousin, who is just my age, and is three years married, has lost her husband, her favorite brother is fatally wounded with three balls and lies in the hospital, and her second brother has a shot in each leg and they don't know whether he will ever be able to walk again. He is a young fellow nineteen years old.

In the first days after the war was declared, I felt as if no punishment could be too hot for Napoleon. The people just gave up everything, and stood in the streets all day long on each side of the railroad track. The trains passed every fifteen minutes, packed with the brave fellows who were going off to lose their lives on a mere pretext. Then there would be one continual cheering all along as they passed, and all the women would cry, and the men would execrate Napoleon. The Prussians don't seem to have any feelings of revenge, but regard the French as a set of lunatics whom they are going to bring to reason. The hatred of Napoleon is intense. They regard him as the leader of a people whom he has willfully blinded, and are determined to make an end of him, if possible. The Prussian army is such a splendid one that it is difficult to imagine that it can be overcome. You see everybody under a certain age is liable to be drafted, and no one is allowed to buy a substitute. So everybody is interested. Bismarck has two sons who are common soldiers, and all the ministers together have twelve sons in the war. Then the King and the Crown Prince being with the army, gives a great

enthusiasm.   The Crown Prince has distinguished himself, and seems to have great military ability.   The King
was very angry with Prince Friedrich Carl, because in
the last battle he exposed one regiment so that it was
completely mowed down.   Only two or three men
escaped.   But it makes one groan for the poor French-
men when one sees these terrible great cannon passing
by.   The largest-sized ones were ordered for the storm-
ing of Metz, and each one requires twenty-four horses
to draw it!

WITH KULLAK.

(93)

CHAPTER VII.

Moving. German Houses and Dinners. The War. The Capture of Napoleon. Kullak's and Tausig's Teaching. Joachim. Wagner. Tausig's Playing. German Etiquette.

BERLIN, *September* 29, 1870.

I must request you in future to direct your letters to No. 30 Königgrätzer Strasse, as we move in three days. The people who live on the floor under us wouldn't bear my practicing for five or six hours daily, and so Frau W. has looked up another lodging. The German houses are about as uncomfortable as can be imagined. Only the newest ones have gas and water-works, or even the ordinary conveniences that *every* house has with us. No carpets on the floors, stiff, straight-backed chairs, precious little fire in cold weather, etc. The rooms have no closets, and one always has to have a great clumsy wardrobe with wooden pegs in it, instead of hooks, so that when you go to take down one dress all the others tumble down, too. In short, the Germans are fifty years behind us. Of course the rich people have superb houses, but I speak now of people in ordinary circumstances. I often look back upon the solid comfort of the Cambridge houses. I think people understand there pretty well how to live. I shall relish a good dinner when I come home, for this is the land where what we call " family

dinners" are unknown. They have *parts* of meals
five times a day, but never a complete one. The meat
is dreadful, and I never can tell what kind of an animal it grows on. They give me two boiled eggs for
supper, so I manage to live, but O! *has* beefsteak
vanished into the land of dreams? and *is* turkey but
the figment of my disordered imagination? They have
delicious bread and butter, but "man cannot live
by bread alone." Mr. F. says that where *he* boards they
give him "pear soup, and cherry soup, and plum
soup!"

Everything here is saddened by this fearful war.
You have no idea how frightful it is. The men on
both sides are just being slaughtered by thousands.
Haven't the Prussians made a magnificent compaign?
I declare, I think it is marvellous what they have done.
The French haven't had the smallest success, and have
had to give up one tremendous stronghold after another.
It is expected that Metz will surrender in about eight
days. It is a terrific place, and was believed to be
impregnable. Over and over again the poor French
have tried to cut through the Prussian army, and just
so often they have been beaten back into the city.
Finally they will have to give over. Their generals
must be shameful, for they have fought to the death,
but they can't make any headway against these formidable Prussians. The German papers say that the
French fire too high, for one thing. They are not
such practiced marksmen as the Germans, and their
balls fly over the enemy's heads. The French are
a savage people, however, and cruelty runs in their

veins. One reads the most awful things, but for the credit of human nature it is to be hoped that the worst of them are not true.

I believe I have not written to you since the capture of the Emperor Napoleon, which of course you heard of as soon as it happened. The Germans, as you may imagine, were completely carried away with the glorious news, and could scarcely believe in their own good fortune. On the 3d of September, when I came out to breakfast, Frau W. called out to me from behind the newspaper, with a face all ablaze with triumph and excitement, " *Der Kaiser Napoleon ist gefangen.* (The Emperor Napoleon is taken.)" "*No!*" said I, for it did not seem possible that anything so great and unexpected *could* have happened. " It is *true*," said she ; " look at this paper, which I just sent out for." The instant I saw that Frau W. had been guilty of the unwonted extravagance of purchasing the morning paper, it became clear to me that Napoleon *must* have been taken prisoner. Generally we do not get the paper till it is a day old, when Frau W. brings it carefully home from her brother's in her capacious bag. He subscribes for it, and after his family have perused it, she borrows it for our benefit—an economical arrangement upon which she frequently congratulates herself.

I fancy there was little work done or business transacted *that* day in Berlin ! After I had finished my coffee, I went and stood by the window and watched the people pour through the streets. Everybody streamed up Unter den Linden past the palace, their

7

faces full of joy. The street boys took an active part in the general jollification, and were as ubiquitous as boys always are when anything extraordinary is going on.   They conceived the brilliant idea of climbing up on the equestrian statue of Frederick the Great, which is just opposite the palace windows.   The Crown Princess, who was looking out, immediately had it announced to them that he who got to the top first should receive a silver cup and some pieces of money. That was all the boys needed. Away they went, struggling and tumbling over each other like a swarm of bees.   At last one little urchin secured the coveted position, and was afterward called up to the palace window to receive the prize.—If the Crown Princess, by the way, were more given to such little acts of generosity, she would be more popular by far, for the Germans sniff at her for being too economical.   They are the closest possible economisers themselves, but they despise the trait in foreigners !

At night there was a grand illumination in honour of the victory, and of course we all went to see it.   Such a time as we had !   The whole city was blazing with light, and all the large firms had put up something brilliant and striking before their places of business.   Stars, eagles, crosses (after the celebrated "iron cross" of Prussia), beside countless tapers, were burning away in every direction, and all the carriages and droschkies in Berlin were slowly crawling along the streets, much impeded by the dense throng of pedestrians crowding through.   All the private houses were lit up with tapers, and thousands of flags were flying.   Over every public building and rail-

road station, and on all the public squares were trans-
parencies in which the substantial form of *Germania*
flourished extensively, leaning upon her shield, and gazing
sentimentally into vacancy. But I always enjoy "Germania." It seems a sort of recognition of the femi-
nine element.

We were in a droschkie, like other people, taking the
prescribed tour round by the Rath-Haus (City-Hall),
and were frequently brought to a stand-still by the crush.
At such times we were the target for all the small boys
standing in our neighbourhood. The "Berlinger Junge"
is almost as famous for his talent for repartee as the
Paris "Gamin." "Do be careful!" said one to me; "you
will certainly tumble out, your carriage is going so
fast." This was intended as a double sarcasm, for in
the first place we were not in a carriage at all, but in a
second-class droschkie, and in the second place we had
been standing stock still for half an hour, and there
was no prospect of getting started for half an
hour more. Many more such little speeches were
addressed to us which we pretended not to hear, though
we were secretly much amused.—It was a strange sort of
feeling to be out in the streets at night with this glare
of light, these crowds of people, and this suppressed
excitement in the air. I thought it gave some idea of
the Day of Judgment.

The women are tremendously patriotic and self-sacri-
ficing, and they seem to be throwing themselves heart
and soul into the war. With the catholicity of the
female sex, however, they could not help taking a peep
at the *French* prisoners when they came on, but went

to the station to see them arrive, and bestowed many little hospitalities upon them in the way of cigars, luncheon,
etc., at all of which the papers were patriotically indignant, and indulged in many sarcasms on the "warm
and sympathetic" reception given by the German women
to their enemies. Quite as many women go into nurs-
ing as was the case in our own war. I know one young
lady who spends her whole time in the hospitals among
the wounded soldiers, who are all the time being sent on
in ambulances. Her name is Fräulein Hezekiel, and she
has received a decoration from the Government.

Just after I wrote you last I went to Kullak, as I
told you I should, and engaged him to give me one
private lesson a week. He looks about fifty, and is
charming. I am enchanted with him. He plays magnificently, and is a splendid teacher, but he gives me
immensely much to do, and I feel as if a mountain
of music were all the time pressing on my head. He
is so occupied that I have to take my lesson from seven
to eight in the evening.

Tausig's conservatory closes on the first of October,
and I feel very sorry, for my three grand friends, Mr.
Trenkel, Mr. Weber and Mr. Beringer, are all going
away, and I shall be awfully lonely without them.
Weber is very handsome, and has the most splendid
forehead I think I ever saw. He composes like an
angel, besides being remarkably clever in every way.
He will be famous some day, I know, and he belongs
to the Music of the Future. Beringer is poetic, passionate and vivid. He has golden hair and golden
eyes, I may say, for they are of a peculiar light hazel,

almost yellow, but with a warmth and sunniness, and often a tenderness of expression that is extremely fascinating. Weber cannot speak English, and as he is from Switzerland, he speaks an entirely different dialect from the Berlinese, so that it took me some time to understand him. He is a perfect child of nature, and has a great deal of humour. He and Beringer are devoted friends, and are about my age. Trenkel is older. He has the blackest hair and eyes, and a dark Italian skin. He is intellectual and highly cultured, and at the same time such a very peculiar character that he interested me greatly. Most of his life has been spent in America: first in Boston, where he seems to know everybody, and afterwards in San Francisco, whither he is about to return. He has been studying with Tausig for two years, and is a heavenly musician, though he hasn't Beringer's great technique and passion. His conception is more of the Chopin order, extremely finely shaded and "filed out," as the Germans have it.

It was so pleasant to have these three musical friends, who all play so much better than I, as they often met and made lovely music in my little room. Weber and Beringer took tea with us only yesterday evening. Weber was in one of his good moods, and played to Beringer and me his most beautiful compositions for ever so long. We settled ourselves comfortably, one in two chairs, the other on the sofa, and enjoyed it. The Andante out of a great sonata he is composing, is perfectly lovely. It is entirely original, and different from any music I have ever heard. Then he

played the second movement of his symphony, and it
is the most exquisite *morceau* you can imagine.   I
asked him to compose a little piece for me, and so
yesterday morning he sat down and wrote seven mazur-
kas, one after the other.   Whether he actually gives
me one is another matter, for, like all geniuses, he is
not very prodigal with his gifts, and is not very easy
to come at.   But I would like to have even four bars
written by him, for he is so individual that it would
be worth keeping.

Weber looks perfectly charming when he plays.
He never glances at the keys, but his large blue eyes
gaze dreamily into vacancy, and his noble brow stands
out white and lofty.   His conception is extremely
musical, but as he only practices when he feels like it
(as he does everything else), he doesn't come up to
the other two.   Tausig burst out laughing at him at
his last lesson.   That individual, by the way, came
back as suddenly as he went off, but announced that
he would give no more lessons except to these favoured
three.   All the rest of us had to go begging.   It didn't
make so much difference to me, as I had already gone
to Kullak, who is now the first teacher in Germany, as
all the greatest virtuosi have given up teaching.

Kullak himself is a truly splendid artist, which I
had not expected.   He used to have great fame here
as a pianist, but I supposed that as he had given up his
concert playing he did not keep it up.   I found, however, that I was mistaken.   His playing does not suf-
fer in comparison with Tausig's even, whom I have
so often heard.   Why in the world he has not contin-

ued playing in public I can't imagine, but I am told
that he was too nervous. Like all artists, he is fascinating, and full of his whims and caprices. He knows
everything in the way of music, and when I take my
lessons he has two grand pianos side by side, and he
sits at one and I at the other. He knows by heart
everything that he teaches, and he plays sometimes
with me, sometimes before me, and shows me all
sorts of ways of playing passages. I am getting no
end of ideas from him. I have enjoyed playing my
Beethoven Concerto so much, for he has played all the
orchestral parts. Just think how exciting to have a
great artist like that play second piano with you!
I am going to learn one by Chopin next.

Kullak is not nearly so terrible a teacher as Tausig.
He has the greatest patience and gentleness, and helps
you on; but Tausig keeps rating you and telling you,
what you feel only too deeply, that your playing *is*
" awful." When Tausig used to sit down in his impatient way and play a few bars, and then tell me to do
it just so, I used always to feel as if some one wished me
to copy a streak of forked lightning with the end of a
wetted match. At the last lesson Tausig gave me,
however, he entirely changed his tone, and was extremely sweet to me. I think he regretted having
made me cry at the previous lesson, for just as I sat
down to play, he turned to the class and made some
little joke about these *"empfindliche Amerikanerinnen*
(sensitive Americans)." Then he came and stood by
me, and nothing could have been gentler than his
manner. After I had finished, he sat down and played

the whole piece for me, a thing he rarely does, introducing a magnificent trill in double thirds, and ending up with some peculiar turn in which he allowed his virtuosity to peep out at me for a moment. Only for a moment though, for he is much too proud and has too much contempt for *Spectakel* to "show off," so he suppressed himself immediately. It was as if his fingers broke into the trill in spite of him, and he had to pull them up with a severe check. Strange, inscrutable being that he is!

BERLIN, *October* 13, 1870.

My room in our new lodging is a charming one. Quite large, and a front one, and there is no *vis-à-vis*. We look right over across the street into Prince Albrecht's Garden. It is very uncommon to have such a nice outlook, particularly in Berlin. But it is so long since I have lived among trees that at first it affected my spirits dreadfully. As I sit by my window and hear the autumn wind rushing through them, and see all the leaves quivering and shaking, and think that they have only a few short weeks more to sway in the breeze, it makes me wretched. I suppose that we shall now have two months of dismal weather.

I wish you were here to counsel me over my dresses. I have just bought two—one for a street dress, and the other for demi-evening toilette, but heaven only knows when they will be done, or how they will fit! You ought to see the biases of the dresses here! They all go zig-zag. The Berlin dressmakers are abomina-

ble. Mrs. ——, of the Legation, told me that when she
first came here she cried over every new dress she had
made, and I could not sufficiently rejoice last winter
that I had got all my things before I sailed. M. E.,
too, who gets all her best things from Paris, told M.
she was never so happy as when her mother sent her
over an "American dress."—" They are *so* comfortable
and *so* satisfactory," said she.

Yesterday I took my fourth lesson of Kullak. He
plays much more to me than Tausig did, and I am
surprised to see how much I have got on in four weeks.
Tausig didn't deign to do more than play occasional
passages, and we had only one piano in the room
where he taught. But at Kullak's there are two grand
pianos side by side. He sits at one and I at the other,
and as he knows everything by heart which he teaches,
as I told you, he keeps playing with me or before me,
so that I catch it a great deal better. Sometimes he
will repeat a passage over and over, and I after him,
like a parrot, until I get it *exactly* right. He has this
excessively finished and elegant fantasia style of playing, like Thalberg or De Meyer. He has great fame
as a teacher, and is perhaps more celebrated in this
respect than Tausig, but I was with Tausig too short
a time to judge personally which teaches the best.

This war is perfectly awful. The men are simply
being slaughtered like cattle. New regiments are all
the time being sent on. The Prussians have taken
over two hundred thousand prisoners, to say nothing
of the killed and wounded. But they lose fearful
numbers themselves also. It is expected in a few days

that Metz will surrender. It is a tremendous strong-hold, and contains an army of fifty thousand men. But isn't it extraordinary how disastrous the war has been to the French? They had an immense army of several hundred thousand men. And then they had all the advantages of position. The Prussians have had to fight their way through all these strong defences one after another. They will soon bombard Paris. As Herr S. says, this war is a disgrace to the governments. He says that they ought to have united against it (America included), and to have said that on such an unjust pretext they would not permit it. I read the other day a most touching letter that was found on the dead body of a common soldier from his old peasant father. He said, " What have we poor people done that the *lieber Gott* visits us with such fearful judgments? When I got thy letter, my dear son, saying that thou art safe come out of the last battle with thy brother, I fell on my knees and thanked God for His goodness." Then he goes on to describe the joy of his mother and sister and sweetheart, and how he read his letter to all the neighbours, " who re-joiced much at thy safety," and his hope and confi-dence that his son would return alive to his old father. But in a few days his son fell in another battle, des-perately wounded. He was carried to the house of a lady who did all she could for him, but he died, and she sent this letter to the paper. Do you get many of the anecdotes in the American papers? Such as that of the three hundred and two horses which, at the usual signal after the battle that called the regiments

together, came back riderless? I think that was very
touching in the poor things.* Or have you heard of
the Frenchman who, when informed that the Emperor
was taken prisoner, coolly replied: *"Moi aussi!"*
But these are already old stories, and you have doubtless heard them. I think one of the worst incidents
of the war is that bomb that fell into a girls' school at
Strasbourg. When one thinks of innocent young
girls having their eyes torn out, and being killed and
wounded, it seems too terrible.—I always pity the poor
horses so much. At the surrender of Sedan, the French
forgot to detach them from the cannon, and to give
them food and drink. Finally, frantic with thirst,
they broke themselves loose and rushed wildly through
the streets. It was said that any body could have a
horse for the trouble of catching him.

BERLIN, *November* 25, 1870.

I went last week to hear Joachim, who lives here,
and is giving his annual series of quartette soirees. Oh!
he is a wonderful genius, and the sublimest artist I
have yet heard. I am amazed afresh every time I
hear him. He draws the most extraordinary *tone*
from his violin, and such a powerful one that it seems
sometimes as if several were playing. Then his ex-

---

* In Mr. Longfellow's Poems of Places is a translation of Gerok's poem
on the subject :—
  " Over three hundred were counted that day
  Riderless horses who joined in the fray,
  Over three hundred saddles, O horrible sight!
  Were emptied at once in that terrible fight."

pression is so marvellous that he holds complete sway
over his audience from the moment he begins till he
ceases. He possesses magnetic power to the highest
degree.

On Saturday night I went to a superb concert given
for the benefit of the wounded. The royal orchestra
played, and as it was in the Sing-Akademie, where the
acoustic is very remarkable, the orchestral performance seemed phenomenal. Generally, this orchestra
plays in the opera house, which is so much larger that
the effect is not so great. The last thing they played
was the "Ritt der Walküren," by Wagner. It was
the first time it was given in Berlin, and it is a wonderful composition. It represents the ride of the Wal-
küre-maidens into Valhalla, and when you hear it it
seems as if you could really see the spectral horses
with their ghostly riders. It produces the most unearthly effect at the end, and one feels as if one had
suddenly stepped into Pandemonium. I was perfectly
enchanted with it, and everybody was excited. The
"bravos" resounded all over the house. Tausig
played Chopin's E minor concerto in his own glorious
style. He did his very best, and when he got through
not only the whole orchestra was applauding him, but
even the conductor was rapping his desk with his baton
like mad. I thought to myself it was a proud position
where a man could excite enthusiasm in the hearts of
these old and tried musicians. As a specimen of his
virtuosity, what do you say to the little feat of playing
the running passage at the end, two pages long, and

which was written for both hands in unison, in octaves instead of single notes?—Gigantic! [Later Kullak gave this great concerto to my sister to study, and as she was struggling with its difficulties he said: "Ah yes, Fräulein, when I think of the time and labour I spent over that concerto in my youth, I could weep *tears of blood!* "]—ED.

Yesterday evening I went to a party at the house of a relative of the M.'s. Madame de Stael was right in saying that etiquette is terribly severe in Germany. It is downright *law*, and everybody is obliged to submit to it. What other people in the world, for example, would insist on your coming at eight and remaining until nearly four in the morning, when the party consists of a dozen or twenty people, almost all of them married and middle-aged, or elderly? I nearly expire of fatigue and ennui, but they would all take it so ill if I didn't go, that there is no escape. Last night I came home with such a dreadful nervous headache from sheer exhaustion, that I could scarcely see. You know in a dancing party the excitement keeps one up, and one doesn't feel the fatigue until afterward. But to sit three mortal hours before supper, and keep up a conversation with a lot of people much older than yourself in whom you have not the slightest interest, and in a foreign language, when you wouldn't be brilliant in your own, and then another long three hours at the supper table, and then *still* an hour or so afterwards, to an American mind is terrible! I always groan in spirit when I think how comfortably I used to jump into the carriage at nine o'clock, in Cambridge, go to the party, and come home at half-past eleven or twelve. These long parties are what the Germans call being "*gemüthlig* (sociable and friendly)." The French would call them "*assommant*," and they would be entirely in the right.

CHAPTER VIII.

Concerts.　Joachim again.　The Siege of Paris.　Peace
Declared.　Wagner.　A Woman's Symphony.
Ovation to Wagner in Berlin.

BERLIN, *December* 11, 1870.

I haven't been doing much of anything lately, except
going to concerts, of which I have heard an immense
number, and all of them admirable.—I wish you *could*
hear Joachim!　I went last night to his third soiree,
and he certainly is the wonder of the age.　Unless I
were to *rave* I never could express him.　One of his
pieces was a quartette by Hadyn, which was perfectly
bewitching.　The adagio he played so wonderfully, and
drew such a pathetic tone from his violin, that it really
went through one like a knife.　The third movement
was a jig, and just the gayest little piece!　It flashed
like a humming bird, and he played every note so dis-
tinctly and so fast that people were beside themselves,
and it was almost impossible to keep still.　It received
a tremendous encore.

Joachim is so bold!　You never imagined such
strokes as he gives the violin—such tones as he brings
out of it.　He plays these great *tours de force*, his fingers rushing all over the violin, just as Tausig dashes
down on the piano.　So free!　And then his conception!!　It is like revealing Beethoven in the flesh, to
hear him.

(111)

I heard a lady pianist the other day, who is becoming very celebrated and who plays superbly. Her name is Fräulein Menter, and she is from Munich. She has been a pupil of Liszt, Tausig and Bülow. Think what a galaxy of teachers! She is as pretty as she can be, and she looked lovely sitting at the piano there and playing piece after piece. I envied her dreadfully. She plays everything by heart, and has a beautiful conception. She gave her concert entirely alone, except that some one sang a few songs, and at the end Tausig played a duet for two pianos with her, in which he took the second piano. Imagine being able to play well enough for such a high artist as he to condescend to do such a thing! It was so pretty when they were encored. He made a sign to go forward. She looked up inquiringly, and then stepped down one step lower than he. He smiled and applauded her as much an anybody. I thought it was very gallant in him to stand there and clap his hands before the whole audience, and not take any of the encore to himself, for his part was as important as hers, and he is a much greater artist. I was charmed with her, though. She goes far beyond Mehlig and Topp, though Mehlig, too, is considered to have a remarkable technique.

I regret so much that M. will have to go back to America without seeing Paris—the most beautiful city in the world! Nobody knows how long the war is going to last. The Prussians have so surrounded Paris that it is cut off from the country, and can't get any supplies. They have eaten up all their meat, and now the French are living upon rats, dogs and cats! Just think how horrid! They catch the rats in the Paris sewers, and cook them in champagne and eat them. (At least that is the story.) It seems perfectly inconceivable. The poor things have no milk, no salt, no butter and no meat. I wonder what they do with all the little babies whose mothers can't nurse them, and with young children. They will not give up, however, for they have bread and wine enough to last all winter, and they declare that Paris is too strong to be taken. Of course if the Prussians remain where they are, eventually Paris will be starved out, and will be obliged to surrender.

It is a difficult position for the Prussians, for they must either bombard the city, or starve it out. If they bombard it, they must be in a situation to begin it from all sides, or else the French will break through their lines, and establish a communication with the rest of France. Now the circle round Paris is twelve miles long, so that it would take an enormous army to keep up such a bombardment, and although the Prussian army *is* enormous, I don't know whether it is equal to that, for the French have so much the advantage of position that they can fire down on the Prussians, and kill them by thousands. On the other hand, if they starve Paris out, the poor soldiers will have to lie out in the cold all winter, and many of them will die from the exposure.

The men are getting very restless from so many weeks of inactivity. Nobody knows how it is to end. The King is opposed to bombardment, for aside from the terrible loss of life it would cause, it seems too

8

inhuman to lay such a splendid city in the dust. Fresh troops are sent on all the time, and every day the trains pass my windows packed with soldiers. It seems as if every man in Germany were being called out, and that looks like bombardment. It is a terrible time, and everybody feels restless and disturbed. One sees few soldiers on the streets except wounded ones. I often meet a young man who is wheeled about in a chair, who has had both legs cut off. The poor fellow looks so sad—and I know of another who has lost both hands and both feet.

It is curious to note the condescending attitude taken by people here toward the French in this war. They never for a moment speak of them as if they were antagonists on equal ground, but always as if they were a set of fools bent on their own destruction, who must be properly chastised and restored to their equilibrium by the Germans. "*Ja!—die Franzosen!*" the Germans will say with a shrug which implies the deepest conviction of their entire imbecility. They admit, however, that the French are an "amusing people," and that "*Paris ist* DOCH *die Welt-Stadt.* (Paris is *the* city of the world.)"

BERLIN, *February* 26, 1871.

I am going to send you a song out of the Meister-sänger, which I think is one of the most beautiful songs I've ever heard. It is called Walther's Traumlied (Walter's Dream Song). The idea of it is that he sees his love in a dream or vision as she will be when

she is his wife. You must begin to sing in a dreamy
way, as if you were in a trance, and then you must
gradually become more and more excited until you
end in a grand gush of passion. You will be quite in
the music of the future if you sing out of the Meist-
ersänger. It is one of Wagner's greatest operas, and
is very beautiful, in my opinion. It caused a grand
excitement when it came out last winter.

The whole musical world is in a quarrel over Wagner. He is giving a new direction to music and is
finding out new combinations of the chords. Half
the musical world upholds him, and declares that in
the future he will stand on a par with Beethoven and
Mozart. The other half are bitterly opposed to him,
and say that he writes nothing but dissonances, and
that he is on an entirely false track. I am on the
Wagner side myself. He seems to me to be a great
genius.—Pity he is such a moral outlaw !

Since I began this letter Paris has capitulated, and
PEACE has been declared. The anxiety and suspense
have lasted so long, however, that the news did not
cause much excitement or enthusiasm. Nothing like
that with which the capture of Napoleon was received.
But that was decidedly *the* event of the war. The
politic Bismarck would not allow the troops to march
triumphantly through Paris, but only permitted them
to pass through as small a corner of it as was consist-
ent with the national honour. This has caused a good
deal of murmuring and discontent among the Germans.
—" Our poor soldiers ! after all their fatigues and hard-
ships, they ought have been allowed the satisfaction of

marching through the city !"—is the general opinion
I hear expressed.   However, they will probably ac-
quiesce in Bismarck's wisdom in not triumphing over
a fallen foe when they come to think it over.   We
are now to have six weeks of mourning for those who
have been killed in the war, and then in May the army
will come back in triumph.   The King is to meet them
at the Brandenburger Gate, and lead them up the
Linden.   All Berlin will be wild with excitement, and
I expect it will be a great sight.   The windows on
Unter den Linden are already selling at enormous
prices for the occasion.

The Germans, by the way, "take no stock" at all in
the King's pious expressions throughout the campaign.
They laugh at him greatly for calling himself vic-
torious "by the grace of God."   "Such a nonsense !"
Herr J. says, contemptuously.

BERLIN, *April* 22, 1871.

I haven't a mortal thing to say, for all the little I
have done I communicated in a letter to N. S.   Kullak has been praising my playing lately, but I cannot
believe in it myself.   I have been learning a Ballade
of Liszt's.   It is beautiful but very hard, and with some
terrific octave passages in it.   It has the double roll of
octaves in it, and this is the first time I ever learned
how it was done.   I am now studying octaves systematically.   Kullak has written three books of them, and
it is an exhaustive work on the subject, and as famous
in its way as the Gradus ad Parnassum.   The first vol-

ume is only the preparation, and the exercises are for each hand separately. There are a lot of them for the thumb alone, for instance. Then there are others for the fourth and fifth fingers, turning over and under each other in every conceivable way. Then there are the wrist exercises, and, in short, it is the most minute and complete work. Kullak himself is celebrated for his octave playing. That I knew when I was in Tausig's conservatory, as Tausig used to tell his scholars that they must study Kullak's Octave School.

Wagner has come to Berlin for a visit, and next week he will have a grand concert, when some of his compositions are to be brought out, and he will, himself, conduct. Weitzmann says that he is a great conductor. I heard his opera of Tannhaüser the other day, and I was perfectly carried away with the overture, which I had not heard for a long time. The orchestra played it magnificently, and I think it quite equal to Beethoven. Wagner's theory is that music is a cry of the mind, and his compositions certainly illustrate it. All other music pales before it in passion and intensity.

Did you read my letter to N. S. in which I told her about Alicia Hund, who composed and conducted a symphony? That is quite a step for women in the musical line. She reminded me of M., as she had just such a high-strung face. All the men were highly disgusted because she was allowed to conduct the orchestra herself. I didn't think myself that it was a very *becoming* position, though I had no prejudice against it. Somehow, a woman doesn't look well with a bâton in her hand directing a body of men.

BERLIN, *May* 18, 1871.

Wagner has just been in Berlin, and his arrival here has been the occasion of a grand musical excitement. He was received with the greatest enthusiasm, and there was no end of ovations in his honour. First, there was a great supper given to him, which was got up by Tausig and a few other distinguished musicians. Then on Sunday, two weeks ago, was given a concert in the Sing-Akademie, where the seats were free. As the hall only holds about fifteen hundred people, you may imagine it was pretty difficult to get tickets. I didn't even attempt it, but luckily Weitzmann, my harmony teacher, who is an old friend of Wagner's, sent me one.

The orchestra was immense. It was carefully selected from all the orchestras in Berlin, and Stern, who directed it, had given himself infinite trouble in training it. Wagner is the most difficult person in the world to please, and is a wonderful conductor himself. He was highly discontented with the Gewandhaus Orchestra in Leipsic, which thinks itself the best in existence, so the Berlinese felt rather shaky. The hall was filled to overflowing, and finally, in marched Wagner and his wife, preceded and followed by various distinguished musicians. As he appeared the audience rose, the orchestra struck up three clanging chords, and everybody shouted *Hoch!* It gave one a strange thrill.

The concert was at twelve, and was preceded by a "greeting" which was recited by Frau Jachmann

Wagner, a niece of Wagner's, and an actress. She was a pretty woman, " fair, fat and forty," and an excellent speaker. As she concluded she burst into tears, and stepping down from the stage she presented Wagner with a laurel crown, and kissed him. Then the orchestra played Wagner's Faust Overture most superbly, and afterwards his Fest March from the Tannhäuser. The applause was unbounded. Wagner ascended the stage and made a little speech, in which he expressed his pleasure to the musicians and to Stern, and then turned and addressed the audience. He spoke very rapidly and in that child-like way that all great musicians seem to have, and as a proof of his satisfaction with the orchestra he requested them to play the Faust Overture under *his* direction. We were all on tiptoe to know how he would direct, and indeed it was wonderful to see him. He controlled the orchestra as if it were a single instrument and he were playing on it. He didn't beat the time simply, as most conductors do, but he had all sorts of little ways to indicate what he wished. It was very difficult for them to follow him, and they had to " keep their little eye open," as B. used to say. He held them down during the first part, so as to give the uncertainty and speculativeness of Faust's character. Then as Mephistopheles came in, he gradually let them loose with a terrible crescendo, and made you feel as if hell suddenly gaped at your feet. Then where Gretchen appeared, all was delicious melody and sweetness. And so it went on, like a succession of pictures. The effect was tremendous.

I had one of the best seats in the house, and could

see Wagner and his wife the whole time. He has an
enormous forehead, and is the most nervous-looking
man you can imagine, but has that grim setting of the
mouth that betokens an iron will. When he conducts
he is almost beside himself with excitement. That is
one reason why he is so great as a conductor, for the
orchestra catches his frenzy, and each man plays under a sudden inspiration. He really seems to be im-
provising on his orchestra.

Wagner's object in coming here was to try and get
his Nibelungen opera performed. ·It is an opera which
requires four evenings to get through with. Did you
ever hear of such a thing? He lays out everything
on such a colossal scale. It reminded me of that story
they tell of him when he was a boy. He was a
great Shakespeare enthusiast, and wanted to write
plays, too. So he wrote one in which he killed off
forty of the principal characters in the last act! He
gave a grand concert in the opera house here, which
he directed himself. It was entirely his own compositions, with the exception of Beethoven's Fifth Symphony, which he declared nobody·understood but himself. That rather took down Berlin, but all had to
acknowledge after the concert that they had never
heard it so magnificently played. He has his own
peculiar conception of it. There was a great crowd,
and every seat had been taken long before. All the
artists were present except Kullak, who was ill. I saw
Tausig sitting in the front rank with the Baroness
von S. There must have been two hundred players in
the orchestra, and they acquitted themselves splen-

didly. The applause grew more and more enthusiastic, until it finally found vent in a shower of wreaths and bouquets. Wagner bowed and bowed, and it seemed as if the people would never settle down again. At the end of the concert followed another shower of flowers, and his Kaiser March was encored. Such an effect! After the tempest of sound of the introduction the drums came in with a sharp tat-tat-tat-tat-tat! Then the brass began with the air and came to a crescendo, at last *blaring* out in such a way as shivered you to the very marrow of your bones. It was like an earthquake yawning before you.

The noise was so tremendous that it was like the roaring of the surf. I never conceived of anything in music to approach it, and Wagner made me think of a giant Triton disporting himself amid the billows and tossing these great waves of sound from one hand to the other. You don't see his face, of course—nothing but his back, and yet you know every one of his emotions. Every sinew in his body speaks. He makes the instruments prolong the tones as no one else does, and the effect is indescribably beautiful, yet he complains that he never *can* get an orchestra to *hold* the tone as they ought. His whole appearance is of arrogance and despotism personified.

By the end of the concert the bouquets were so heaped on the stage in front of the director's desk, that Wagner had no place left big enough to stand on without crushing them. Altogether, it was a brilliant affair, and a great triumph for his friends. He has a great many bitter enemies here, however. Joachim is one of them, though it seems unaccountable that a man of his musical gifts should be. Ehlert is also a strong anti-Wagnerite, and the Jews hate him intensely.—Perhaps his character has something to do with it, for he has set all laws of honour, gratitude and morality at defiance all his life long. It is a dreadful example for younger artists, and I think Wagner is depraving them. In this country everything is forgiven to audacity and genius, and I must say that if Germany can teach *us* Music, we can teach *her* morals!

CHAPTER IX.

Difficulties of the Piano. Triumphal Entry of the Troops.
Paris.

BERLIN, *June* 25, 1871.

I have been learning Beethoven's G major Concerto
lately, and it is the most horribly difficult thing I've
ever attempted. I have practiced the first movement
a whole month, and I can't play it any more than I
can fly. If you hear Miss Mehlig play it, I trust you
will take in what a feat it is. Kullak gave me a regular rating over it at my last lesson, and told me I
must stick to it till I *could* play it. It requires the
greatest rapidity and facility of execution, and I get
perfectly desperate over it. Kullak took advantage
of the occasion to expand upon all the things an artist
must be able to do, until my heart died within me.
"What do you know of double thirds?" said he. I
had to admit that I knew nothing of double thirds,
and then he rushed down the piano like lightning
from top to bottom in a scale in double thirds, just as
if it were a common scale.

In one respect Kullak is a more discouraging teacher
than Tausig, for Tausig only played occasionally
before you, where it was absolutely necessary, and con-
tented himself with scolding and blaming. Kullak,
on the contrary, doesn't scold much, but as he plays
continually before and with you, with him you see

(123)

how the thing *ought* to be done, and the perception
of your own deficiencies stands out before you merci-
lessly. My constant thought is, "When *will* my passages pearl? When *will* my touch be perfectly equal?
When *will* my octaves be played from a lightly-hung
wrist? When *will* my trill be brilliant and sustained?
When *will* my thumb turn under and my fourth finger over without the slightest perceptible break?
When *will* my arpeggios go up the piano in that
peculiar *roll* that a genuine artist gives?" etc., etc.
All this gives a heavy heart, and so disinclines me to
write that you must excuse my frequent silences.

We are having such a horrid cold summer that I
sit and shiver all the time. I wish we could have a
little of the hot weather you speak of. I have put on
a muslin dress only once. Berlin is a very severe cli-
mate, I think.

The week before last was the triumphal entry or
"Einzug" of the troops. They all went past my window, so I had a full view of them. The Emperor had
made immense preparations, for he is very proud of
his army. All along the Königgrätzer Strasse (the
street we live in), to the Brandenburger Gate, a distance of two or three miles, were set tall poles at intervals of a few feet, connected by wreaths of green.
These were painted red and white, and had gilded pin-
nacles; they were surmounted by the Prussian flag,
which is black and white, with a black eagle in the
centre. About half way down the poles was set a coat
of arms, with the flags of the older German States
grouped about it. As they were of different colours,

the effect was very gay, and they made a triumphal
path of waving banners for the troops to pass under.
All along the last part of the Königgrätzer Strasse,
before you come to the Linden, were set the French
cannon which were captured, and on them was printed
the name of the place where the battle was, and one
read on them "Metz, Sedan, Strasburg," etc.   All up
the Linden, too, the way for the soldiers was hemmed
in on each side with cannon.   The mitrailleuses interested me the most, because they had thirty bores in
each one, and could fire as many balls in succession.
In this way, you see, a single cannon could *rain* shot.
Luckily the French aim so badly that they couldn't
have killed half so many Prussians as they expected.
On every Platz (as the Germans call the squares), were
columns and statues set up, and enormous scaffolds for
people to sit on, all decked out with flags and coloured
cloth.   In short, the whole city was got up in gala
array, and looked as gay as possible.

Of course there were thousands of strangers who had
come on to see it, and the streets were crowded.   For
about a week beforehand there was one continual stream
of people going by our house, and a long line of carriages and droschkies as far as one could see, creeping
along at a snail's pace behind each other.   I got worn out
with the noise and confusion long before the eventful
day came.   When it *did* arrive, already at six o'clock in
the morning, when I looked out of my window, the walls
of Prince Albrecht's garden opposite were covered with
boys and men, and there they had to sit until nearly twelve
o'clock, with their legs dangling down, and nothing to eat

or drink, before the procession came by, and *then* it
took four hours to pass! Such is German endur-
ance, and a still more striking instance of it was shown
by an orchestra stationed on the sidewalk opposite my
window. There were no seats or awnings for them, and
there they stood on the stones in the hot sun for fully
six hours, playing every little while on those heavy
French horns and trumpets. Just imagine it! I was
astonished that there was no scaffold erected for them
to sit on, and wondered how the poor fellows could *stand*
it.

Just before eleven o'clock the gate of Prince Albrecht's
garden flew open, and out he rode, accompanied by a
large suite, and they remained there awaiting the Emperor, who was to ride by on his way to meet the troops.
I wish you could have seen them in their superb uniforms,
seated on their magnificent horses. They looked like
knights of the olden time, with their embroidered saddle-
cloths and gay trappings. Preceding the Emperor came
the Empress and all the ladies of the royal family in
about ten carriages, each one with six horses and the
Empress's with eight. The ladies were gorgeously dressed,
of course, in light coloured silks with lace over-dresses.
Then came the Emperor and his escort, riding slowly and
majestically along. The enthusiasm was immense as they
passed by, and they were indeed a proud sight. Bismarck,
Moltke and Von Roon rode in one row by themselves. Bismarck looked very imposing in his uniform entirely of
white and silver, with enormous top-boots, and a brazen
helmet surmounted by a silver eagle. There was every
variety of uniform, and the Crown Prince looked very

handsome in his. He is a splendid-looking man, with a very soldierly bearing, and he rides to perfection.

The royal party went out to the parade ground, where they met the army, and then returned at the head of it, riding very slowly. Then, for four hours, the soldiers poured by at a very quick step. If you could have seen that *river* of men roll along, you would have some idea of the strength of this nation. They were tall for the most part, and their helmets and guns glittered in the sun. They were dressed in their old uniforms, just as they came from the field of battle. The people showered wreaths and bouquets upon them as they passed, and every man presented a festal appearance with his helmet crowned, a bouquet on the point of his bayonet, and flowers in his button hole. The Emperor's way was literally carpeted with flowers, and his grooms rode behind him picking them up, and hanging the wreaths upon their saddle-bows. Bismarck, Moltke and Von Roon and all the men of mark during the war were similarly favoured.

The army marched along at an astonishingly quick pace. I was surprised to see them walk so fast, heavily laden as they were with their guns and knapsacks and blankets, etc. Many of them had been marching a good part of the night to get to the place of rendezvous, and they had had a parade early in the morning. A good many of them fainted and had to be carried out of the ranks, and eight of them died ! It was the hottest day we have had this summer.—I was the most interested in the Uhlanen. They were the greatest terror of the French, and were light cavalry with no arms except

a large pistol and a lance. Just below the head of the
lance was a little Prussian flag attached, and nearly every
one was splashed with the blood of some poor Frenchman. When one looked at those terrible spikes, it
seemed a most dreadful death, and I don't wonder that
the French lost all courage at the sight of them. You
see, being on horseback and so lightly armed, the Uhlanen could go about like lightning, and were able to
appear suddenly at the most unexpected points. As I
was not on the Linden I did not see the army received at
the Brandenburger Gate by the four hundred young
ladies dressed in white, so I can't give you any account
of *that*. Bismarck, who always knows what to do, took
a handful of wreaths from his saddle-bow, and flung
them smilingly over among the welcoming maidens. He
is a courtly creature. I was nearly dead from just looking out of my window, and listening to the continual
music of the bands, and I did not get over the fatigue
and nervous excitement for several days; but I was very
fortunate to be able to see it from the house, for many
persons who had to sit on the scaffolds were dreadfully
burned, and were thrown into a fever by it. You see they
weren't allowed to put up their parasols, as that obscured
the view of the people behind them. I had one friend
who suffered awfully with her face, and did not sleep for
three nights. She said it was as if she had been burnt
by fire, and the whole skin peeled off.

July 4th.—As usual, it is over a week since I began
this letter, and I have just decided to start at once on a
summer journey with Mrs. and Miss V. N., Mr. P. and
Mrs., Mr. and Miss S. Kullak is away for his vaca-

tion, so I shall lose no lessons. We shall go first to Cologne and then to Bonn and Coblentz and down the Rhine. Perhaps we shall get as far as Heidelberg. We got one of those return tickets, which makes the journey very cheap; only you are limited to a certain time. We expect to be gone until the 1st of August. I intend to walk a great deal between the different points. Where the scenery is picturesque we shall occasionally walk from station to station. We take no baggage except a little bag (which we sling over our backs with straps), containing a change of linen and a brush and comb and tooth brush. We shall wear the same dress all the time and have our linen washed at the hotel. I thought it was a good chance for me, and as we shall be a party of embryo artists, we expect to go along in the Bohemian and happy-go-lucky style of our class. I think of writing a novel on the way! Won't it be romantic? Only, unluckily for Miss S. and myself, we shall have no adorers, as Mr. P. and Miss V. G. are engaged, and Mr. S. is only about eighteen!

Just before the Einzug I was at a party at the Bancroft's, and was standing near a doorway talking to one of N.'s class-mates in Harvard, when a portly gentleman pushed very rudely between us and stood there talking to Mr. Bancroft, who was on the other side of me. We gazed at him for a minute before we went on with our conversation. Presently the gentleman took his leave and bustled away. "That was the Duke of Somerset," said Mr. Bancroft to me. I was rather surprised, for I had just been thinking to my-

9

self, "What an unmannerly creature you are!"—I suppose he had come on to the Einzug.

Triumphant Berlin, by the way, is rather a contrast to Paris under the Commune. Such a horrible time as they have been having there! It is enough to make one's blood run cold to think of it. What insane barbarians they are—and the worst of it is the part the women take in it. I saw a picture of Thiers' house which they burnt down. It was a magnificent mansion, and crammed full of exquisite works of art. Mr. Bancroft grieved over it, for he had dined there, and knew what treasures it contained. He said it was one of the most beautiful houses he had ever been in. —And then the idea of pulling down the column of the Place Vendome! Napoleon had built it from cannon which he had captured in his great battles and melted down, so that in a special manner it was a monument of their victories over other nations. There is a stupidity about them which makes them perfectly pitiable.

[In 1848 Saint Beuve wrote the following almost prophetic words: "Nothing is 'swifter to decline in crises like the present (the Revolution of 1848) than civilization. In three weeks the result of many centuries are lost. Civilization, life, is a thing learned and invented. * * * * After years of tranquility men are too forgetful of this truth; they come to think that culture is innate, that it is the same thing as nature. But in truth barbarism is but a few paces off and begins again as soon as our hold is slackened."] —Ed.

CHAPTER X.

A Rhine Journey. Frankfort. Mainz. Sail down the Rhine.
Cologne. Bonn. The Seven Mountains. Worms.
Spire. Heidelberg. Tausig's Death.

ROLANDSECK AM RHEIN, *July* 14, 1871.

You will be surprised to get this letter, dated from
a little village on the Rhine, and I shall proceed to
tell you how I came here, if the vilest of vile paper
and pens will permit. I wrote a letter to L. just before I left Berlin, in which I informed her that I
meant to go on a little trip with a party of friends, as
Berlin in summer is malarious, and I felt the need of
a change.

Thursday a week ago we left Berlin and rode
straight through to Frankfort. It was a long journey, and lasted from six o'clock in the morning until
ten at night. I got up at four in the morning in a
most halcyon frame of mind. In fact, I felt as if I were
going to get married, owing to my putting on everything new from top to toe! The laundress had
made such ravages upon my linen that I found myself
suddenly obliged to replenish throughout, and consequently I arrayed myself with great satisfaction in
new stockings, new under-clothes, new flannel, new
skirts, new hat, new veil and new shoes to *boot!* I
put on my black silk short suit, took my bag and

shawl, and sallied to the station, where I found the others waiting for me.

It was a lovely ride from Berlin to Frankfort, and having been shut up in a city for nearly two years, the country appeared perfectly charming and new to me, and every little smiling tuft of daisies had a special significance. I don't know whether you stopped at Frankfort on your travels. I fell dead in love with it, and liked it better than any part of Germany I have seen. It is such a quiet town and has such an air of elegance, and there are such lovely walks all about. Everything looks so clean, and the streets are so handsomely laid out, and then there are no *smells*, as there are in Berlin. The river flows all along the outside of the city, and the promenade along it is delightful. I went to see the house where my adorable Goethe was born, and afterward walked over the bridge over which he used to go to school. There was a gilded cock perched upon it, which he used to be very fond of as a child. We saw his statue, and then visited the Museum where was Danecker's great masterpiece, Ariadne sitting on the Panther. It is the most exquisite thing, and it is cut out of one solid block of Carrara marble. Through a pink curtain a rosy light is thrown on it from above, which gives the marble a delicious tinge. Strange that he should have risen to such a poetic conception, and never done anything afterwards of importance.

We went into a great room where life-size pictures of all the Emperors of Germany were. Some of them are very handsome men, and the Latin mottoes underneath are very funny. One of them was: "If you don't know how to hold your tongue, you'll never know the right place to speak." I hope P. will keep L. well at her Latin and her history, and teach her something about architecture and mythology, for these one needs to know when one travels abroad. We only stayed one day in Frankfort, for there isn't a great deal to be seen there. The afternoon we spent in walking about and in sitting on logs by the river-side. Oh, what a sweet place one of those beautiful villas by the swiftly flowing river would be to live in!

We left Frankfort at seven P. M., and rode to Mainz, which is only a ride of two hours, I believe. As we came over the railroad bridge into the town, we got our first glimpse of the Rhine, and it was a splendid sight. Our hotel was very near the river, and as our rooms were front rooms, and three stories up, we had a magnificent view of it. In the evening it was so fascinating to watch the lights on the water and the boats plying up and down, that it was long before we could make up our minds to leave the windows and go to bed. At Mainz we saw our first cathedral. It is six hundred years old, and had suffered six times by fire, but it was very fine, notwithstanding. We spent a long time studying it out. Afterwards we visited another church and ascended a tower which was built 30, B. C. It seemed almost as firm as the day it was finished. The view from it is magnificent, and the top of it is all overgrown with harebells, golden rod and grass. It was very picturesque.

On Sunday evening we took the boat for Cologne

which we reached at four o'clock in the afternoon.
Oh, that sail down the Rhine was too delicious! The
weather was perfect, and everything seemed to me like
a fairy tale. It is one of the most beautiful parts of
the Rhine, and it was too lovely to see those old castles
in every degree of ruin, jutting out over the steep
rocks, so high in the air, and then the vineyards slop-
ing down the hillsides to the water's edge. The whole
lay of the land was so exquisite. I didn't wonder that
it is so celebrated, and that so much has been written
about it. A funny old Englishman came and sat beside me, and we had a long conversation, pretty much
as follows:

Englishman.—" England is no doubt the finest
country in the world. You know the people there are
so enormous rich, they can do as they please." " Ah,
indeed," said I, " have you travelled much in Germany?" " O yes! I've been all over Germany. I
come up the Rhine every year," said he. " It's all very
pretty when you've never seen it before, but it's nothing to me now." " Have you been to Berlin?" asked
I. " O yes," said he. " Shouldn't want to live there.
Your Prussians are so confounded arrogant. They
think they're the greatest people in the world." " How
did you like Dresden?" said I. "Stupid hole," said
he. " Leipsic?" " Dull town." " Stuttgardt?" " Quite
pretty." " Kissingen?" " 'Orrible place, nothing but
fanatics; every other day a Saint's day, and the shops
shut up." " Wiesbaden?" " Very fine place." " Ems?"
" Never been to Hems." " Mainz?" " Nasty hole."
" Cologne?" " Stinking place." " Munich?" " Dread-

ful unhealthy. They have fevers there, typhus, etc. *I* call 'em fevers." "How do you like the Rhine wines?" "Don't like them at all. It's very seldom a man gets to drink a decent glass of wine here. I don't drink 'em at all. I like a glass of port." "Beer?" "O, the German beer isn't fit to drink. The English beer is the best in the world. German beer is 'orrible bad stuff. Nothing but slops,—slops!" Here I burst out laughing, for his flattering descriptions were too much for me. He gave me a quizzical look and said, "Well, I'm glad I made you laugh. You're from America, aren't you?" "Yes," said I. "Very unhealthy place, I'm told." "Indeed? I never heard so," said I. "O yes, *very!*" said he. Then he went off, and after a long while he returned. "I've been asleep," said he, "I've slept two hours and a half, all through the fine scenery." "*What!*" said I, "don't you enjoy it?" "No, I don't enjoy it at all." Then he told me he lived in Rotterdam, and that I must come to Holland. He was very complaisant over the Dutch, whom he said were "nice, decent people, like the English. There's nothing of the German in them," said he, "they're quite another people—not so en-*thu*si-*as*tic,"—with a contemptuous air. We got out at Cologne, and he went on to his dear Rotterdam. So I saw him no more.

Oh! isn't the Cologne Cathedral magnificent? It quite took my breath away as I entered it. The priests were just having vespers as we went in, and there was scarcely a person in the cathedral beside. It was so solemn and so touching to see them all by themselves intoning the prayers, their voices swelling and falling in that vast place. And when the superb organ struck up, and they began to sing a hymn, so wildly sweet, with an interlude most beautifully worked up at the end of each line by the organist—as we sat there under those great arches which soar up to such an immense height, I felt as if I were in Heaven.

ANDERNACH, *July* 16, 1871.

I believe I left off in my last with our arrival at Cologne, of which I saw very little, as I was extremely tired, and remained at the hotel. The Cathedral was, of course, the main point of interest, and that I saw thoroughly, as I went to it twice, and spent a number of hours each time. I was entirely carried away by its beauty and grandeur, as everybody must be. The descriptions I had heard and the photographs I had seen of it didn't prepare me at all. The *height* of the great pile is one of the most astounding things, I think. The three and four story houses about it look like huts beside it. Beside the Cathedral I only saw the church where the eleven thousand virgins are buried, but that was more curious than beautiful.—I was much taken down by the shops in Cologne, which I think much finer than the Berlin ones, and saw no end of things in the windows I should like to have bought. The cravats alone quite turned my head !

We only spent two days in Cologne, and then sailed for Bonn, which is but a very short distance. Here we were in a hotel directly upon the river, and I had a sweet little room quite to myself. The view up and down the river was superb, and we could see the Seven Mountains most beautifully. Bonn is the most quiet, sleepy little town you can imagine, and just the place to study, I should think. We saw the house where Beethoven was born, a little yellow, two-story house, and then we visited the Minster, which is nine hundred years old. We saw there a tomb devoted to the memory of the first architect of the Cologne Cathedral, with his statue lying upon it. He had a severely beautiful face, and I could very well imagine him capable of such a great conception. We had great difficulty in getting a dinner at Bonn, as, being a university town, the students gobble up everything. Finally, we found a little restaurant where they got us up one, consisting of steak and potatoes. After dinner I went to walk with Mr. S. and we ate cherries all the way, and finally sat down on a bench by the river's side, where we had an enchanting view. Then we went back to the hotel, and I went directly to bed. It was delicious to lie there and hear the little waves washing up outside my window. It is just the place for a honey-moon—so out of the world as it seems, and with none of the activity and bustle of other cities.

At six o'clock the next morning we took the boat, and in about half an hour we landed at a little town on the side of the river opposite to Bonn, and began our pedestrian tour through the Seven Mountains, of which we ascended and descended four. They were all very steep and difficult to climb, and it reminded me of my trip to Mount Mansfield, years ago, only *then* we had horses.

We spent the night on one of them, the Löwen-berg (Lion-mountain). This was a funny experience, as all we five ladies had to sleep in one room, and in one great bed of straw made up on the floor. The fleas bit us all night, so we did not sleep *too* much. I mentioned the little fact to the servant next day, to which she replied, " Yes, when you are, n't used to fleas and bed-bugs, it *is* hard to sleep !" I agreed with her perfectly !—Our walk was enchanting in spite of the difficulty of the ascent, and of the fact that all of us had satchels slung over our shoulders, and a shawl and umbrella to carry, which made locomotion rather difficult. We were in the sylvan shades, following delicious footpaths scented with flowers, and with the birds singing and trilling as loud as they could over our heads.

It was heavenly on the Löwenberg, for the view was glorious on every side, and it seemed as if we were on the highest peak in the universe. I sat for hours looking over the lovely country and following the meanderings of the Rhine. The atmospheric effects produced by the sunset were wonderful, and when it got to be nine o'clock we saw the lights twinkle up one by one from the distant villages below like little earth-stars—reflections of the heavenly ones above. The last mountain we ascended was the Drachenfels (Dragon-rock), and a fearful pull it was. The three others had been so easy, comparatively, that we none of us knew what we were in for. Soon found out, though ! It was like trying to go up a wall, it was so steep. But when we got up we were rewarded, for the view was superb, and there was an interesting old Roman ruin up there. We wandered all about, and

got an excellent dinner, and then came down late in the
afternoon, took a row boat and rowed across the Rhine
to Rolandseck—a fashionable watering place, and as
charming as German towns have a way of being.

GOTHA, *July* 27, 1871.

Since I wrote you from Andernach I have been travelling steadily. The whole party except Mrs. V. N. and
myself made a pedestrian tour along the Rhine from
Rolandseck to Bingen, a distance of sixty miles. I
started to walk, but when I had gone fifteen miles I gave
out, and was glad to take the boat. Mrs. V. N. was an
invalid and couldn't walk, so I took charge of her, and
we would travel on together. When we got to the station where we had agreed to wait for the others, I would
seat her somewhere with the bags of the party piled up
around her, and then I would make a sortie, look at the
hotels, and engage our rooms.

We saw the Rhine from Cologne to Worms very thoroughly—for we kept stopping all along. It is truly magnificent, and nothing can be more interesting and picturesque than those old ruined castles which look as if
they had grown there. Bingen is the sweetest place, and
just the spot to spend a summer. We travelled from
there to Worms, which is a delightful old city. We
were there only an hour or two, but the walk from the
boat to the cars was through the prettiest part of it; I
should judge, and was very romantic, through winding
walks overshadowed with trees. We saw that great Luther
monument there, which is most imposing. The exterior

of the Cathedral is splendid, and in quite another style
of architecture from the Cologne Cathedral. From
Worms we went to Spire, in order to see the Cathedral
there, which is superb, and very celebrated. It was
founded in 1030 by Conrad the Second, as a burial place
for himself and his successors. It has no stained windows at all, even in the chancel, which surprised me, but
the frescoes and the whole interior colouring are gorgeous in the extreme. It is in the Romanesque style of
architecture, and is so entirely different from the Cologne
Cathedral that it was very interesting, but there's nothing equal to the Gothic, after all.

From Spire we went to Heidelberg. I was
enchanted with Heidelberg. It is the most romantic
and beautiful place I was ever in. The Castle is the
prince of ruins. I had made up my mind all along
that I was going to enjoy myself at Heidelberg, for
my friend Dr. S. was studying there, and I knew I
should have him to go about with. So I had been
urging the party to go there from the first. As soon
as we arrived, off I went to find him, which I soon
accomplished. He was very glad to see me, and put
himself at once at my disposal. You know the S.'s
used to live at Heidelberg, among other places, so he
knows it all by heart. After dinner we all went up to
the Castle, of course. I was very sorry that I had
never read Hyperion. We had to ascend a long hill
before we got to it, but the weather was perfect, so we
didn't mind. It is so high up that the view of the
town and of the Neckar winding through it, with the
wooded hills on the opposite shore, is panoramic.

The Castle itself is an enormous ruin, and very richly ornamented. Ivy two hundred years old climbs over it in great luxuriance. We passed through a gateway over which stand two stone knights which are said to change places with each other at midnight, and there are all sorts of charming stories like that connected with the place. We saw a beautifully carved stone archway which was put up in a single night, in honour of somebody's birthday, and a monument with an inscription over it stood in one corner of the grounds, stating that here had stood some distinguished personage (I always forget all the names, unluckily, but "the *principle* remains the same"), when the Castle was being besieged by the French. Two balls came from opposite directions, passed close by him, and struck against each other, miraculously leaving him unharmed!

After we had walked around the outside of the Castle sufficiently we went inside. It took us a long time to go over it, it was so large. We saw the stone dungeon, which was called the "Never Empty," because somebody was always confined there—a dreadful hole, and it must have been in perfect darkness—and we saw the great Heidelberg cask which had a scaffolding on the top of it big enough to dance a quadrille on. But the finest of everything was the ascending of the tower. Just as we got to the top of it, and had begun to take in the magnificent scenery, an orchestra at a little distance below struck up Wagner's " Kaiser March." It was the one touch which was needed to make the *ensemble* perfect. On one side the landscape lay far below us, with the silver river winding through it; on the other the hills rose behind the Castle to an immense height, and with the greatest boldness of outline. The tops were thickly wooded, and lower down the trees were beautifully grouped, and the velvety turf rolled and swelled to the foot of the Castle. The sun was just setting in a clear sky, and cast long shadows athwart the scene, and I thought I had never seen anything more striking. Then to hear Wagner's Kaiser March by a well-trained orchestra come soaring up, made a combination such as one gets perhaps not more than once in a life-time.

The march is superb, so pompous and majestic, and with delicious melodies occasionally interwoven through it. Wagner's melodies are so heavily and intoxicatingly sweet, that they are almost narcotic. His music excites a set of emotions that no other music does, and he is a great original. It has the power of expressing longing and aspiration to a wonderful degree, and it always seems to me as if two impulses were continually trying to get the mastery. The one is the embodiment of all those vague yearnings of the soul to burst its prison house, and the other is the cradling of the body in the lap of pleasure. I always feel as if I should like to swoon away when I hear his compositions. Then his harmonies are so strangely seductive, so complicated, so "grossartig," as the Germans say, and so peculiar! Oh, I have an immense admiration for him! He thinks that music is not the impersonation of an idea, but that it *is* the idea.

But to return to the Castle.—We stayed up in the

tower for some time, and then we made the tour of the
interior.   Afterwards we walked and sat about until
all the party thought it was time to go back to the hotel.   Dr. S. and I thought we would stay up there to
supper.   So we went where the orchestra was playing,
which was in an enclosed space near the Castle.   We
took our seats at a little table in the open air, and
ordered a delicious little supper, also

> " A bottle·of wine
> To make us shine "

in *conversation !*—and so glided by the most ideal evening, as far as surroundings go, that I ever spent.

In our hotel at Heidelberg I kept hearing a man
play splendidly in the room below us, and every time
we passed his door it was open, and we could partly
see the interior of a charming room with a grand piano
in it, at which he was seated.   A pretty woman was
always lying back in the corner of the sofa listening to
him, apparently.   The presence of a large wax doll indicated that there must be a child about, and the perfume of flowers stole through the open doorway.   My
interest was at once excited in these people, and I said
to myself as I heard this gentleman practice every day,
" This must be some artist passing the summer here
and getting up his winter programme."   Accordingly,
on Sunday afternoon when he was playing beautifully,
I roused myself up and enquired of a servant who he
was.   " Nicolai Rubinstein, from St. Petersburg," replied she.   He is the brother of the great Anton Rubinstein, and is nearly as fine a pianist.   I know a
scholar of Tausig's who had studied with him, and
Tausig had a high opinion of him.

Oh, isn't it *dreadful?*   When we were at Bingen we saw the news of Tausig's DEATH in the paper !   He died at Leipsic, on the 17th of July, of typhus fever, brought on by over-taxing his musical memory.   It was a dreadful blow to me, as you may imagine, and when I think of his wonderful playing silenced forever, and comparatively in the beginning of his career, I cannot get reconciled to it.   If you could have heard those matchlessly trained fingers of his, you would be able to sympathize with me on the subject.   I had counted so on hearing him next winter, for he gave no concerts in Berlin last winter.   He was only thirty-one years old !

CHAPTER XI.

Eisenach. Gotha. Erfurt. Andernach. Weimar. Tausig.

Well, here I am back in smelly old Berlin! I really hated to leave Heidelberg, it was such a paradisiacal spot, but we saw so much that was beautiful afterwards, that my impression of it has become a little dimmed. From Heidelberg we went to Eisenach, its rival in a different way, for here we went over the Wartburg—the Castle famous for having been the dwelling of the holy St. Elizabeth, and where Luther translated the Bible and spent ten months of his life disguised as a knight. I saw his room, a bare and comfortless hole, but with a splendid view from the windows. The Castle is in good repair, and is a noble pile. I suppose the Duke of Weimar spends some time there every summer, as it looks as if it were lived in. It is endlessly interesting. There is a lovely little chapel in it where Luther used to preach, with everything left in just as it was in his time—a little gem. The Wartburg is on a very high hill, and the views from it are superb. Among other things to be seen from it is the Venusberg, which is the mountain Wagner has introduced in his famous opera of Tannhäuser. He was so carried away by the Wartburg when he concealed himself near it, as he was being pursued by the government to be arrested as a revolutionary, twenty years ago, that

10   (145)

he never rested until he had united the legends of St. Elizabeth and of the Venusberg in his opera. Liszt, also, wrote an oratorio on St. Elizabeth as *his* tribute to the Wartburg.

From Eisenach we went to Gotha, a lovely place, all shaded with trees, and surmounted by a very imposing castle, with two immense towers. It is an enormous edifice, and is surrounded by a magnificent park, through which goes the slowly winding river. I believe that Gotha belongs to the Duke of Saxe-Coburg, brother of the Queen of England, or something. At all events, in the middle of this river is an island where the ducal family is buried, and it is so thickly planted with trees whose boughs hang over the water, that their graves are quite shrouded from the vulgar eye. Pretty idea! The river laps lazily against the grassy slope which covers the princely ones, and the wind rushing through the trees, sings their dirge.

From Gotha we went to Erfurt, where we only spent one night, in order to see the Cathedral. Erfurt is an Undine of a place, full of running streams and bridges and mills roaring all about you. I saw one street with a brook rippling down the very middle of it at a most rattling pace, and at every little distance two or three stepping stones by which to cross it. Just think how fascinating for children! I longed to stay and have a good play there myself. The Erfurt Cathedral is much smaller than those of Spire and Cologne, but the exterior is wonderfully beautiful. The transept is a masterpiece, and has fifteen enormous windows of rich old stained glass going round it. The nave did not please me so well, because in addition to its not being very rich, the side aisles were of equal height with the main body of the Cathedral, and were not sufficiently marked off from it to prevent the roof's looking like a ceiling. I believe the side aisles were of equal height with the main aisle in the Cologne Cathedral, but the archways and pillars cut them off more, so that it had a different effect.—I am more interested in cathedrals than anything else, and should like to travel all over Europe and see all the different ones. There is a lovely old church at Andernach, Roman Catholic, as most of the churches on the Rhine are. I went there to church one Sunday morning, and stayed through the service. They had the most powerful church music I've ever heard. There was an excellent boy choir which sang in unison and led the congregation, *every person* of which joined in. The organ was fine, as was also the organist, and the singing was so universal that the old church walls rang again. The priest preached an excellent sermon, too—the best I have heard in Germany.

BERLIN, *August* 31, 1871.

Germany is a most lovely country, and perfectly delicious to travel through. I believe I have described all the places we went to excepting Weimar. Weimar is delightful, and *so* interesting, because Goethe and Schiller, Wieland and Herder lived there, and everything is connected with them, and especially with the first two. There are many fine statues in the little

city, and a delicious great park along the river which
was laid out under Goethe's superintendence.—One
group of Goethe and Schiller standing together in
front of the theatre is magnificent. One hardly knows
which to admire the most, Goethe, with his courtly
mein and commanding features, or Schiller, with his
extreme ideality and his head a little thrown back as
if to take in inspiration direct from the sky. It is
a most striking conception.

The palace of the Grand Duke of Weimar is the
principal "show" of the place. It is filled with the
richest works of art, and is beautifully frescoed in
rooms devoted each to a particular author, and representing his most celebrated works.   There is the
Goethe room, and the Wieland room, etc.   The Wieland room is the most charming thing.   The frescoes on the walls are all illustrative of his "Oberon,"
which is his most celebrated work, and one picture
represents what happened when Oberon blew his horn.
You must know that when Oberon blows his horn
everybody is obliged to dance.   So in this picture he
is represented blowing it in a convent, and all the fat
friars and nuns are dancing away like mad. They
look so serious, and as if they didn't want to do it at
all, but their feet *will* fly up in the air in spite of them.
The nuns' slippers scarcely stick on, and it looks so
absurd ! I was as highly amused at it as the mischievous Oberon himself must have been, so delicately has
the artist touched it off.   There was another design
representing a band of nymphs dancing in the sky,
hand in hand in the twilight, and it was the most

graceful thing!—Their delicate little bare feet with every pretty turn a foot could have, their clothes and hair streaming in the breeze, and every attitude so airy. It was *lovely!* The Goethe frescoes were by another painter, and not so fine, but I prefer pictures to frescoes. Only one suite of the ducal rooms was frescoed. The others had superb pictures by the old masters, many of them originals.

The Duke is an artist himself, and designs a great many pretty things. For instance, he designed the large candelabra which stood on each side of one of the doorways,—Cupid peeping through a wreath of thistles and nettles. He was kneeling on one knee, and pushing them aside with each hand. It was all done in gilt metal and made a very dainty conceit, beside being a good illustration of the pains of love! I think the Duke probably designed some of the picture frames, for they were peculiarly rich and artistic; for instance, the frames of the original cartoons of Leonardo da Vinci's Last Supper were entirely composed of the leaves and flowers of the calla lily. The leaves lapped one over the other, and here and there a lily was laid between. The flowers were done in a different coloured gilding from the leaves. They were *very* beautiful. The pictures were not all hung together, so as to confuse your eye, but here a gem and there a gem—and O, I saw the most bewitching little statue there that ever I saw in my life! The subject was "Little Red Riding Hood," and it stood in the corner of one of the great salons. It was about two feet high, and represented the most fascinating little girl you can imagine, clothed in the wolf's skin, which hung down behind and had formed the little hood. The child herself was quite indescribable—the daintiest little creature, with the most captivating expression of innocence and roguishness. If she looked like that I should have followed the wolf's example and eaten her up! It was really a perfect little *pearl* of a statue. I would give anything to possess it. In short, I wish the Duke of Weimar were my intimate friend, for he must be a man worth knowing. Now, if I could only play like Liszt!—I don't wonder Liszt spends so much of his time in Weimar. I am getting perfectly crazy to hear him, by the way, for everybody says there is nobody in the world like him, and that he is the only artist who combines *everything*. He does not play in public any more, but Weitzmann says that he is amiability itself, and that it would probably not be difficult for me to get an opportunity to hear him in private.

In the palace I also saw the little boudoir of the Duchess. It was all panelled in white satin, and the furniture was of the richest white brocaded silk. The window frames were of malachite, and one looked out through the single great plate of glass on to the beautiful park, and the winding river spanned by a bridge which suggests immediately to your mind, "Walk over me into the Garden of Paradise, for I was made for your express benefit!" The park lies on each side of this little river Ilm, and Goethe's exquisite taste has given it more a look of nature than of art. It seems as if you were walking in a delicious meadow, the

trees being sometimes grouped together, sometimes
growing thickly along the water's edge. You go
in and out of sunshine and shadow, and here and
there are dusky little retreats, and, to borrow
Goldsmith's elegant style, — "the winding walks
assume a natural sylvage." Some distance up the
river, on the side of a gentle hill, was a small house in
the woods where Goethe used to live in summer.
Here he slept sometimes, and farther up the hill
was a summer house where he took his coffee after
dinner. To the left of this summer house he had had
made a long alley-way or vista of trees whose tops met
overhead and formed a leafy ceiling. It was like a
cloister, and here he could pace up and down and muse.
It was a delightful idea. To the right of the summer
house was a small garden, and beyond that was a path
which wound through the wood down to the path below.
In one of the rocks there Goethe had had a little poem
cut. I was sorry afterward that I hadn't copied it, it
was so pretty.—But it was such a charming place to
read and study, and it seemed to give me a better
impression of him than anything else.

I saw a piano in the Duke's palace upon which
Beethoven had played. It was a funny little instrument of about five octaves, but it was so wheezy with
age that there wasn't much tone to be got out of it.
After we had finished looking at the palace, we went
over to see the ducal library. Here I saw a superb
bust of Goethe as a young man. It was so handsome
that it spurns description. He must have been a
perfect Apollo. I also saw a likeness of him painted

upon a cup by some great artist, for which he sat
thirty-four times! The old librarian, who had known
Goethe, said that it was *exactly* like him, and the min-
iature painting was so wonderful that when you looked
at it with a magnifying glass it was only finer and
more accurate instead of less so! There was also a
most noble bust of the composer Glück. The face
was all scarred with small-pox, so that the cast must
must have been moulded from his features after death,
but I never saw such a living, animated, likeness in
marble. It looked as if it were going to speak to you.
There was a funny toy there, nearly three hundred
years old. It was a drummer boy, with a little baby
strapped on his back. The librarian wound him up,
and then he beat his drum lustily, rolled his eyes from
side to side, and wagged his head, while the baby
on his back hopped up and down. Whenever little
children see it, it scares them, and they begin to cry.
It had on a red flannel coat, and hasn't had a new one
since it was made.—"Nearly three hundred years old,
and never had a new coat," is worse than when C.
P. bought himself a trunk, and went round the
house saying, "Twenty-seven years old, and been in
twenty-three states of the Union, and *never* had a
new trunk before!"

Goethe's house is not exhibited, which I think
highly inexcusable in the Goethe family, but Schiller's
is. So we saw that, and what a contrast it was to the
ducal palace!—You go to a small yellow house on one
of the principal streets, enter a little hall by a little
door, go up two flights of a little stair-case, and in the

very low-ceilinged third story was Schiller's home—
"home" I say, and the *whole* of it, so please take it in!
The first room you enter is a sort of ante-room where
photographs are now sold. The next room was the
parlour, and of late years it has been comfortably furnished by the ladies of Weimar in the usual cheap
German taste. The third room was Schiller's study,
with an infinitesimal fourth room, or large closet,
opening from it, which was his sleeping apartment. The study is precisely as he left it, and
nothing could be more bald and bare. No carpet on the floor, the three windows slightly festooned at the top with a single breadth of Turkey red,
his own portrait and a few wretched prints on the walls
—in short, such a sordid habitation for such a soaring
nature as seemed almost incredible! His writing table,
with a globe, inkstand, and pens upon it, stands at one
window, and his wife's tiny little piano with her guitar
on top, is against the wall. There are two or three
chairs, and a wash-stand with a minute washing appa-
ratus. In one corner is the tiny unpainted wooden
bedstead on which he died; a bed not meant to stretch
out in, but to lie, as Germans do, half reclining, and
so low, narrow, plain and mean that I never saw anything like it. In it and hanging on the wall over it
are wreaths which leading German actresses have
brought there as votive offerings to their great national
dramatist, their white satin ribbons yellowing by time.
At the foot of the stair-case as you go out, you see the
little walled-up garden at the back of the house where
the poet loved to sit.

After getting through with the abodes of the living, we visited the ducal vault where Goethe and Schiller are buried. It is the crypt of a sort of temple built in the old secluded cemetery in Weimar, and in it all the coffins are laid in rows on supporters. Goethe and Schiller lie apart from the others, side by side, near the foot of the stair-case leading down into the crypt. Their coffins, especially Schiller's, are covered with wreaths and bouquets brought by strangers and laid there. Schiller's had on it a garland of silver leaves presented by the women of Hamburg, and another of leaves of green gauze or crape, on every one of which was worked in gold thread the name of one of his plays. A great actress had made it herself as her tribute to his genius. From all I observe, I should judge that the German people love Schiller much more than they do Goethe. The dukes and duchesses lie farther back in the vault in their red velvet coffins, quite unnoticed. So much better is genius than rank! Hummel is buried also in the cemetery, which is the most beautiful I ever saw—not stiff and "arranged" like ours, but so natural! with over-grown foot-paths, and with much fewer and simpler grave-stones and monuments, and many more vines and flowers and roses creeping over the graves. We went to Hummel's grave, and had I been Goethe and Schiller I should much rather have been buried out of doors like him, amid this sweet half-wild, half-gentle nature, than in that dismal vault.

Speaking of Hummel reminds me of Tausig's death. Was it not terrible that he should have died so young!

Such an enormous artist as he was! I cannot get reconciled to it at all, and he played only twice in Berlin last winter.

He was a strange little soul—a perfect misanthrope. Nobody knew him intimately. He lived all the last part of his life in the strictest retirement, a prey to deep melancholy. He was taken ill at Leipsic, whither he had gone to meet Liszt. Until the ninth day they had hopes of his recovery, but in the night he had a relapse, and died the tenth day, very easily at the last. His remains were brought to Berlin and he was buried here. Everything was done to save him, and he had the most celebrated physicians, but it was useless. So my last hope of lessons from him again is at an end, you see! I never expect to hear such piano-playing again. It was as impossible for him to strike one false note as it is for other people to strike right ones. He was absolutely infallible. The papers all tell a story about his playing a piece one time before his friends, from the notes. The music fell upon the keys, but Tausig didn't allow himself to be at all disturbed, and went on playing through the paper, his fingers piercing it and grasping the proper chords, until some one rushed to his aid and set the notes up again. Oh, he was a wonder, and it is a tragic loss to Art that he is dead. He was such a *true* artist, his standard was so immeasurably high, and he had such a proud contempt for anything approaching clap-trap, or what he called *Spectakel*. I have seen him execute the most gigantic difficulties without permitting himself a sign of effort beyond an almost imperceptible compression of one

corner of his mouth.—And then his touch! Never
shall I forget it!—that *rush* of silver over the keys.
However, he entirely overstrained himself, and his
whole nervous system was completely shattered long
before his illness.   He said last winter that the very
idea of playing in public was unbearable to him, and
after he had announced in the papers that he would
give four concerts, he recalled the announcement on the
plea of ill health.   Then he thought he would go to
Italy and spend the winter.   But when he got as far
as Naples, he said to himself, "*Nein, hier bleibst du
nicht* (No, you won't stay here) ;" and back he came
to Berlin.   He doesn't seem to have known what he
wanted, himself; his was an uneasy, tormented,
capricious spirit, at enmity with the world.   Perhaps
his marriage had something to do with it.   His wife
was a beautiful artist, too, and they thought the world
of each other, yet they couldn't live together.   But
Tausig's whole life was a mystery, and his reserve was
so complete that nobody could pierce it.   If I had only
been at the point in music two years ago that I am
now, I could have gone at once into his class.   His
scholars were most of them artists already, or had got
to that point where they had pretty well mastered the
technique.   A number of them came out last winter,
and the little Timanoff played duets with Rubinstein
for two pianos, at St. Petersburg.

Since my return I have gone into the first class in
Kullak's conservatory, instead of taking private lessons
of him.   I think it will be of use to me to hear his
best pupils play.

CHAPTER XII.

Dinner-Party and Reception at Mr. Bancroft's.   Auction at
Tausig's House.   A German Christmas.
The Joachims.

BERLIN, *October* 2, 1871.

This week I have been to a dinner-party at the Bancroft's.   There were several eminent Germans there,
and I was taken out by Bötticher, the Herr who has
arranged all the casts in the Museum, and who knows
everything about Art.   He couldn't speak a word of
English, so we *Germaned* it.   We talked about Sap-
pho all through dinner, and he gave me several details
about that young woman which I did not know before.
As C. used to say, we had one of those dinners " such
as you read about in the Arabian Nights," topping off
with a glass of my favourite Tokay, which, I regret to
say, I so prolonged the pleasure of drinking, that
finally the signal was given to adjourn to the drawing-
room, and I was obliged to leave my glass standing
half full, to be swallowed by the waiter as soon as my
back was turned.   Sad, but true !

On another evening, at a Bancroft reception, I
talked with a Miss R., who was charming.   She is
twenty-two or three, I should think, very pretty
and extremely elegant, and with the most delicious way of speaking you can imagine.   Such softness of manner and such a delightfully pitched voice,

and then along with this perfect repose, such a
vivid way of describing things! I was immensely
taken with her, and was delighted to have her for a
countrywoman. She gave me a wonderful account
of the Island of Java. I had a lot of questions to ask
her, for you remember how persistently I read that
book by a naturalist (Wallace) who went to Java in
search of the Bird of Paradise. Miss R. is so extremely intelligent, and yet so unassuming; and then
this high-bred manner.—I did not have time to hear
her talk half enough, and, unfortunately, her party
went away the next day.

The other day was an auction in poor little Tausig's
house, and all his furniture was sold. It was very
handsome, all of solid oak, beautifully carved. He
had spent five thousand thalers on it. His wardrobe
was sold, too, and I don't know how many pairs of his
little boots and shoes were there, his patent leather
concert boots among others. His little velvet coat
that he used to wear went with the rest. I saw it
lying on a chair. I came home quite ill, and was
laid up two days. It was the fatigue, I suppose, and
miserable reflections. I wanted to buy a picture, but
they were all sold in a lot. He had excellent ones of
all the great composers, down to Liszt and Wagner,
hanging over his piano in the room where he always
played. Kullak deplores Tausig's death very deeply.
He had visited him in Leipsic two days before he was
taken ill, and said no one would have dreamed that
Tausig was going to die, he looked so well. Kullak
said Tausig was one of the three or four great *special*

pianists. " Who will interpret to us so again?" said he ; and I echoed, sadly enough, " Who, indeed?"

Kullak, by the way, is a wonderfully *finished* teacher. He is a great friend of Liszt's, and Liszt has taught him a good many things. I doubt, however, how M. will fare with him, if she is only going to be here a year. My experience is that it takes fully a year to get started under a first class master. These great teachers won't take a pupil raw from America, still less trouble themselves with a scholar who cannot immediately comprehend. I have written her to-day a three-sheet letter in which I have set forth the disadvantages of Germany in a sufficiently forcible manner to prevent her feeling disappointed if she still insists upon the journey. I have come to the conclusion that I am no criterion as to other people's impressions. Unless people have an enthusiasm for art I don't see the least use in their coming abroad. If they cannot appreciate the *culture* of Europe, they are much better off in America. There is no doubt whatever that as to the *comfort* of every-day life, we are a long way ahead of every nation, unless perhaps the English, whom, however, I have not seen.

———

BERLIN, *December* 25, 1871.

To-day is Christmas-day, and I have thought much of you all at home, and have wondered if you've been having an apathetic time as usual. I think we often spend Christmas in a most shocking fashion in America, and I mean to revolutionize all that when I get

back.   So long a time in Germany has taught me better.   Here it is a season of universal joy, and *every-*
body enters into it.   Last night we had a Christmas
tree at the S.'s, as we always do.   We went there at
half past six, and it was the prettiest thing to see in
every house, nearly, a tree just lighted, or in process
of being so.   As a separate family lives on each floor,
often in one house would be three trees, one above the
other, in the front rooms.   The curtains are always
drawn up, to give the passers-by the benefit of it.   They
don't make a fearful undertaking of having a Christmas tree here, as we do in America, and so they are
attainable by everybody.   The tree is small, to begin
with, and nothing is put on it except the tapers and
bonbons.   It is fixed on a small stand in the centre of
a large square table covered with a white cloth, and
each person's presents are arranged in a separate pile
around it.   The tree is only lighted for the sake of
beauty, and for the air of festivity it throws over the
thing.—After a crisp walk in the moonlight (which
I performed in the style of "Johnny-look-up-in-the
air," for I was engaged in staring into house-windows,
so far as it was practicable), we sat down to enjoy a
cup of tea and a piece of cake.   I had just begun my
second cup, when, Presto ! the parlour doors flew open,
and there stood the little green tree, blossoming out
into lights, and throwing its gleams over the well-laden
table.   There was a general scramble and a search
for one's own pile, succeeded by deep silence and suspense while we opened the papers.   Such a hand shaking and embracing and thanking as followed ! conclud-

ing with the satisfactory conviction that we each had
"just what we wanted." Germans do not despise the
utilitarian in their Christmas gifts, as we do, but, between these and their birthday offerings, expect to be
set up for the rest of the year in the necessaries of life
as well as in its superfluities. Presents of stockings,
under-clothes, dresses, handkerchiefs, soaps—nothing
comes amiss. And every one *must* give to every one
else. That is LAW.

I have just heard a young artist from Vienna who
made a great impression on me. His name is Ignaz
Brühl. He is quite exceptional, and has not only a
brilliant technique, but also a peculiar and beautiful
conception.—But the best concert I have heard this
season was one given by Clara Schumann a week ago
last Monday. She was assisted by Joachim and his
wife, and *that* galaxy is indeed unequalled. Frau
Joachim sings deliciously. Not that her voice is so
remarkable. You hear such voices all the time. But
she manages it consummately, and sings German songs
as no one but a German *could* sing them. Indeed I
never heard any woman approach her in unobtrusive
yet perfect art. She does not take you by storm, and
when I first came here I did not think much of her,
but every time I hear her I am struck with how exquisite it is. Every word takes on a meaning, and on this
account I think you have to understand the language
before you can realize the beauty of it. One of her
songs was Schumann's "Spring Song," with that rapid
agitato accompaniment, you know.—She came out and
started off in it with a half breath and a tremor just

11

like a bird fluttering up out of its nest, and then went up on a portamento with *such* abandon !—like the bird soaring off in its flight. I never *shall* forget that effect ! Of course it carried you completely away.

Beside singing so admirably she is a beauty—a sort of baby beauty—and when she comes out in a pale pink silk, contrasting with her dark hair and revealing her imperial neck and arms, she is ravishing. I've been told she wasn't anything remarkable when Joachim married her. No doubt dwelling with such a genius has developed her. They say that Joachim has had such a happy life that he wants to live for-ever ! He certainly does overtop everything. On this occasion he played Beethoven's great Kreutzer Sonata for violin and piano, with Clara Schumann, and I thought it the *most magnificent performance I ever heard !* I perfectly adore Joachim, and consider him the wonder of the age. It is simple ecstasy to listen to him.

CHAPTER XIII.

Visit to Dresden. The Wiecks. Von Bülow. A Child Prodigy. Grantzow, the Dancer.

BERLIN, *February* 10, 1872.

A week ago last Monday I went to Dresden with J. L. to visit B. H. We got there at about five in the afternoon, and were met at the station by B.'s maid, who conducted us straightway to their house in Christian Strasse. B. and Mrs. H. received us with the greatest cordiality, and we had a splendid time. I came home only the day before yesterday, and J. is still there. The H.'s have a charming lodging, and Mrs. H. is a capital housekeeper. The *cuisine* was excellent, and you can imagine how I enjoyed an American breakfast once more, after nothing but "rolls and coffee" for two years. B. did everything in her power to amuse us, and she is the soul of amiability. She kept inviting people to meet us, and had several tea-parties, and when we had no company she took us to the theatre or the opera. She invited Marie Wieck (the sister of Clara Schumann) to tea one night. I was very glad to meet her, for she is an exquisite artist herself, and plays in Clara Schumann's style, though her conception is not so remarkable. Her touch is perfect. At B.'s request she tried to play for us, but the action of B.'s piano did not suit her, and she presently got up, saying that she could do nothing on that instrument, but that if we would come to *her*, she would play for us with pleasure.

I was in high glee at that proposal, for I was very anxious to see the famous Wieck, the trainer of so many generations of musicians. Fräulein Wieck appointed Saturday evening, and we accordingly went. B. had instructed us how to act, for the old man is quite a character, and has to be dealt with after his own fashion. She said we must walk in (having first laid off our things) as if we had been members of the family all our lives, and say, "Good-evening, Papa Wieck,"— (everybody calls him Papa). Then we were to seat ourselves, and if we had some knitting or sewing with us it would be well. At any rate we must have the apparent intention of spending several hours, for nothing provokes him so as to have people come in simply to call. "What!" he will say, "do you expect to know a celebrated man like me in half an hour?" then (very sarcastically), "perhaps you want my autograph!" He hates to give his autograph.

Well, we went through the prescribed programme. We were ushered into a large room, much longer than it was broad. At either end stood a grand piano. Otherwise the room was furnished with the greatest simplicity. My impression is that the floor was a plain yellow painted one, with a rug or two here and there. A few portraits and bas-reliefs hung upon the walls. The pianos were of course fine. Frau Wieck and "Papa" received us graciously. We began by taking tea, but soon the old man became impatient, and said, "Come! the ladies wish to perform (*vortragen*) something before me, and if we don't begin we shan't accomplish anything." He *lives* entirely in music, and has a class of girls whom he instructs every evening for nothing. Five of these young girls were there. He is very deaf, but strange to say, he is as sensitive as ever to every musical sound, and the same is the case with Clara Schumann. Fräulein Wieck then opened the ball. She is about forty, I should think, and a stout, phlegmatic-looking woman. However, she played superbly, and her touch is one of the most delicious possible. After hearing her, one is not surprised that the Wiecks think nobody can teach touch but themselves. She began with a nocturne by Chopin, in F major. I forgot to say that the old Herr sits in his chair with the air of being on a throne, and announces beforehand each piece that is to be played, following it with some comment: *e. g.*, "This nocturne I allowed my daughter Clara to play in Berlin forty years ago, and afterward the principal newspaper in criticising her performance, remarked: 'This young girl seems to have much talent; it is only a pity that she is in the hands of a father whose head seems stuck full of queer new-fangled notions,'—so new was Chopin to the public at that time." That is the way he goes on.

After Fräulein Wieck had finished the nocturne, I asked for something by Bach, which I'm told she plays remarkably. She said that at the moment she had nothing in practice by Bach, but she would play me a *gigue* by a composer of Bach's time,—Haesler, I think

she said, but cannot remember, as it was a name
entirely unknown to me. It was very brilliant, and
she executed it beautifully. Afterward she played the
last movement of Beethoven's Sonata in E flat major,
but I wasn't particularly struck with her conception
of that. Then we had a pause, and she urged me to
play. I refused, for as I had been in Dresden a week
and had not practiced, I did not wish to sit down and
not do myself justice. My hand is so stiff, that as
Tausig said of himself (though of him I can hardly
believe it), "When I haven't practiced for fourteen days
I can't do anything." The old Herr then said, "Now
we'll have something else;" and got up and went to
the piano, and called the young girls. He made three
of them sing, one after the other, and they sang very
charmingly indeed. One of them he made improvise
a *cadenza*, and a second sang the alto to it without
accompaniment. He was very proud of that. He exercises his pupils in all sorts of ways, trains them to sing
any given tone, and "to skip up and down the ladder,"
as they call the scale.

After the master had finished with the singing,
Fräulein Wieck played three more pieces, one of which
was an exquisite arrangement by Liszt of that song by
Schumann, *"Du meine Seele."* She ended with a
gavotte by Glück, or as Papa Wieck would say, "This
is a gavotte from one of Glück's operas, arranged by
Brahms for the piano. To the superficial observer the
second movement will appear very easy, but in *my*
opinion it is a very hard task to hit it exactly." I happened to know just how the thing ought to be played,

for I had heard it three times from Clara Schumann herself. Fräulein Wieck didn't please me at all in it, for she took the second movement twice as quickly as the first. "Your sister plays the second movement much slower," said I. "*So?*" said she, "I've never heard it from her." She then asked, "So slow?" playing it slower. "Still slower?" said she, beginning a third time, at my continual disapproval. "*Streng im Tempo* (in strict time)", said I, nodding my head oracularly. "*Väterchen.*" called she to the old Herr, "Miss Fay says that Clara plays the second movement *so* slow," showing him. I don't know whether this correction made an impression, but he was then *determined* that I should play, and on my continued refusal he finally said that he found it very strange that a young lady who had studied more than two years in Tausig's and Kullak's conservatories shouldn't have *one* piece that she could play before people." This little fling provoked me, so up I jumped, and saying to myself, "*Kopf in die Höhe, Brust heraus,—vorwärts!*" (one of the military orders here), I marched to the piano and played the fugue at the end of Beethoven's A flat Sonata, Op. 110. They all sat round the room as still as so many statues while I played, and you cannot imagine how dreadfully nervous I was. I thought fifty times I would have to stop, for, like all fugues, it is such a piece that if you once get out you never can get in again, and Bülow himself got mixed up on the last part of it the other night in his concert. But I got well through, notwithstanding, and the old master was good enough to commend me warmly.

He told me I must have studied a great deal, and asked me if I hadn't played a great many *Etuden*. I informed him in polite German " He'd better believe I had !"

I should like to study with the Wiecks in my vacation next summer if they would take me. Perhaps I may. They are considered somewhat old-fashioned in their style, and I shouldn't wish to exchange Kullak for them, but they are *such* veterans that one could not help getting many valuable ideas from them. Papa Wieck used to be Bülow's master before he went to Liszt.

Did I tell you how carried away with Bülow I was? He is magnificent, and just between Rubinstein and Tausig. I am going to hear him again on Saturday, and then I'll write you my full opinion about him. He is famous for his playing of Beethoven, and I wish you could have heard the Moonlight Sonata from him. One thing he does which is entirely peculiar to himself. He runs all the movements of a sonata together, instead of pausing between. It pleased me very much, as it gives a *unity* of effect, and seems to make each movement beget the succeeding one.

BERLIN, *May* 30, 1872.

I wish L. were here studying piano with Kullak's son. He has one little fairy of a scholar ten years old. Her name is Adele aus der Ohe—(isn't that an old knightly name?)—and it is the most astonishing thing to hear that child play ! I heard her play a concerto of Beethoven's the other day with orchestral accompaniment and a great cadenza by Moscheles, absolutely *perfectly*. She never missed a note the whole way through. I suppose she will become, like Mehlig, a great artist. But perhaps, like her, she won't have a great conception, but will do everything mechanically. One never can tell how these child-prodigies will turn out.—Please don't form any exalted ideas of *my* playing! I'm a pretty stupid girl, and go forward slowly. I never expect to play as Miss Mehlig does. If I can ever get up to Topp, I shall be satisfied. You wouldn't believe how long it takes to get to be a virtuoso unless you tried it. Mehlig, you know, studied steadily for ten years, under the *best* of teaching all the time, and she had probably more talent to start with than I have. Miss V. and Mr. G. have been here *five* years studying steadily, and they are no farther than I am now. Not so far. It makes all the difference in the world what kind of hand and wrist a person has. Mine, you know, were pretty stiff, and then it is a great disadvantage to begin studying after one is grown up. One ought to be learning while the hand is forming.

I am just now learning that A minor concerto of Schumann's that Topp played at the Handel and Haydn Festival in Boston. The cadenza is tough, I can tell you. That is the worst of these concertos. There is always a grand cadenza where you must play all alone and "make a splurge." I don't know how it feels to be left all at once without any support from the orchestra. It is bad enough when Kullak

lies back in his chair and ceases accompanying me.
He plays with me on two pianos, and I get so excited
that my wrists tremble. He is a magnificent pianist,
and his technique is perfect. There's nothing he
can't do. Like all artists, he is as capricious and exasperating as he can be, and, as the Germans say, he
is " *ein Mal im Himmel und das nächste Mal im Kel-
ler* (one time in heaven and the next time in the cel-
lar) !" He has a deep rooted prejudice against Americans, and never loses an opportunity to make a
mean remark about them, and though he has some
remarkably gifted ones among his scholars, he always
insists upon it that the Americans have no real talent.
As far as I know anything about his conservatorium
just now, his *most* talented scholars are Americans.
There is a young fellow named Sherwood, who is only
seventeen years old, and he not only plays splendidly
but composes beautifully, also. In my own class Miss
B. and I are far ahead of all the others. Kullak will
praise us very enthusiastically, and then when some
one plays particularly badly in the class he will say to
them, " Why, Fräulein, you play exactly as if you
came from America." It makes Miss B. and me so
indignant that we don't know what to do. Of course we
can't say anything, for he addresses this remark in a
lofty way to the whole class. Miss V. couldn't
bear Kullak, and the other day, when she and Mr. G.
were taking leave of him to go to America, she let him
see it. He said to her, " And when shall I see you
again ?" "*Never*," exclaimed she ! We have only one
way of revenging ourselves, and that is when he gives

us the choice of taking one of his compositions or a piece by some one else, always to take the other person's. For instance, he said to me, "Fräulein, you can take Schumann's concerto or *my* concerto." I immediately got Schumann's.

The other night I went to see a great ballet-dancer. Her name is Fräulein Grantzow, and she is the court dancer at St. Petersburg, where I've heard that the ballet surpasses everything of the kind in the world. This danseuse is a wonder, and they say there has never been such dancing since the days of Fanny Ellsler. She has the figure of a Venus, and the most expressive face imaginable. When she dances, it is not only dancing, but a complete representation of character, for she plays a rôle by her motions just the same as if she were an actress. I have seen many a ballet, but I never conceived what an art dancing is before. I saw her in "Esmeralda," a ballet which is arranged from Victor Hugo's romance and modified for the stage. Fräulein Grantzow took the part of Esmeralda. In the first act a man is condemned to death, but is pardoned on condition that one of the women present will promise to marry him. The women, represented by about fifty ballet dancers, come up one after the other, contemplate the poor victim, pirouette round him, and reject him in turn with a gesture of contempt. At last Esmeralda (a gypsy) comes dancing along, asks what is the matter, and on being told, has compassion on the poor wretch, and promises to marry him in order to save him from his fate.

When the time came for Grantzow to appear, the

crowd of dancers suddenly divided, and she bounded
out from the back of the stage. *Such* an appari-
tion as she was! In the first place her toilettes sur-
passed everything, and she appeared in a fresh dress
in every act. In this first one she had on a most dazzling shade of green gauze for her skirt. From her
waist fell a golden net-work, like a cestus, with littl¡
golden tassels all round. She wore a little scarlet
satin jacket all fringed with gold coins, and a broad
golden belt, pointed in front, clasped her waist. On
her head was a tiny scarlet cap, also fringed with coins,
and she had some golden bangles round her neck. In
her hand was a tambourine from which depended four
knots of coloured ribbons with long ends. Shaking
her tambourine high in the air, out she sprang like a
panther, made one magnificent circuit all round the
stage, and after executing an immensely difficult *pas*
with perfect ease, she suddenly posed to the audience
in the most ravishing and impossible attitude and with
the most captivating grace conceivable. Anything like
her *élan*, her *aplomb*, I never saw. Such a daring creature! Well, I cannot tell you all the things she did.
She is a perfect Terpsichorean genius. All through
the first act she danced very slowly, merely to show
her wonderful grace, and the beauty and originality of
her positions. She had a way of folding her arms over
her breast and dancing with a dreamy step that was
quite different from anybody else, and it produced an
entrancing effect. Through the second and third acts
she made a regular crescendo, just to display her technique and show what she could do. All the other

dancers seemed like blocks of wood in comparison with her.—Fräulein Grantzow is said to be between thirty-five and thirty-eight years old. As the papers said, her art shows the perfection that only maturity can give. The men are all crazy over her, as you may imagine, and she was showered with bouquets as large as the top of a barrel. The play of her features was as extraordinary as the play of her muscles. Her whole being seemed to be the soul of motion.

CHAPTER XIV.

A Rising Organist. Kullak. Von Bülow's Playing.
A Princely Funeral. Wilhelmj's Concert.
A Court Beauty.

BERLIN, *July* 1, 1872.

Since I have been here X. has gradually developed into a great organ player, and I fancy he is now one of the first organ virtuosi in the world. His musical activity is immense, and I don't doubt he will be one of the great musical authorities here by the time he is a few years older. He is a good-hearted little demon, the incarnation of German dirt and good humour, and he pretends to be desperately devoted to me. Last Sunday he was at M.'s and went home with us afterward. Generally I go in front with A. or Herr J. and let X. give his arm to M., but this time I accorded him the honour of taking it myself. He is about a foot shorter than I am, but he trotted along by my side in a state of high satisfaction, and asked me what he should play at this concert. I told him he might play the G Minor Prelude and Fugue, as I had just taken it, *"but,"* said I, "mind you play it well, for I shall study it very hard during the next fortnight, and I shall know if you strike one false note. I'll allow you six faults, but if you make one more I'll beat you." This amused him highly, but he said, "It is a very com-

plicated fugue, and it isn't so easy to play it perfectly,
with all the pedal passages.   What will you do for me
if I come off without making *one* fault?"   I told him
there was plenty of time to think about that, and I
didn't believe he could.   I have no doubt that he *will*
play it magnificently, but I love to plague him.   I wish
that his department were secular rather than church
music, for if he were only a conductor of an orchestra,
or something of that sort, he could give me many a lift.
He doesn't dare play the piano any more since I played
to him a few times.   He used nearly to kill me with his
extemporizations, for he has no memory, and so he
always had to extemporize.   I generally went off into
a secret convulsion of laughter when he went bang!
bang! Donner and Blitz!—splaying all over the key-
board.   It was the funniest thing I ever heard, and when
I heard him burst forth in such grand style on the organ, I was perfectly amazed, and couldn't reconcile
it with his piano playing at all.   He is a great reader,
of course, and can transpose at sight, and all that sort
of thing.   I've known him to play accompaniments at
sight in a great concert in the Dom and transpose
them at the same time!

July 6.—You ask me why I gave up going to the
Wiecks in Dresden this summer.—Because they make
everybody begin at the very beginning of their system
and go through it before they give them a piece, and
at my stage of progress that would be losing time.
They think nobody can teach touch but themselves,
but Kullak is a much greater musician, and I should
not be willing to exchange him for Fräulein Wieck,

who does not begin to equal him in reputation. Much as Kullak enrages me, I have to admit that he is a great master, and that he is thoroughly capable of developing artistic talent to the utmost. He makes Miss B. so provoked that she had very strong thoughts of going to Stuttgardt. The Stuttgardt conservatorium is so crowded that it is very difficult to get admission. Lebert (Mehlig's master,) sent word on her writing to enquire, that he would only take her on condition that she brought him a letter from Kullak authorizing her leaving him, as Kullak was a personal friend of his own, and so great an artist, that only the most important reasons could justify her giving up his instructions! Of course that put the stopper on any such movement.

I've always forgotten to describe Bülow's playing to you, and it is now so long since I heard him that my impressions of it are not so vivid. He has the most forcible style I ever heard, and phrases wonderfully. It is like looking through a stereoscope to hear him. All the points of a piece seem to start out vividly before you. He makes me think of Gottschalk a little, for he is full of his airs. His expression is proud and supercilious to the last degree, and he looks all round at his audience when he is playing. He always has two grand pianos on the stage, one facing one way, and one the other, and he plays alternately on both. His face seems to say to his audience, " You're all cats and dogs, and I don't care what you think of my playing." Sometimes a look of infinite humour comes over it, when he is playing a rondo or anything gay. It is

very funny.   He has remarkable magnetic power, and
you feel that you are under the sway of a tremendous
will.   Many persons find fault with his playing, because
they say it is pure intellect (*der reine Verstand*) but
I think he has too much passion to be called purely
intellectual.   Still, it is always passion controlled.   Beethoven has been the grand study of his life, and he
playes his sonatas as no one else does.

If he goes to America next winter, you *must* hear
him thoroughly, *coûte que coûte*.   So I advise you to
be saving up your pennies, and be sure to get a place
near the piano so that you can see his face, for it is a
study.   I always sit in the second or third row here.

————

BERLIN, *October* 27, 1872.

This week has been quite an eventful one.   It began
on Monday with the funeral of Prince Albrecht, the
youngest brother of the Emperor, and it was a very
imposing spectacle.   I was in hopes that Mr. B. would
send me a card of admission to the Dom, where the serv-
ices were to be held, but as he didn't, I was obliged to
content myself with a sight of the procession and general arrangement outside.   I took my stand on a wagon
with H., and we got an excellent view.   There was a
roadway built of wood from the royal Castle to the Dom,
carpeted with black, over which the procession was to
pass.   We waited about an hour before it came along,
but we were pretty well amused by the gorgeous equipages and liveries of the different diplomatic corps
which dashed past.

12

We were on the opposite side of the canal which
separated us from the square in front of the Dom.
On the right of the Dom is the Castle, and the Museum
is on the left. All this square was surrounded by
military, for as Prince Albrecht was a Field-Marshal,
the funeral had a military character. They were beautifully arranged, the cavalry on one side and the
infantry on the other, and the different uniforms were
contrasted with each other so as to make the best
effects in colour. Both horses and men stood as if
they were carved out of marble, with the greatest pre-
cision of position. A little before eleven the royal
carriages rolled past from the palace to the Castle,
with their occupants. Presently the bells began to toll,
and exactly at eleven the procession started. The Gardes
du Corps, which is the Crown Prince's regiment, preceded the coffin, dressed in white and silver uniforms,
with glittering brass helmets surmounted by silver
eagles. The coffin itself was borne on a catafalque,
and drawn by eight horses covered with black velvet
trappings. It was yellow, and was surmounted by a
crown of gold. On it was laid the Prince's sword, helmet, etc., and some flowers. I was too far away to
distinguish the personages that followed. Of course
the Emperor was nearest, and all were on foot. Behind the coffin the Prince's favorite horse was led, sad-
dled and bridled. All the servants of his household
walked together in silver liveries and with large tri-
angular hats with long bands of crape hanging down
behind. The band played a chorale, "Jesus, my Refuge," and the bells kept tolling all the while. At the

door of the Dom, the procession was received by the clergy officiating. The coffin was so heavy that it was rolled down a platform of boards put up for the purpose. Then it was lifted by sixteen bearers, the glittering cortége closed round it, and they all swept it at the open portal.

We waited until the end of the service, as it was a short one, in order to hear the eight rounds of firing by the artillery. It was interesting to see how exactly they all fired the instant the signal was given. First the musketry on one side, and then the musketry on the other, in answer to it. The officers galloped and curveted about on their fiery steeds, and finally, the cannon went boom—boom. The sharp crack of the rifles made you start, but the sullen roar of the cannon made you shudder. It gave you some idea of a battle.

Tuesday night I went to a concert given by a new star in the musical world, a young violinist named Wilhelmj. He is only twenty-six years old, and is already said to be one of the greatest virtuosi living, perhaps *the* greatest of the romantic school, for Joachim belongs to the severe classic. All the artists and critics and many of the aristocracy turned out to hear him. It was his first appearance in Berlin, and as I looked round the audience and picked out one great musician after another, I fairly trembled for him. Joachim and de Ahna were both present, among others, and my adorable Baroness von S. swept in late, looking more exquisite than ever in black lace over black silk, with jet ornaments, and her lovely hair curled and done up high on her aristocratic little head.

She was all in mourning for the Prince, even to a
black lace fan with which she occasionally shaded her
eyes, so that her peach-bloomy cheek was just to be
discerned through it.   She is a charming pianist herself, I've heard, and is a great patroness of music and
musicians, especially of the "music of the future,"
and its creators.   I see her at all the concerts.   When
her face is in perfect repose she has the most charming
expression and a sort of celestial look in her deep-
set blue eyes.   She is what the French call *spirituelle*,
and the Germans *geistreich*, but we've no word in our
language that just describes her.

Well, as I was saying, my head got quite dizzy with
thinking what a trial it was to play before such an audience, but Wilhelmj seemed to differ from me, for he
came confidently down the steps with the dignified
self-poise of an artist who is master of his instrument,
and who knows what he can do.   He is extremely
handsome, with regular features, massive overhanging
forehead, and with an expression of power and self-con-
tainment.   He looked a perfect picture as he stood there
so quietly and played.   He hadn't gone far before he
made a brilliant cadenza that took down the house, and
there was a general burst of applause.   His *tone* (which
is the grand thing in violin-playing) was magnificent,
and his technique masterly.   He didn't play with that
tenderness of feeling and wonderful variety of expression
that Joachim does, but it was as if he didn't care to
affect people in that way.   It made me think of Tausig on the piano.   He played with the greatest intensity and *aplomb*, and the strings seemed actually to

seethe. People were taken by storm. The second piece was a concerto by Raff. Wilhelmj was in the midst of the Andante, and was sawing our hearts with every saw of his bow, when suddenly a string snapped under the strain of his passionate fingers. He instantly ceased playing, and retired up the steps to the back of the stage to put on another string. Unfortunately he had not brought along an extra one in his pocket, and had to borrow one from one of the orchestra. Weitzmann, who in his youth was himself an eminent concert violinist, was amazed at Wilhelmj's temerity. "What *rashness*," exclaimed he, "and the G string, too!" (one of the most important). After a pause Wilhelmj came down and began again, but the string was so out of tune that he retired a second time. He must have been furious inwardly, one would think, and at his *Berlin* début, too! but he came down the third time with the utmost imperturbability, and got through the concerto. The whole effect of the concert was spoiled, though, and he had also to change the solos he had intended playing, so as to avoid the G string as much as possible. Instead of the lovely Chopin Nocturne in D flat (his own arrangement), he played an Aria by Bach. He did it so wonderfully that I was really startled.—I never shall forget the *nuances* he put into his trill. But at his second concert, where he *did* give the Nocturne, it was evident that the romantic is his great forte, and on a first appearance, and before his large and critical audience, he should have been heard in that *genre*.*

* This letter, which was published in *Dwight's Journal of Music*, is the one alluded to on p. 193.

CHAPTER XV.

The Boston Fire.   Aggravations of Music Study.   Kullak.
Sherwood.   Hoch Schule.   A Brilliant American.
German Dancing.

BERLIN, *November* 24, 1872.

All the papers over here have been ringing with the
Boston fire, the horse pestilence, shipwrecks, explosions,
etc., until I feel as if all America were going to the bad.
What an awful calamity that fire is!   I can't take it in
at all.   All the Germans are wondering what our fire
companies are made of that such conflagrations *can* take
place.   They say it would be an impossibility *here,*
where the organization is so perfect.   The men are
trained to the work for years, and are on the spot in a
twinkling, knowing just what to do.   They are as fully
convinced of their super-excellence in the Fire Department as in every other, and nothing can make them
believe that if two or three of their little fire-engines had
been there, and worked by *their* firemen, the Chicago
and Boston fires could not have been put out!   You
know their machines are pumped by *hand,* too, instead
of by steam, as ours are, which makes the assumption
all the more ludicrous.   It reminds me of a German
party I was at once, where our war was the subject of
conversation.   "Oh, you don't know anything about
fighting over there," said one gentleman, nodding at me
patronizingly across the table.   "If you had had two or

three of *our* regiments, with one of *our* generals, your war would have been finished up in no time !"

I've had *such* a vexation to-day that I'm really quite beside myself ! I was to play the first movement of my Rubinstein Concerto in the conservatory with the orchestra. I've been straining every nerve over it for several weeks, practicing incessantly, and had learned it perfectly. When I played it in the class the other day it went beautifully, and I think even Kullak was satisfied. Well, of course I was anticipating playing it with the orchestra before an audience, with much pleasure, and hoped I was going to distinguish myself. Music-director Wuerst and Franz Kullak always take charge of these orchestra lessons, sometimes one directing and sometimes the other. I got up early this morning, and practiced an hour and a half before I went to the conservatory, and I was there the first of all who were to play concertos. I spoke to Wuerst and told him what I was to play, and he said "All right." Wouldn't you have thought now, that he would have let me play first? Not a bit of it. He first heard the orchestra play a stupid symphony of Hadyn's, which they might just as well have left out. Then he began screaming out to know if Herr Moszkowski was there? Herr Moszkowski, however, was *not* there, and I began to breathe freer, for he is a finished artist, and has been studying with Kullak for years, and plays in concerts. Of course if he had played first, it would have been doubly hard for me to muster up my courage, and you would have thought that Wuerst would have taken that into consideration. As Moszkowski was absent, I thought I certainly should be called up next, but another

girl received the preference.   She played extremely well,
and Wuerst paid her his compliments, and then took his
departure, leaving Franz Kullak to conduct.   Then one
of my class played Beethoven's G major concerto most
wretchedly.   Poor creature, she was nervous and frightened, and couldn't do herself any sort of justice.   At
last it was over, and at last Franz Kullak sung out, "We
will now have Rubinstein's concerto in D minor."

I got up, went to the piano, wiped off the keys,
which were completely *wet* from the nervous fingers
of those who had preceded me, and was just going to
sit down, when a young fellow approached from the
other side with the same intention.   "O, Fräulein
Fay, you have the same concerto?   Very well, you can
play it the *next* time.   To-day Herr So-and-So plays
it!"   Now, did you ever know anything so provoking?
I hoped at least that the young fellow would play it
well, and that I should learn something, but he perfectly *murdered* it, and there I had to sit through it
all, with the piece tingling at my fingers ends—and
now there's no knowing *when* I shall play it, as the
orchestra lessons are so seldom and so uncertain.   I
hope there will be one two weeks from to-day, but
even so I probably shan't do half so well as I should
have done to-day, for the freshness will be all out of
the piece, and I've practiced it so much *now* that I
hate the sound of it, and can't bear to waste any more
time over it.   Such is life!   I thought this time that
I had taken every precaution to ensure success, for I
had risen early every day, and eaten no end of the
"bread of carefulness," and the result is—nothing at

all! Not even a failure. It is the more to be regretted as to-day was the first Sunday of the month,
and I wanted to go to church, especially as the bad
weather kept me at home for two Sundays. However,
I'm determined I *will* play the concerto *yet*, if I stake
"*Kopf und Kragen* (head and collar)" on it, as the
Germans say.—But oh, the difficulty of doing *anything*
at all in this world!

December 18, 1872.—*At last* I played my Rubinstein concerto a week ago Sunday with the orchestra,
and had the pleasure of being told by Scharwenka
that I had had a brilliant success. Franz Kullak said
that my octave passages were superbly played, and
Moszkowski (who, to my surprise, was playing first
violin) applauded. So I was complimented by the
three of whom I stood most in awe. Scharwenka and
Moszkowski are both finished artists and exquisite
composers, and play a great deal in concerts this winter. Scharwenka is very handsome. He is a Pole,
and is very proud of his nationality. And, indeed,
there *is* something interesting and romantic about
being a Pole. The very name conjures up thoughts
of revolutions, conspiracies, bloody executions, masked
balls, and, of *course*, grace, wit and beauty! Scharwenka certainly sustains the traditions of his race as
far as the latter qualification is concerned. I never
talked with him, as I have but a bowing acquaintance
with him, so I don't know what sort of a *mind* he has,
but I find myself looking at him and saying to myself
with a certain degree of satisfaction, " He is a Pole."
Why I should have this feeling I know not, but I

seem to be proud of knowing Poles!—Scharwenka has a clear olive complexion, oval face, hazel eyes (I *think*) and a mass of brown silky hair which he wears long, and which falls about his head in a most picturesque and attractive fashion. He always presides over the piano at the orchestral lessons in the conservatory on Sunday mornings, and supplies those parts which are wanting. When concertos are performed he accompanies. He has a delightful serenity of manner, and sits there with quiet dignity, his back to the windows, and the light striking through his fluffy hair. He plays beautifully, and composes after Chopin's manner. Perhaps he will do greater things and develop a style of his own by and by. Every winter he gives a concert in Berlin in the Sing-Akademie.

By the way, I would not advise your paying any attention to what G. says about music. She is incapable of forming a correct judgment on the subject, and she used to provoke me to death with her ignorant and sweeping criticisms. I continually set her right, but to hear her go on about music and musicians is much like hearing S. R. and the M. crowd talk about art. What *can* be easier or more absurd, than to set yourself up and say that "nobody satisfies you." *Stuff!*—As for Kullak, I think a master must be judged by the number of players he turns out. In the two years that I have studied with him he has formed six or eight artists to my knowledge, beside no end of pupils who play extremely well. People come to him from all over the world, and as an artist himself he ranks first class.

I must tell you about a new acquaintance I've just made, a Mr. P., a Harvard man, very fascinating, very brilliant, a great swell, and the most perfect *dancer* I ever saw. I first met this phœnix at a dinner, when he fairly sparkled. He seemed to have the history of all countries at his tongue's end, and went through revolutions and reigns in the most rapid way. We had an animated discussion over the Germans, whom he loathes and despises, and he brought up all the historical events he could to justify his disgust. I was on the defensive, of course. "They've no *delicacy*," said P., in his emphatic way, and I had to give in there. Indeed, I can imagine that to a fastidious creature like him, imbued, too, with all the Southern chivalry, the Germans would be startling, to say the least. "Why," he cried, "they help you at table with their own forks after they've been eating with them! What do you think my host did to-day? He took a piece of meat that he had begun to eat, from *his own plate!* and put it on to mine with *his own fork!!* saying, 'Try this, this is a good piece!'—His intentions were excellent, but it never occurred to him that I shouldn't be delighted to eat after him."—P. can't bear it when the waiters at the restaurants pretend to think him a lord and address him as "Herr Graf." "I'll teach them to *Herr Graf* me," he said between his teeth, lowering his head, his eyes flashing dangerous fire. But it is quite likely that they do suppose him a lord, for he looks it, "every inch."

I met him again at a reception, and was having a most charming conversation with him about Goethe, whom he was dissecting in his keen way, when in came Mr. and Mrs. N. I knew at once that there was an end of our delightful talk, for though Mrs. N. has a most fascinating and high-bred husband herself, and is, moreover, extremely jealous of him, she is never content unless the most agreeable man in the room is devoted to her, also. Sure enough, she came straight toward us, and took occasion to whisper some senseless thing in my ear. Of course Mr. P. had to offer her his seat. She was, however, not quite bare-faced enough to take it, but she had succeeded in breaking the tête-à-tête and in distracting his attention. Soon after another gentleman came up to speak to me, Mr. P. bowed, and for the rest of the evening he was pinned to Mrs. N.'s side. Such are the satisfactions of parties! Either one does not meet any one worth talking to, or the conversation is sure to be interrupted. It takes these women of the world, like Mrs. N., to get the plums out of the pudding.

However, seeing him dance gave me almost as much pleasure as talking with him. He has this air of having danced millions of Germans, and is grace and elegance incarnate. Just at the end of the party, he asked me for a turn, and we took three long ones. I never enjoyed dancing so much. He manages to annihilate his legs entirely, and his arm, though strong, is so light that you feel yourself borne along like a bubble, and are only conscious that you are sustained and guided. He inspired me so that I danced really well, but when he complimented me, I basely refrained from letting him know it was all owing to him! By a funny coincidence he is the son of that elegant Mrs. P. who was on the steamer with me, and his father is very prominent in politics. I remember perfectly the pride with which Mrs. P. spoke to me of this son, and how slightly interested I was. He accompanied her to the steamer, and in fact the first time I saw her was when Mr. T., who was standing by me on the deck, said, "That was a *mother's* kiss," as she rapturously embraced him on taking leave. I didn't notice Mr. P. at all, though he says he remembers me perfectly standing there. He is going, or has gone, to Russia, and from there he will rejoin his family in Paris. That is the worst of being abroad. Charming people pass over your path like comets and disappear never to be seen again.

By the way, I now feel equal to anything in the shape of a German dance. Perhaps that may seem to you a trifling statement; but little do you know on the subject if it does. If you've ever read "Fitz Boodle's Confessions," you will remember that he represents the German dancing as a thing fearful and wonderful to the inexperienced, and how the match between him and Dorothea was broken off by his falling with her during the waltz, and rolling over and over. Here *everybody* dances, old and young, and you'll see fat old married ladies waddle off with their gray and spindle-shanked husbands. Declining doesn't help you in the least, and you are liable to be whisked off without notice by some old fellow who revolves with you like lightning on the tips of his toes, his coat-tails flying at an angle of considerably *more* than

forty-five degrees. Reversing is unknown, and consequently you see the room go spinning round with you.

I always thought, though, that if one *could* take
their steps, it might be pretty good fun. So, after a
pause of three years, I finally concluded this winter
to go to some German balls and try it again. The
first one I attended was an artists' ball. There was
first a little concert (at which I played), then a supper at ten o'clock, and then the dancing began. The
dancing cards were handed round at supper, and my
various acquaintances came up to ask me for different
dances. The first one asked me for the Polonaise.
"Delighted!" said I;—not that I had the remotest
idea what a " polonaise " was, but I was determined not
to flinch. The second engaged me for the "Quadrille
à la Cour," and the third for the "Rheinlaender," etc.,
etc. I assented to everything with outward alacrity,
but with some inward trepidation, for I thought it
rather a bold stroke to get up at a large ball and
attempt to dance a string of things I had never heard
of! However, I was in luck. The Polonaise turned
out to be merely walking, but in different figures, and
this, before the conclusion of it, makes you continually change partners until you have promenaded and
spoken with every one of the opposite sex in the room.
This is to get the whole party acquainted. When you
finally get back to your own partner, it breaks up with
a waltz, and so ends.

My partner was a young artist, half painter, half
musician, and a very intelligent and in fact charming
talker. Like most artists, his dress was rather at

sixes and sevens. He had on a swallow-tailed coat, but it did not fit him, so I conclude it was borrowed or hired for the occasion. It was so wide, and so long, that when I saw him dancing with some one else, I thought I must have made a laughable figure with him, for he was small into the bargain. However, he had that sunny, happy-go-lucky way about him that all artists have when they're in good humour, and he was a capital dancer. When I came back to him at the end of the Polonaise I started off with a mental "Now for it," for the waltz was the thing I was most afraid of; but to my surprise, I got on most beautifully. Emboldened by success, I went on recklessly. "Rheinlaender" turned out to be the schottisch, and "Quadrille à la Cour" the lancers, so I was all right. They had to be danced in the German sense of the word, of course, but with courage it is possible to do it. Since this ball I have been to two others, and am now pronounced by the gentlemen to be a finished dancer. I don't know how I learned, but it seemed to come to me with a sudden inspiration.

CHAPTER XVI.

A German Professor. Sherwood. The Baroness von S.
Von Bülow. A German Party. Joachim.
The Baroness at Home.

BERLIN, *February* 25, 1873.

At Mr. P.'s we had a charming dinner the other day,
which was as sociable as possible, though we sat thirteen at table. Think what an oversight! I believe
though, that I was the only one who perceived it. I sat
next to a German professor, who is said to speak sixty-
four languages! He had a little compact head, which
looked as if it were stuffed and crammed to the utmost.
I reflected a long time which of his sixty-four languages I should start him on, but finally concluded that
as I spoke English with tolerable fluency we would
confine ourselves to that! He was perfectly delightful
to talk to, as all these German *savans* are, and I got
a lot of new ideas from him. He had been writing
a pamphlet on the subject of love, as considered in
various ancient and modern languages, and in it
he proves that the passion of love used to be quite
a different thing from what it is now. All this ideality
of sentiment is entirely modern.

My friend Miss B. is playing exquisitely now, and
Sherwood is going ahead like a young giant. To-day
Kullak said that Sherwood played Beethoven's E flat
major concerto (the hardest of all Beethoven's con-

certos) with a perfection that he had rarely heard equalled. So much for being a genius, for he is still under twenty, and has only been abroad a year or two. But he studied with our best American master, William Mason, and played like an artist before he came. But, then, Sherwood has one enormous advantage that no master on earth can bestow, and that is, perfect confidence in himself. There's nothing like having faith in yourself, and I believe *that* is the kind of faith that "moves mountains."

At Mr. Bancroft's grand party for Washington's birthday, last Friday, he presented me to the Baroness von S., but without telling her that I was the person who wrote that letter about her and Wilhelmj that M. published without my knowledge in *Dwight's Journal*. She was as exquisite as I thought she would be, and is the most bewitching creature! She is just such a woman as Balzac describes—like Honorine, for instance. She has *"l'oeil plein de feu,"* etc., and is grace and sentiment personified.

She was dressed in white silk, cut square neck and trimmed with a lot of little box-plaited ruffles round the bottom. Round her throat was a black velvet ribbon, with a necklace of magnificent pearls fastened to it in festoons and a diamond pendant in the middle. She greeted me with a ceremonious bow, and began the conversation by complimenting me on an accompaniment I had been playing. I told her I was studying music here, and that I had been in Tausig's conservatory a year. As soon as I mentioned him we got on delightfully, for she was his favourite pupil, and

3

we talked a good deal about him and Bülow. She
said she had heard Tausig play everything he ever
learned, she thought, and that only a fortnight before his death, he was at her house and played Chopin's
first Sonata. The last movement comes after the
well-known Funeral March (which forms the Adagio)
and is very peculiar. It is a continual running movement with both hands in unison, and it is played all
muffled, and with the soft pedal. Kullak thinks that
Chopin meant to express that after the grave all is
dust and ashes, but the Baroness said that Tausig
thought Chopin meant to represent by it the ghost of
the departed wandering about. On this occasion,
when Tausig had finished playing it, he turned and
said to her, "That seems to me like the wind blowing
over my grave." A fortnight later he was dead! I
asked her if it were not dreadful that such an artist
should have died so young. The most pained look
came into her beautiful eyes, and she said, "I have
never been able to reconcile myself to it."

The conversation continued in the most charming
manner until von Moltke came up to speak to her on
one side and Mr. Bancroft on the other offered his
arm to lead her into the supper-room. "Did you tell
her?" whispered Mr. Bancroft. "No; how could I?"
said I. "*You* ought to tell her." So I imagine
he did tell her, as they went into supper, that I was
the young lady who had described her in the paper.
I did not have a chance to approach her again until
just as I was going home. She was standing in the
door-way of an ante-room with Mr. Bancroft, wrapped

in her opera cloak and waiting for her carriage to be announced. I bade Mr. Bancroft good-night, and as I passed her she put out her hand and said to me with a meaning look, in her little hesitating English, "I am so happy to have met you." I told her I owed her an apology, which I hoped to make another time. "Oh, no," said she, smilingly, "I am very thankful." —I suppose she meant "very much flattered," or something of that kind.

I heard two tremendous concerts of Bülow's lately. Oh, I do hope you'll hear him some day! He is a colossal artist. I never heard a pianist I liked so well. He has such perfect mastery, and yet such comprehension and such sympathy. Among other things, he played Beethoven's last Sonata. Such a magnificent one as it is! I liked it better than the Appassionata.

The other night I went to a party at a General von der G.'s. It was a "dreadfully" elegant set of people—all countesses, Vons and generals' wives. Stiff, oh, *how* stiff! I felt as if the ladies did me a personal favor every time they spoke to me. They were very handsomely dressed, and wore their family jewels. There was a great deal of music, and a certain old Herr von K. sat on a sofa and nodded his head *à la* connoisseur, while the officers stood round and scarcely dared to wink. The formality did not abate till we adjourned to the supper-room, when, as is always the case in German parties, everybody's tongue suddenly became loosed.— Germans are the happiest people *at* supper, and the most wretched before it, that you ever saw. Their parties are *always* "just so." So many hours of propriety beforehand,—the ladies all by themselves round a centre-table in one room, the young girls discreetly sandwiched in between with their embroidery, and talking on the most limited subjects in the most "papa, potatoes, poultry, prunes and prism" manner—and the men in the other room playing cards. On this occasion, when we went into supper, there was one large central table covered with the feast, and then there were little tables standing about, whither you could retire with your prey when you had once secured it. I got something, and betook myself to a table in the corner, whither a young artist, also Miss B. and an officer, the son of the celebrated General von W., who won the battle of something, speedily followed me. The artist, Herr Meyer, sat opposite me, and I began to jabber with him, unmindful of the officer, as I had previously tried him on every subject in the known world without being able to extract a reply. We gradually collected a miscellaneous array of plates full of things, when I dropped one of my spoons on the floor. I picked it up, laid it aside, and began eating out of one of my other plates. Presently the officer, who had been glaring at me all the while out of his uniform, rose solemnly and went to the centre-table and returned. Suddenly I became aware, by my light being obscured, that he was standing opposite me on the other side of the table. I glanced up, and remarked that he had a spoon in his thumb and finger. As he did not offer it, however, it did not occur to me that it was for me, so I went on eating. After a minute I looked up again, and he was still standing as if he were pointing a gun, the spoon between thumb and finger. At last it dawned upon me that he had brought it for me, so I took it out of his hand and thanked him, whereupon he resumed his seat. I was so overcome by this unheard-of act of gallantry on the part of an aristocrat! and an officer!! that I felt I must say something worthy of the occasion. So after a few minutes I remarked to him, "Everything tastes very sweet out of *this* spoon!"—Total silence and impassibility of countenance on his part.—Miss B., who was sitting opposite, remarked mischievously, "That was entirely lost, my dear," and I was so depressed by my failure that I subsided and did not try to kindle him again.

BERLIN, *April* 14, 1873.

Colonel B. told me some weeks ago, that Kullak had told him I was ready for the concert room, and that he would like to have me play at court. If this is his real opinion *I* have no evidence of it, for he knows I am anxious to play in concert before I leave Germany, and yet he does nothing whatever to bring me forward. It is very discouraging. In this conservatory there is no stimulus whatever. One might as well be a machine.

I propose to go to Weimar the last of this week. It seems very strange that I shall actually know Liszt at last, after hearing of him so many years. I am wild to see him! They say everything depends upon the humour he happens to be in when you come to him. I

hope I shall hit upon one of his indulgent moments.
Every one says he gives no lessons. But I hope at least
to play to him a few times, and what is more important,
to hear *him* play repeatedly. Happy the pianist who
can catch even a faint reflection of his wonderful style !

Not long ago Mr. Bancroft invited me to drive out
to Tegel, Humboldt's country-seat, near here, with the
Joachims, and so I had a three hours conversation with
that idol ! He is the most modest, unpretending man
possible. To hear him talk you wouldn't suppose he
could play at all. I've always said to myself that if anything would be heaven, it would be to play a sonata with
Joachim, but have supposed such a thing to be unattain-
able—these master-artists are so proud and unapproachable. But I think now it might not have been so difficult
after all, he is so lovely. Joachim was very quiet during
the first part of the excursion, and I couldn't think how
I could get him to talk. At last I mentioned Wagner,
whom I knew he hated. His eyes kindled, and he roused
up, and after that was animated and interesting all the
rest of the time ! He said that "Wagner was under the
delusion that he was the only man in the world that
understood Beethoven ; but it happened there *were* other
people who could comprehend Beethoven as well as he,"
—and indeed, it is difficult to conceive of any one under-
standing Beethoven any better than Joachim.

Joachim is quite as noble and generous to poor artists
as Liszt is, and constantly teaches them for nothing. He
has the greatest enthusiasm for his class in the Hoch
Schule, and I shouldn't think that any one who wishes
to study the violin would *think* of going any where else.

They say that Joachim possesses beautiful social qualities, also, and has the faculty of entertaining in his own house charmingly. He brings out what there is in every one without apparently saying anything himself.

The Baroness von S. had seemed so cordial and friendly at Mr. Bancroft's on account of the letter you had published in *Dwight's Journal of Music*, that I finally made up my mind to the daring act of calling on her in order to ask her for a letter of introduction to Liszt. She lives in a palace belonging to the Empress. There is a deep court in front of it, with lions on the gateway. Before the door stood a soldier on guard. As I approached, one of the Gardes du Corps (the Crown Prince's regiment) emerged from the entrance. He was dressed all in white and silver, with big top boots, and his helmet surmounted by a silver eagle. He was an officer, and of course all the officers in this regiment belong to the flower of the nobility. I was rather awed by his imposing appearance, and advanced timidly to the doors, which were of glass, and pulled the bell. A tall phantom in livery appeared, as if by magic, and signed to me to ascend the grand staircase. The walls of it were all covered with pictures. I went up, and was received by another tall phantom in livery. I asked him "if the Frau Excellency was to be spoken." He took my card, and discreetly said, "he would see," at the same time ushering me into an immense ball-room, where he requested me to be seated. It was furnished in crimson satin, there were myriads of mirrors, and the floor was waxed. I took refuge in a corner of it, feeling very small indeed. Those few minutes of waiting were extremely

uncomfortable, for I didn't know what she would say to
my request, as I had only seen her that one time at Mr.
Bancroft's, and was not sure that she would not regard
my coming as a liberty. People are so severe in their
ideas here.

At last the servant returned and said she would receive
me, and led the way across the ball-room to a door
which he opened for me to enter. I found myself in a
large, high room, also furnished in crimson, and in the
centre of which stood two pianos nestled lovingly
together. The Baroness was not there, however, and I
saw what seemed to be an endless succession of rooms
opening one out of the other, the doors always opposite
each other. I concluded to "go on till I stopped,"
and after traversing three or four, I at last heard a
faint murmur of voices, and entered what I suppose is
her *boudoir*. There my divinity was seated in a little
crimson satin sofa, talking to an old fellow who sat on
a chair near her, whom she introduced as Herr Professor Somebody. He had a small, well-stuffed head,
and a pale, observant eye that seemed to say, "I've
looked into everything"—and I should think it *had*
by the way he conversed.

The Baroness was attired in an olive-coloured silk,
short, and fashionably made. She was leaning forward as she talked, and toying with a silver-sheathed
dagger which she took from a table loaded with costly
trifles next her. She rose as I came in, and greeted
me very cordially, and asked me to sit down on the
sofa by her. I explained to her my errand, and she immediately said she would give me a letter with the great-

est pleasure. We had a very charming conversation about artists in general, and Liszt in particular, in which the little professor took a leading part. He showed himself the connoisseur he looked, and gradually diverged from the art of music to that of speaking and reading, which he said was the most difficult of all the arts, because the tone was not there, but had to be made. He said he had never heard a perfect speaker or reader in his life. He descanted at great length upon the art of speaking, and finally, when he paused, the Baroness took my hand and said, " Where do you live?" I gave her my address, and she said she would send me the letter. I then rose to go, and she assured me again she would say all she could to dispose Liszt favourably towards me. I thanked her, and said good-bye. She waited till I was nearly half across the next room, and then she called after me, " I'll say lots of pretty things about you!" That was a real little piece of coquetry on her part, and she knew that it would take me down! She looked so sweet when she said it, standing and smiling there in the middle of the floor, the door-way making a frame for her. A few days afterward I met her in the street, and she told me she had enjoined it upon Liszt to be amiable to me, " but," she added, with a mischievous laugh, " I didn't tell him you wrote so well for the papers." Oh, she is too fascinating for anything !—She seems just to float on the top of the wave and never to think. Such exquisite perception and intelligence, and yet lightness !

The last excitement in Berlin was over the wedding

of Prince Albrecht (the son of the one whose funeral I saw) with the Princess of Altenburg. When she arrived she made a regular entry into the city in a coach all gold and glass, drawn by eight superb plumed horses. A band of music went before her, and she had an escort all in grand equipages. As she sat on the back seat with the Crown Princess, magnificently dressed, and bowing from side to side, you rubbed your eyes and thought you saw Cinderella!

WITH LISZT.

(203)

CHAPTER XVII.

Arrives in Weimar. Liszt at the Theatre. At a Party. At his own House.

WEIMAR, *May* 1, 1873.

Last night I arrived in Weimar, and this evening I have been to the theatre, which is very cheap here, and the first person I saw, sitting in a box opposite, was Liszt, from whom, as you know, I am bent on getting lessons, though it will be a difficult thing I fear, as I am told that Wiemar is overcrowded with people who are on the same errand. I recognized Liszt from his portrait, and it entertained and interested me very much to observe him. He was making himself agreeable to three ladies, one of whom was very pretty. He sat with his back to the stage, not paying the least attention, apparently, to the play, for he kept talking all the while himself, and yet no point of it escaped him, as I could tell by his expression and gestures.

Liszt is the most interesting and striking looking man imaginable. Tall and slight, with deep-set eyes, shaggy eyebrows, and long iron-gray hair, which he wears parted in the middle. His mouth turns up at the corners, which gives him a most crafty and Mephistophelean expression when he smiles, and his whole appearance and manner have a sort of Jesuitical elegance and ease. His hands are very narrow, with long and slender fingers that look as if they had twice as many joints as other people's. They are so flexible and supple that it makes you nervous to look at them. Anything like the polish of his manner I never saw. When he got up to leave the box, for instance, after his adieux to the ladies, he laid his hand on his heart and made his final bow,—not with affectation, or in mere gallantry, but with a quiet courtliness which made you feel that no other way of bowing to a lady was right or proper. It was most characteristic.

But the most extraordinary thing about Liszt is his wonderful variety of expression and play of feature. One moment his face will look dreamy, shadowy, tragic. The next he will be insinuating, amiable, ironical, sardonic; but always the same captivating grace of manner. He is a perfect study. I cannot imagine how he must look when he is playing. He is all spirit, but half the time, at least, a mocking spirit, I should say. I have heard the most remarkable stories about him already. All Weimar adores him, and people say that women still go perfectly crazy over him. When he walks out he bows to everybody just like a King! The Grand Duke has presented him with a house beautifully situated on the park, and here he lives elegantly, free of expense, whenever he chooses to come to it.

WEIMAR, *May* 7, 1873.

There isn't a piano to be had in Weimar for love or money, as there is no manufactory, and the few there were to be disposed of were snatched up before I got here. So I have lost an entire week in hunting one

up, and was obliged to go first to Erfurt and finally
to Leipsic, before I could find one—and even that was
sent over as a favour after much coaxing and persua-
sion. I felt so happy when I fairly saw it in my room!
As if I had taken a city! However, I met Liszt two
evenings ago at a little tea-party given by a friend and
protégée of his to as many of his scholars as have arrived, I being asked with the rest. Liszt promised to
come late. We only numbered seven. There were
three young men and four young ladies, of whom three,
including myself, were Americans. Five of the number had studied with Liszt before, and the young men
are artists already before the public.

To fill up the time till Liszt came, our hostess made
us play, one after the other, beginning with the latest
arrival. After we had each "exhibited," little
tables were brought in and supper served. We
were in the midst of it, and having a merry time, when
the door suddenly opened and Liszt appeared. We all
rose to our feet, and he shook hands with everybody
without waiting to be introduced. Liszt looks as if
he had been through everything, and has a face *seamed*
with experience. He is rather tall and narrow, and
wears a long abbé's coat reaching nearly down to his
feet. He made me think of an old time magician
more than anything, and I felt that with a touch of
his wand he could transform us all. After he had
finished his greetings, he passed into the next room
and sat down. The young men gathered round him
and offered him a cigar, which he accepted and began
to smoke. We others continued our nonsense where

we were, and I suppose Liszt overheard some of our brilliant conversation, for he asked who we were, I think, and presently the lady of the house came out after Miss W. and me, the two American strangers, to take us in and present us to him.

After the preliminary greetings we had some little talk. He asked me if I had been to Sophie Menter's concert in Berlin the other day. I said yes. He remarked that Miss Menter was a great favourite of his, and that the lady from whom I had brought a letter to him had done a good deal for her. I asked him if Sophie Menter were a pupil of his. He said no, he could not take the credit of her artistic success to himself. I heard afterwards that he really had done ever so much for her, but he won't have it said that he teaches! After he had finished his cigar, Liszt got up and said, "America is now to have the floor," and requested Miss W. to play for him. This was a dreadful ordeal for us new arrivals, for we had not expected to be called upon. I began to quake inwardly, for I had been without a piano for nearly a week, and was not at all prepared to play to him, while Miss W. had been up since five o'clock in the morning, and had travelled all day. However, there was no getting off. A request from Liszt is a command, and Miss W. sat down, and acquitted herself as well as could have been expected under the circumstances. Liszt waved his hand and nodded his head from time to time, and seemed pleased, I thought. He then called upon Leitert, who played a composition of Liszt's own most beautifully. Liszt commended him and patted him on the back. As soon as Leitert had finished, I slipped off into the back room, hoping Liszt would forget all about me, but he followed me almost immediately, like a cat with a mouse, took both my hands in his, and said in the most winning way imaginable, "*Mademoiselle, vous jouerez quelque-chose, n'est-ce-pas?*" I can't give you any idea of his *persuasiveness*, when he chooses. It is enough to decoy you into anything. It was such a desperate moment that I became reckless, and without even telling him that I was out of practice and not prepared to play, I sat down and plunged into the A flat major Ballade of Chopin, as if I were possessed. The piano had a splendid touch, luckily. Liszt kept calling out " Bravo " every minute or two, to encourage me, and somehow, I got through. When I had finished, he clapped his hands and said, "Bravely played." He asked with whom I had studied, and made one or two little criticisms. I hoped he would shove me aside and play it himself, but he didn't.

Liszt is just like a monarch, and no one dares speak to him until he addresses one first, which I think no fun. He did not play to us at all, except when some one asked him if he had heard R. play that afternoon. R. is a young organist from Leipsic, who telegraphed to Liszt to ask him if he might come over and play to him on the organ. Liszt, with his usual amiability, answerd that he might. "Oh," said Liszt, with an indescribably comic look, "he improvised for me a whole half-hour in this style,"—and then he got up and went to the piano, and without sitting down he

14

played some ridiculous chords in the middle of the key-
board, and then little trills and turns high up in the
treble, which made us all burst out laughing. Shortly
after I had played I took my leave. Liszt had gone
into the other room to smoke, and I didn't care to follow him, as I saw that he was tired, and had no intention of playing to us. Our hostess told Miss W. and
me to "slip out so that he would not perceive it."
Yesterday Miss W. went to see him, and he asked her
if she knew that Miss " Fy," and told her to tell me to
come to him. So I shall present myself to-morrow,
though I don't know how the lion will act when I
beard him in his den.

WEIMAR, *May* 21, 1873.

Liszt is so *besieged* by people and so tormented with
applications, that I fear I should only have been sent
away if I had come without the Baroness von S.'s letter of introduction, for he admires her extremely, and
I judge that she has much influence with him. He
says "people fly in his face by dozens," and seem to
think he is "only there to give lessons." He gives *no*
paid lessons whatever, as he is much too grand for
that, but if one has talent enough, or pleases him, he
lets one come to him and play to him. I go to him
every other day, but I don't play more than twice a
week, as I cannot prepare so much, but I listen to the
others. Up to this point there have been only four in
the class besides myself, and I am the only new one.
From four to six P. M. is the time when he receives

his scholars. The first time I went I did not play to him, but listened to the rest. Urspruch and Leitert, the two young men whom I met the other night, have studied with Liszt a long time, and both play superbly. Fräulein Schultz and Miss Gaul (of Baltimore), are also most gifted creatures.

As I entered Liszt's salon, Urspruch was performing Schumann's Symphonic Studies—an immense composition, and one that it took at least half an hour to get through. He played so splendidly that my heart sank down into the very depths. I thought I should never get on *there!* Liszt came forward and greeted me in a very friendly manner as I entered. He was in very good humour that day, and made some little witticisms. Urspruch asked him what title he should give to a piece he was composing. *"Per aspera ad astra,"* said Liszt. This was such a good hit that I began to laugh, and he seemed to enjoy my appreciation of his little sarcasm. I did not play that time, as my piano had only just come, and I was not prepared to do so, but I went home and practiced tremendously for several days on Chopin's B minor sonata. It is a great composition, and one of his last works. When I thought I could play it, I went to Liszt, though with a trembling heart. I cannot tell you what it has cost me every time I have ascended his stairs. I can scarcely summon up courage to go there, and generally stand on the steps awhile before I can make up my mind to open the door and go in!

This day it was particularly trying, as it was really my first serious performance before him, and he speaks

so very indistinctly that I feared I shouldn't understand his corrections, and that he would get out of
patience with me, for he cannot bear to explain. I
think he hates the trouble of speaking German, for
he mutters his words and does not half finish his sen-
tences. Yesterday when I was there he spoke to me
in French all the time, and to the others in German,
—one of his funny whims, I suppose.

Well, on this day the artists Leitert and Urspruch,
and the young composer Metzdorf, who is always hanging about Liszt, were in the room when I came. They
had probably been playing. At first Liszt took no
notice of me beyond a greeting, till Metzdorf said to
him, "Herr Doctor, Miss Fay has brought a sonata."
"Ah, well, let us hear it," said Liszt. Just then he left
the room for a minute, and I told the three gentlemen
that they ought to go away and let me play to Liszt
alone, for I felt nervous about playing before them.
They all laughed at me and said they would not budge
an inch. When Liszt came back they said to him,
"Only think, Herr Doctor, Miss Fay proposes to send
us all home." I said I could not play before such
great artists. "Oh, that is healthy for you," said Liszt,
with a smile, and added, "you have a very choice audience, now." I don't know whether he appreciated
how nervous I was, but instead of walking up and
down the room as he often does, he sat down by me
like any other teacher, and heard me play the first
movement. It was frightfully hard, but I had studied
it so much that I managed to get through with it
pretty successfully. Nothing could exceed Liszt's

amiability, or the trouble he gave himself, and instead of frightening me, he inspired me. Never was there such a delightful teacher! and he is the first sympathetic one I've had. You feel so *free* with him, and he develops the very spirit of music in you. He doesn't keep nagging at you all the time, but he leaves you your own conception. Now and then he will make a criticism, or play a passage, and with a few words give you enough to think of all the rest of your life. There is a delicate *point* to everything he says, as subtle as he is himself. He doesn't tell you anything about the technique. That you must work out for yourself. When I had finished the first movement of the sonata, Liszt, as he always does, said "Bravo!" Taking my seat, he made some little criticisms, and then told me to go on and play the rest of it.

Now, I only half knew the other movements, for the first one was so extremely difficult that it cost me all the labour I could give to prepare that. But playing to Liszt reminds me of trying to feed the elephant in the Zoological Garden with lumps of sugar. He disposes of whole movements as if they were nothing, and stretches out gravely for more! One of my fingers fortunately began to bleed, for I had practiced the skin off, and that gave me a good excuse for stopping. Whether he was pleased at this proof of industry, I know not; but after looking at my finger and saying, "Oh!" very compassionately, he sat down and played the whole three last movements himself, That was a great deal, and showed off all his powers. It was the first time I had heard him, and I don't know which was the most

extraordinary,—the Scherzo, with its wonderful lightness and swiftness, the Adagio with its depth and
pathos, or the last movement, where the whole key-
board seemed to "*donnern und blitzen* (thunder and
lighten)." There is such a vividness about everything
he plays that it does not seem as if it were mere music
you were listening to, but it is as if he had called up a
real, living *form*, and you saw it breathing before your
face and eyes. It gives *me* almost a ghostly feeling to
hear him, and it seems as if the air were peopled with
spirits. Oh, he is a perfect wizard! It is as interesting to see him as it is to hear him, for his face changes
with every modulation of the piece, and he looks exactly as he is playing. He has one element that is
most captivating, and that is, a sort of delicate and
fitful mirth that keeps peering out at you here and
there! It is most peculiar, and when he plays that way,
the most bewitching little expression comes over his
face. It seems as if a little spirit of joy were playing
hide and go seek with you.

On Friday Liszt came and paid me a visit, and even
played a little on my piano.—Only think what an honour! At the same time he told me to come to him
that afternoon and play to him, and invited me also to a
matinee he was going to give on Sunday for some
countess of distinction who was here for a few days.
None of the other scholars were asked, and when I entered the room there were only three persons in it beside Liszt. One was the Grand Duke himself, the
other was the Countess von M. (born a Russian Princess), and the third was a Russian minister's wife.

They were all four standing in a little knot, speaking in French together. I had no idea who they were, as the Grand Duke was in morning costume, and had no star or decoration to distinguish him. I saw at a glance, however, that they were all swells, and so I didn't speak to any of them, luckily, though it was an even chance that I had not said something to avoid the awkwardness of standing there like a post, for I had been told beforehand that Liszt never introduced people to each other. Liszt greeted me in a very friendly manner, and introduced me to the countess, but she was so dreadfully set up that it was impossible to get more than a few icy words out of her. I was thankful enough when more people arrived, so that I could retire to a corner and sit down without being observed, for it was a very uncomfortable situation to be standing, a stranger, close to four fashionables and not dare to speak to *any* of them because they did not address me.

After the company was all assembled, it numbered eighteen persons, nearly all of whom were titled. I was the only unimportant one in it. Liszt was so sweet. He kept coming over to where I sat and talking to me, and promised me a ticket for a private concert where only his compositions were to be performed. He seemed determined to make me feel at home. He played five times, but no *great* work, which was a disappointment to me, particularly as the last three times he played duetts with a leading Weimar artist named Lassen, who was present. He made me come and turn the leaves. Gracious! how he *does* read! It is very difficult to turn for him, for he reads ever so far ahead of what he is playing, and takes in fully five bars at a glance, so you have to guess about where you *think* he would like to have the page over. Once I turned it too late, and once too early, and he snatched it out of my hand and whirled it back.—Not quite the situation for timorous me, was it?

May 21.—To-day being my birthday, I thought I must go to Liszt by way of celebration. I wasn't really ready to play to him, but I took his second Ballade with me, and thought I'd ask him some questions about some hard places in it. He insisted upon my playing it. When we came in he looked indisposed and nervous, and there happened to be a good many artists there. We always lay our notes on the table, and he takes them, looks them over, and calls out what he'll have played. He remarked this piece and called out "*Wer spielt diese grosse mächtige Ballade von mir?* (Who plays this great and mighty ballad of mine?)" I felt as if he had asked "Who killed Cock Robin?" and as if I were the one who had done it, only I did not feel like "owning up" to it quite so glibly as the sparrow had, for Liszt seemed to be in very bad humour, and had roughed the one who had played before me. I finally mustered up my courage and said "*Ich*," but told him I did not know it perfectly yet. He said, "No matter; play it." So I sat down, expecting he would take my head off, but, strange to say, he seemed to be delighted with my playing, and said that I had "quite touched him." Think of that from Liszt, and when I was playing his own composition! When I went out he accompanied me to the door, took my hand in both of his and said, " To-day you've covered yourself with glory!" I told him I had only *begun* it, and I hoped he would let me play it again when I knew it better. "What," said he, " I must pay you a still greater compliment, must I?" "Of course," said I. " *Il faut vous gâter?*" "*Oui,*" said I. He laughed.

CHAPTER XVIII.

Liszt's Drawing-room. An Artist's Walking Party. Liszt's
Teaching.

WEIMAR, *May* 29, 1873.

I am having the most heavenly time in Weimar,
studying with Liszt, and sometimes I can scarcely realize that I am at that summit of my ambition, to be
his pupil! It was the Baroness von S.'s letter that
secured it for me, I am sure. He is so overrun with
people, that I think it is a wonder he is civil to
anybody, but he is the most amiable man I ever knew,
though he *can* be dreadful, too, when he chooses, and
he understands how to put people outside his door
in as short a space of time as it can be done. I go to
him three times a week. At home Liszt doesn't wear
his long abbé's coat, but a short one, in which he
looks much more artistic. His figure is remarkably
slight, but his head is most imposing.—It is *so* delicious in that room of his! It was all furnished and
put in order for him by the Grand Duchess herself.
The walls are pale gray, with a gilded border running
round the room, or rather two rooms, which are divided,
but not separated, by crimson curtains. The furniture is crimson, and everything is so *comfortable*—such
a contrast to German bareness and stiffness generally.
A splendid grand piano stands in one window (he
receives a new one every year). The other window is

always wide open, and looks out on the park. There is a dove-cote just opposite the window, and the doves promenade up and down on the roof of it, and fly about, and sometimes whirr down on the sill itself. That pleases Liszt. His writing-table is beautifully fitted up with things that all match. Everything is in bronze—ink-stand, paper-weight, match-box, etc., and there is always a lighted candle standing on it by which he and the gentlemen can light their cigars. There is a carpet on the floor, a rarity in Germany, and Liszt generally walks about, and smokes, and mutters (he can never be said to *talk*), and calls upon one or other of us to play. From time to time he will sit down and play himself where a passage does not suit him, and when he is in good spirits he makes little jests all the time. His playing was a complete revelation to me, and has given me an entirely new insight into music. You cannot conceive, without hearing him, how poetic he is, or the thousand *nuances* that he can throw into the simplest thing, and he is equally great on all sides. From the zephyr to the tempest, the whole scale is equally at his command.

But Liszt is not at all like a master, and cannot be treated like one. He is a monarch, and when he extends his royal sceptre you can sit down and play to him. You never can ask him to play anything for you, no matter how much you're dying to hear it. If he is in the mood he will play, if not, you must content yourself with a few remarks. You cannot even offer to play yourself. You lay your notes on the table, so he can see that you *want* to play, and sit down. He takes a turn up and down the room, looks at the music, and if the piece interests him, he will call upon you. We bring the same piece to him but once, and but once play it through.

Yesterday I had prepared for him his *Au Bord d'une Source.* I was nervous and played badly. He was not to be put out, however, but acted as if he thought I had played charmingly, and then he sat down and played the whole piece himself, oh, *so* exquisitely! It made me feel like a wood-chopper. The notes just seemed to ripple off his fingers' ends with scarce any perceptible motion. As he neared the close I remarked that that funny little expression came over his face which he always has when he means to surprise you, and he suddenly took an unexpected chord and extemporized a poetical little end, quite different from the written one.—Do you wonder that people go distracted over him?

Weimar is a lovely little place, and there are most beautiful walks all about. Ascension being a holiday here, all we pianists made up a walking party out to Tiefurt, about two miles distant. We went in the afternoon and returned in the evening. The walk lay through the woods, and was perfectly exquisite the whole way. As we came back in the evening the nightingales were singing, and I could not help wishing that P. were there to hear them, as he has such a passion for birds. There are cuckoos here, too, and you hear them calling "cuckoo, cuckoo." Metzdorf and I danced on the hard road, to the edification of all the others. In Tiefurt we partook of a magnificent collation consisting of a mug of beer, brown bread and sausage! Some of the party preferred coffee, among whom was Metzdorf, who made us laugh by sticking the coffee-pot into his inside coat pocket as soon as he had poured out his first cup, in order to make sure that the others didn't take more than their share; he would coolly take it out, help himself, and put it back again. The servant who waited got frightened, and thought he was going to steal it. Afterwards when we were playing games and wanted the door shut, the host came and opened it, and would not allow us to shut it, because he said we might carry off something! How's that!

WEIMAR, *June* 6, 1873.

When I first came there were only five of us who studied with Liszt, but lately a good many others have been there. Day before yesterday there came a young lady who was a pupil of Henselt in St. Petersburg. She is immensely talented, only seventeen years old, and her name is Laura Kahrer. It is a very rare thing to see a pupil of Henselt, for it is very difficult to get lessons from him. He stands next to Liszt. This Laura Kahrer plays everything that ever was heard of, and she played a fugue of her own composition the other day that was really vigorous and good. I was quite astonished to hear how she had worked it up. She has made a grand concert tour in Russia. I never saw such a hand as she had. She could bend it backwards till it looked like the palm of her hand turned inside out. She was an interesting little creature, with dark eyes and hair, and one could see by her Turkish necklace and numerous bangles that she had been making money. She played with the greatest *aplomb*, though her touch had a certain roughness about it to my ear. She did not carry me away, but I have not heard many pieces from her.

However, all playing sounds barren by the side of Liszt, for *his* is the living, breathing impersonation of poetry, passion, grace, wit, coquetry, daring, tenderness and every other fascinating attribute that you can think of! I'm ready to hang myself half the time when I've been to him. Oh, he is the most phenomenal being in every respect! All that you've heard of him would never give you an idea of him. In short, he represents the whole scale of human emotion. He is a many-sided prism, and reflects back the light in all colours, no matter how you look at him. His pupils *adore* him, as in fact everybody else does, but it is impossible to do otherwise with a person whose genius flashes out of him all the time so, and whose character is so winning.

One day this week, when we were with Liszt, he was in such high spirits that it was as if he had suddenly become twenty years younger. A student from the Stuttgardt conservatory played a Liszt Concerto. His name is V., and he is dreadfully nervous. Liszt kept up a little running fire of satire all the time he was playing, but in a good-natured way. I shouldn't have minded it if it had been I. In fact, I think it would have inspired me; but poor V. hardly knew whether

he was on his head or on his feet.   It was too funny.
Everything that Liszt says is so striking.   For instance,
in one place where V. was playing the melody rather
feebly, Liszt suddenly took his seat at the piano and
said, " When *I* play, I always play for the people in
the gallery [by the gallery he meant the cock-loft,
where the rabble always sit, and where the places cost
next to nothing], so that those persons who pay only
five groschens for their seat also hear something."
Then he began, and I wish you could have heard him !
The sound didn't seem to be very *loud*, but it was penetrating and far-reaching.   When he had finished, he
raised one hand in the air, and you seemed to see all
the people in the gallery drinking in the sound.   That
is the way Liszt teaches you.   He presents an *idea* to
you, and it takes fast hold of your mind and sticks
there.   Music is such a real, visible thing to him, that
he always has a symbol, instantly, in the material
world to express his idea.   One day, when I was playing, I made too much movement with my hand in a
rotatory sort of a passage where it was difficult to
avoid it.   " Keep your hand still, Fräulein," said Liszt ;
"*don't make omelette.*"   I couldn't help laughing, it
hit me on the head so nicely.   He is far too sparing
of his playing, unfortunately, and, like Tausig, only
sits down and plays a few bars at a time, generally.
It is dreadful when he stops, just as you are at the
height of your enjoyment, but he is so thoroughly
blasé that he doesn't care to show off, and doesn't like
to have any one pay him a compliment.   Even at the
court it annoyed him so that the Grand Duchess told

people to take no notice when he rose from the piano.

On the same day that Lizst was in such high good-humour, a strange lady and her husband were there who had made a long journey to Weimar, in the hope of hearing him play. She waited patiently for a long time through the lesson, and at last Liszt took compassion on her, and sat down with his favourite remark that " the young ladies played a great deal better than he did, but he would try his best to imitate them," and then played something of his own so wonderfully, that when he had finished we all stood there like posts, feeling that there was *nothing* to be said. But he, as if he feared we might burst out into eulogy, got up instantly and went over to a friend of his who was standing there, and who lives on an estate near Weimar, and said, in the most commonplace tone imaginable, " By the way, how about those eggs? Are you going to send me some?" It seems to be not only a profound bore to him, but really a sort of sensitiveness on his part. How he can bear to hear *us* play, I cannot imagine. It must grate on his ear terribly, I think, because everything *must* sound expressionless to him in comparison with his own marvellous conception. I assure you, no matter how beautifully we play any piece, the minute Liszt plays it, you would scarcely recognize it! His touch and his peculiar use of the pedal are two secrets of his playing, and then he seems to dive down in the most hidden thoughts of the composer, and fetch them up to the surface, so that they gleam out at you one by one, like stars!

The more I see and hear Liszt, the more I am lost in amazement! I can neither eat nor sleep on those days that I go to him. All my musical studies till now have been a mere going to school, a preparation for him. I often think of what Tausig said once: "Oh, compared with Liszt, we other artists are all blockheads." I did not believe it at the time, but I've seen the truth of it, and in studying Liszt's playing, I can see where Tausig got many of his own wonderful peculiarities. I think he was the most like Liszt of all the army that have had the privilege of his instruction.—I began this letter on Sunday, and it is now Tuesday. Yesterday I went to Liszt, and found that Bülow had just arrived. None of the other scholars had come, for a wonder, and I was just going away, when Liszt came out, asked me to come in a moment, and introduced me to Bülow. There I was, all alone with these two great artists in Liszt's *salon!* Wasn't *that* a situation? I only stayed a few minutes, of course, though I should have liked to spend hours, but our conversation was in the highest degree amusing while I *was* there. Bülow had just returned from his grand concert tour, and had been in London for the first time. In a few months he had given one hundred and twenty concerts! He is a fascinating creature, too, like all these master artists, but entirely different from Liszt, being small, quick, and airy in his movements, and having one of the boldest and proudest foreheads I ever saw. He looks like strength of will personified. Liszt gazed at "his Hans," as he calls him, with the fondest pride, and seemed perfectly

15

happy over his arrival. It was like his beautiful
courtesy to call me in and introduce me to Bülow instead of letting me go away. He thought I had come
to play to him, and was unwilling to have me take
that trouble for nothing, though he must have wished
me in Jericho. You would think I paid him a hundred dollars a lesson, instead of *his* condescending to
sacrifice his valuable time to *me* for nothing.

CHAPTER XIX.

Liszt's Expression in Playing.　Liszt on Conservatories.
　　Ordeal of Liszt's Lessons.　Liszt's Kindness.

WEIMAR, *June* 19, 1873.

In Liszt I can at last say that my ideal in *something*
has been realized.　He goes far beyond all that I
expected.　Anything so perfectly beautiful as he looks
when he sits at the piano I never saw, and yet he is
almost an old man now.*　I enjoy him as I would an
exquisite work of art.　His personal magnetism is
immense, and I can scarcely bear it when he plays.
He can make me cry all he chooses, and that is saying
a good deal, because I've heard so much music, and
never have been affected by it.　Even Joachim, whom
I think divine, never moved me.　When Liszt plays
anything pathetic, it sounds as if he had been through
everything, and opens all one's wounds afresh.　All
that one has ever suffered comes before one again.
Who was it that I heard say once, that years ago he
saw Clara Schumann sitting in tears near the platform, during one of Liszt's performances?—Liszt
knows well the influence he has on people, for
he always fixes his eyes on some one of us when he
plays, and I believe he tries to wring our hearts.
When he plays a passage, and goes *pearling* down the
key-board, he often looks over at me and smiles, to see
whether I am appreciating it.

* Liszt was born in 1811.

(227)

But I doubt if he feels any particular emotion himself, when he is piercing you through with his rendering. He is simply hearing every tone, knowing exactly what effect he wishes to produce and how to do it. In fact, he is practically two persons in one—the listener and the performer. But what immense self-command that implies! No matter how fast he plays you always feel that there is "plenty of time"—no need to be anxious! You might as well try to move one of the pyramids as fluster *him*. Tausig possessed this repose in a technical way, and his touch was marvellous; but he never drew the tears to your eyes. He could not wind himself through all the subtle labyrinths of the heart as Liszt does.

Liszt does such bewitching little things! The other day, for instance, Fräulein Gaul was playing something to him, and in it were two runs, and after each run two staccato chords. She did them most beautifully, and struck the chords immediately after. "No, no," said Liszt, "after you make a run you must wait a minute before you strike the chords, as if in admiration of your own performance. You must pause, as if to say, 'How nicely I did that.'" Then he sat down and made a run himself, waited a second, and then struck the two chords in the treble, saying as he did so "Bra-*vo*," and then he played again, struck the other chord, and said again "Bra-*vo*," and positively, it was as if the piano had softly applauded! That is the way he plays everything. It seems as if the piano were speaking with a *human* tongue.

Our class has swelled to about a dozen persons now,

and a good many others come and play to him once or twice and then go. As I wrote to L. the other day, that dear little scholar of Henselt, Fräulein Kahrer, was one, but she only stayed three days. She was a most interesting little creature, and told some funny stories about Henselt, who she says has a most violent temper, and is very severe. She said that one day he was giving a lesson to Princess Katherina (whoever that is), and he was so enraged over her playing that he snatched away the music, and dashed it to the ground. The Princess, however, did not lose her equanimity, but folded her arms and said, "Who shall pick it up?" And he had to bend and restore it to its place.

I've never seen Liszt look angry but once, but then he was terrific. Like a lion! It was one day when a student from the Stuttgardt conservatory attempted to play the Sonata Appassionata. He had a good deal of technique, and a moderately good conception of it, but still he was totally inadequate to the work—and indeed, only a *mighty* artist like Tausig or Bülow ought to attempt to play it. It was a hot afternoon, and the clouds had been gathering for a storm. As the Stuttgardter played the opening notes of the sonata, the tree-tops suddenly waved wildly, and a low growl of thunder was heard muttering in the distance. "Ah," said Liszt, who was standing at the window, with his delicate quickness of perception, "a fitting accompaniment." (You know Beethoven wrote the Appassionata one night when he was caught in a thunder-storm.) If Liszt had only played it himself, the whole thing would have been like a poem. But he walked up and down the room and forced himself to listen, though he could scarcely bear it, I could see. A few times he pushed the student aside and played a few bars himself, and we saw the passion leap up into his face like a glare of sheet lightning. Anything so magnificent as it was, the little that he *did* play, and the startling individuality of his conception, I never heard or imagined. I felt as if I did not know whether I were "in the body or out of the body." —GLORIOUS BEING! He is a two-edged sword that cuts through everything.

The Stuttgardter made some such glaring mistakes, not in the notes, but in rhythm, etc., that at last Liszt burst out with, "You come from Stuttgardt, and play like *that!*" and then he went on in a tirade against conservatories and teachers in general. He was like a thunder-storm himself. He frowned, and bent his head, and his long hair fell over his face, while the poor Stuttgardter sat there like a beaten hound. Oh, it was awful! If it had been I, I think I should have withered entirely away, for Liszt is always so amiable that the contrast was all the stronger.—"*Aber das geht Sie nichts an* (But this does not concern you)," said he, in a conciliatory tone, suddenly stopping himself and smiling. "*Spielen Sie weiter* (Play on)."—He meant that it was not at the student but at the conservatories that he had been angry.

Liszt hasn't the nervous irritability common to artists, but on the contrary his disposition is the most exquisite and tranquil in the world. We have been there inces-

santly, and I've never seen him ruffled except two or
three times, and then he was tired and not himself, and
it was a most transient thing.   When I think what a
little savage Tausig often was, and how cuttingly sarcastic
Kullak could be at times, I am astonished that Liszt so
rarely loses his temper.   He has the power of turning
the best side of every one outward, and also the most
marvellous and instant appreciation of what that side is.
If there is *anything* in you, you may be sure that Liszt
will know it.   Whether he chooses to let you think he
does, may, however, be another matter.

WEIMAR, *July* 15, 1873.

Liszt is such an immense, inspiring force that one has
to try and stride forward with him at double rate,
even if with double expenditure, too !   To-day I'm more
dead than alive, as we had a lesson from him yesterday
that lasted four hours.   There were twenty artists present,
all of whom were anxious to play, and as he was in high
good-humour, he played ever so much himself in between.
It was perfectly magnificent, but exhausting and exciting
to the last degree.   When I come home from the lessons I
fling myself on the sofa, and feel as if I never wanted to
get up again.   It is a fearful day's work every time I go
to him.   First, four hours' practice in the morning.
Then a nervous, anxious feeling that takes away my appe-
tite, and prevents me from eating my dinner.   And then
several hours at Liszt's, where one succession of concertos,
fantasias, and all sorts of tremendous things are played.
You never know before whom you must play there, for

it is the musical headquarters of the world. Directors of conservatories, composers, artists, aristocrats, all come in, and you have to bear the brunt of it as best you can. The first month I was here, when there were only five of us, it was quite another matter, but now the room is crowded every time.

Liszt gave a matinee the other day at which I played a "Soirée de Vienne," by Tausig—awfully hard, but very brilliant and peculiar. I don't know how I ever got through it, for I had only been studying it a few days, and didn't even know it by heart, nor had I played it to Liszt. He only told me the evening before, too, about eight o'clock—"To-morrow I give a matinee; bring your Soirée de Vienne." I rushed home and practiced till ten, and then I got up early the next morning and practiced a few hours. The matinee was at eleven o'clock. First, Liszt played himself, then a young lady sang several songs, then there was a piece for piano and flute played by Liszt and a flutist, and then I came. I was just as frightened as I could be! Metzdorf (my Russian friend) and Urspruch sat down by me to give me courage, and to turn the leaves, but Liszt insisted upon turning himself, and stood behind me and did it in his dexterous way. He says it is an art to turn the leaves properly! He was *so* kind, and whenever I did anything well he would call out *"charmant!"* to encourage me. It is considered a great compliment to be asked to play at a matinee, and I don't know why Liszt paid it to me at the expense of others who were there who play far better than I do—among them a young lady from Norway, lately come, who is a most *superb* pianist. She was a pupil of Kullak's, too, but it is four years since she left him, and she has been concertizing a good deal. Yesterday she played Schumann's A minor concerto magnificently. I was surprised that Liszt had not selected her, but one can never tell what to expect from Liszt. With him "nothing is to be presumed on or despaired of"—as the proverb says. He is so full of moods and phases that you have to have a very sharp perception even to begin to understand him, and he can cut you all up fine without your ever guessing it. He rarely mortifies any one by an open snub, but what is perhaps worse, he manages to let the rest of the class know what he is thinking while the poor victim remains quite in darkness about it!—Yes, he can do very cruel things.

After all, though, people generally have their own assurance to thank, or their own want of tact, when they do not get on with Liszt. If they go to him full of themselves, or expecting to make an impression on *him*, or merely for the sake of saying they have been with him, instead of presenting themselves to sit at his feet in humility, as they ought, and learn whatever he is willing to impart—he soon finds it out, and treats them accordingly. Some one once asked Liszt, what he would have been had he not been a musician. "The first diplomat in Europe," was the reply. With this Machiavellian bent it is not surprising that he sometimes indulges himself in playing off the conceited or the obtuse for the benefit of the bystanders. But the real *basis* of his nature is compassion. *The bruised reed he does not break, nor the humble and docile heart despise!*

Fräulein Gaul tells a characteristic story about the "Meister," as we call Liszt.   When she first came to him a year or two ago, she brought him one day Chopin's B flat minor Scherzo—one of those stock pieces that every artist *must* learn, and that has also been thrummed to death by countless tyros.   Liszt looked at it, and to her fright and dismay cried out in a fit of impatience, "No, I *won't* hear it!" and dashed it angrily into the corner.   The next day he went to see her, apologized for his outburst of temper, and said that as a penance for it he would force himself to give her not one, but two or three lessons on the Scherzo, and in the most minute and careful manner—which accordingly he did!   Fancy any music teacher you ever heard of, so humbling himself to a little girl of fifteen, and then remember that Tausig, the greatest of modern virtuosi, said of Liszt, "No mortal can measure himself with Liszt.   He dwells upon a solitary height."

But you need not fear that I am "giving up American standards" because I reverence Liszt so boundlessly. Everything is topsy-turvy in Europe according to *our* moral ideas, and they don't have what we call "men" over here.   But they *do* have artists that we cannot approach!   It is as a Master in Art that I look at and write of Liszt, and his mere presence is to his pupils such stimulus and joy, that when I leave *him* I shall feel I have left the best part of my life behind!

CHAPTER XX.

Liszt's Compositions. His Playing and Teaching of Beethoven. His "Effects" in Piano-playing. Excursion to Jena. A New Music Master.

WEIMAR, *July* 24, 1873.

Liszt is going away to-day. He was to have left several days ago, but the Emperor of Austria or Russia (I don't know which), came to visit the Grand Duke, and of course Liszt was obliged to be on hand and to spend a day with them. He is such a grandee himself that kings and emperors are quite matters of course to him. Never was a man so courted and spoiled as he! The Grand Duchess herself frequently visits him. But he never allows anyone to ask him to play, and even she doesn't venture it. That is the only point in which one sees Liszt's sense of his own greatness; otherwise his manner is remarkably unassuming.

Liszt will be gone until the middle of August, and I shall be thankful to have a few weeks of repose, and to be able to study more quietly. With him one is at high pressure all the time, and I have gained a good many more ideas from him than I can work up in a hurry. In fact, Liszt has revealed to me an entirely new idea of piano-playing. He is a wonderful *composer*, by the way, and that is what I was unprepared for in him. His oratorio of *Christus* was brought out here this summer, and many strangers and celebrities came to hear it, Wagner

among others. It was magnificent, and one of the
noblest, and decidedly the grandest oratorio that I ever
heard. I've never had time to write home about it, for
I felt that it required a dissertation in itself to do it justice. I wish it could be performed in Boston, for his
orchestral and choral works, I am sorry to say, make
their way very slowly in Germany. " Liszt helped Wagner," said he to me, sadly, "but who will help Liszt?
though, compared with Opera it is as much harder for
Oratorio to conquer a place as it is for a pianist to
achieve success when compared to a singer." So he
feels as if things were against him, though his heart and
soul are so bound up in sacred music, that he told me it
had become to him "the only thing worth living for."
He really seems to care almost nothing for his piano-
playing or for his piano compositions.

And yet, what beauty is there in those compositions!
In Berlin I had always been taught that Liszt was a
would-be composer, that he could not write a melody,
that he had no originality, and that his compositions
were merely glitter to dazzle the eyes of the public.
How unjust and untrue have I found all these asser-
tions to be! Here I have an opportunity of hearing
his piano works *en masse,* and day by day (since all
the young artists are playing them), and my previous
ideas have been entirely reversed. If Liszt is *anything,*
he is *original.* One can see that at a glance, simply
by imagining his music taken out. Where is there
anything that would fill its place? When artists wish
to make an "effect" and stir up the public—"to fuse
the leaden thousands," as Chopin expressed it—what

do they play? LISZT!—Not only is his music brilliant
—not only does he pour this wealth of pearls and diamonds down the key-board, but his pieces rise to great
climaxes, are grandiose in style, overleap all bound-
aries, and whirl you away with the vehemence of passion. Then what lightness of touch in the lesser *mor-
ceaux*, where he is often the acme of tenderness, grace
and fairy-like sportiveness, while in the melancholy
ones, what subtle feeling after the emotions curled up
in the remote corners of the heart! They are so rich in
harmony, so weird, so wild, that when you hear them
you are like a sea-weed cast upon the bosom of the
ocean. And then what could be more deep and poetic
than Liszt's transcriptions of Schubert's and Wagner's
songs? They are altogether exquisite. Finally, Liszt's
compositions stand the severest test of merit. They
wear well. You can play them a long time and never
weary of them. In short, they embrace every element
except the classic, and the question is, whether these
airy or intense ideas that appeal to you through their
veils of shimmer and sheen are not a sort of classics
in their own way!

Liszt's Christus is arranged for piano for four hands,
and I wish I had it, and also Bülow's great edition of Beethoven's sonatas—Oh! you cannot *conceive*
anything like Liszt's playing of Beethoven. When *he*
plays a sonata it is as if the composition rose from the
dead and stood transfigured before you. You ask
yourself, "Did *I* ever play that?" But it bores him
so dreadfully to hear the sonatas, that though I've
heard him teach a good many, I haven't had the cour-

age to bring him one. I suppose he is sick of the sound
of them, or perhaps it is because he feels obliged to be
conscientious in teaching Beethoven!

When one of the young pianists brings Liszt a sonata, he puts on an expression of resignation and generally begins a half protest which he afterward thinks
better of.—"Well, go on," he will say, and then he
proceeds to be very strict. He always teaches Beethoven with notes, which shows how scrupulous he is
about him, for, of course, he knows all the sonatas by
heart. He has Bülow's edition, which he opens and
lays on the end of the grand piano. Then as he walks
up and down he can stop and refer to it and point out
passages, as they are being played, to the rest of the
class. Bülow probably got many of his ideas from
Liszt. One day when Mr. Orth was playing the Alle-
gro of the Sonata Op. 110, Liszt insisted upon having
it done in a particular way, and made him go back
and repeat it over and over again. One line of it is
particularly hard. Liszt made every one in the class
sit down and try it. Most of them failed, which
amused him.—"Ah, yes," said he, laughing, "when I
once begin to play the pedagogue I am not to be out-
done!" and then he related as an illustration of his
"pedagogism" a little anecdote of a former pupil of
his, now an eminent artist. "I liked young M. very
much," said he. "He played beautifully, but he was
inclined to be lazy and to take things easily. One
morning he brought me Chopin's E minor concerto,
and he rather skimmed over that difficult passage in the
middle of the first movement as if he hadn't taken the

trouble really to study it. His execution was not clean. So I thought I would give him a lesson, and I kept him playing those two pages over and over for an hour or two until he had mastered them. His arms must have been ready to break when he got through! At the next lesson there was no M. I sent to know why he did not appear. He replied that he had been out hunting and had hurt his arm so that he could not play. At the lesson following he accordingly presented himself with his arm in a sling. But I always suspected it was a stratagem on his part to avoid playing, and that nothing really ailed him. He had had enough for one while," added Liszt, with a mischievous smile.

On Monday I had a most delightful téte-â-téte with Liszt, quite by chance. I had occasion to call upon him for something, and, strange to say, he was alone, sitting by his table and writing. Generally all sorts of people are up there. He insisted upon my staying a while, and we had the most amusing and entertaining conversation imaginable. It was the first time I ever heard Liszt really talk, for he contents himself mostly with making little jests. He is full of *esprit*. We were speaking of the faculty of mimicry, and he told me such a funny little anecdote about Chopin. He said that when he and Chopin were young together, somebody told him that Chopin had a remarkable talent for mimicry, and so he said to Chopin, "Come round to my rooms this evening and show off this talent of yours." So Chopin came. He had purchased a blonde wig ("I was very blonde at that time," said

Liszt), which he put on, and got himself up in one of
Liszt's suits. Presently an acquaintance of Liszt's came
in, Chopin went to meet him instead of Liszt, and
took off his voice and manner so perfectly, that
the man actually mistook him for Liszt, and made an
appointment with him for the next day —"and there I
was in the room," said Liszt. Wasn't that remarkable?

Another evening I was there about twilight and
Liszt sat at the piano looking through a new oratorio,
which had just come out in Paris upon "Christus,"
the same subject that his own oratorio was on. He
asked me to turn for him, and evidently was not interested, for he would skip whole pages and begin again,
here and there. There was only a single lamp, and
that rather a dim one, so that the room was all in
shadow, and Liszt wore his Merlin-like aspect. I asked
him to tell me how he produced a certain effect he
makes in his arrangement of the ballad in Wagner's
Flying Dutchman. He looked very "*fin*" as the
French say, but did not reply. He never gives a direct
answer to a direct question. "Ah," said I, "you won't
tell." He smiled, and then immediately played the
passage. It was a long arpeggio, and the effect he made
was, as I had supposed, a pedal effect. He kept the
pedal down throughout, and played the beginning of
the passage in a grand *rolling* sort of manner, and
then all the rest of it with a very pianissimo touch,
and so lightly, that the continuity of the arpeggios was
destroyed, and the notes seemed to be just *strewn* in,
as if you broke a wreath of flowers and scattered them

according to your fancy. It is a most striking and beautiful effect, and I told him I didn't see how he ever thought of it. "Oh, I've invented a great many things,"said he,indifferently—"*this*,for instance,"—and he began playing a double roll of octaves in chromatics in the bass of the piano. It was very grand, and made the room reverberate. "Magnificent," said I. "Did you ever hear me do a storm?" said he. "No." "Ah, you ought to hear me do a storm! Storms are my *forte!*" Then to himself between his teeth, while a weird look came into his eyes as if he could indeed rule the blast, "*Da* KRACHEN *die Bäume* (Then *crash* the trees!)"

How ardently I wished he *would* "play a storm," but of course he *didn't,* and he presently began to trifle over the keys in his *blasé* style. I suppose he couldn't quite work himself up to the effort, but that look and tone told how Liszt *would* do it.—Alas, that we poor mortals here below should share so often the fate of Moses, and have only a glimpse of the Promised Land, and that without the consolation of being Moses! But perhaps, after all, the vision is better than the reality. We see the *whole land,* even if but at a distance, instead of being limited merely to the spot where our foot treads.

Once again I saw Liszt in a similar mood, though his expression was this time *comfortably* rather than *wildly* destructive. It was when Fräulein Remmertz was playing his E flat concerto to him. There were two grand pianos in the room, and she was sitting at one, and he at the other, accompanying and interpolating as he felt disposed. Finally they came to a

16

place where there were a series of passages beginning
with both hands in the middle of the piano, and going
in opposite directions to the ends of the key-board,
ending each time in a short, sharp chord. *"Alles
zum Fenster hinaus werfen* (Pitch everything out of
the window)," said he, in a cozy, easy sort of way, and
he began playing these passages and giving every chord
a whack as if he *were* splitting everything up and fling-
ing it out, and that with such enjoyment, that you felt
as if you'd like to bear a hand, too, in the work of general demolition! But I never shall forget Liszt's look
as he so lazily proposed to "pitch everything out of
the window." It reminded me of the expression of a
big tabby-cat as it sits and purrs away, blinking its
eyes and seemingly half asleep, when suddenly — ! — !
out it strikes with both its claws, and woe be to whatever is within its reach! Perhaps, after all, the secret
of Liszt's fascination is this power of intense and wild
emotion that you feel he possesses, together with the
nost perfect control over it.

Liszt sometimes strikes wrong notes when he plays,
but it does not trouble him in the least. On the contrary, he rather enjoys it. He reminds me of one of
the cabinet ministers in Berlin, of whom it is said that
he has an amazing talent for making blunders, but a
still more amazing one for getting out of them and
covering them up. Of Liszt the first part of this is
not true, for if he strikes a wrong note it is simply because he chooses to be careless. But the last part of
it applies to him eminently. It always amuses him
instead of disconcerting him when he comes down

LISZT MAKING A MISTAKE. 243

squarely *wrong*, as it affords him an opportunity of displaying his ingenuity and giving things such a turn that the false note will appear simply a key leading to new and unexpected beauties. An accident of this kind happened to him in one of the Sunday matinees, when the room was full of distinguished people and of his pupils. He was rolling up the piano in arpeggios in a very grand manner indeed, when he struck a semi-tone short of the high note upon which he had intended to end. I caught my breath and wondered whether he was going to leave us like that, in mid-air, as it were, and the harmony unresolved, or whether he would be reduced to the humiliation of correcting himself like ordinary mortals, and taking the right chord. A half smile came over his face, as much as to say— "Don't fancy that *this* little thing disturbs me,"—and he instantly went meandering down the piano in harmony with the false note he had struck, and then rolled deliberately up in a second grand sweep, *this* time striking true. I never saw a more delicious piece of cleverness. It was so quick-witted and so exactly characteristic of Liszt. Instead of giving you a chance to say, "He has made a mistake," he forced you to say, "He has shown how to get out of a mistake."

Another day I heard him pass from one piece into another by making the finale of the first one play the part of prelude to the second. So exquisitely were the two woven together that you could hardly tell where the one left off and the other began.—Ah me! *Such* a facile grace! *Nobody* will ever equal him, with those rolling basses and those flowery trebles. And then his Adagios ! When you hear him in one of *those*, you feel that his playing has got to that point when it is purified from all earthly dross and is an exhalation of the soul that mounts straight to heaven.

WEIMAR, *August* 8, 1873.

The other day we all made an excursion to Jena, which is about three hours' drive from here. We went in carriages in a long train, and pulled up at a hotel named The Bear. There we took our second breakfast. There was to be a concert at five in a church, where some of Liszt's music was to be performed. After breakfast we went to the church, where Liszt met us, and the rehearsal took place. After the rehearsal we went to dinner. We had three long tables which Liszt arranged to suit himself, his own place being in the middle. He always manages every little detail with the greatest tact, and is very particular never to let two ladies or two gentlemen sit together, but always alternately a lady and a gentleman. "*Immer eine bunte Reihe machen* (Always have a little variety)," said he. The dinner was a very entertaining one to me, because I could converse with Liszt and hear all he said, as he was nearly opposite me. I was in very high spirits that day, and as Kellerman, Bendix and Urspruch were all near me, too, we had endless fun. We had new potatoes for dinner, boiled with their skins on, and Liszt threw one at me, and I caught it. There was another young artist there from Brussels named Gurickx, whom I didn't know, because he spoke only French, and as I do not speak it, we had never exchanged words in the class. I wasn't paying any attention to him, therefore, when suddenly my left-hand neighbour touched my arm. I looked round and he handed me a flower made of bread "from Monsieur Gurickx." I wish you could have seen it! It had the effect of a tube rose. Every little leaf and petal was as delicately turned as if nature herself had done it. The bread was fresh, and Gurickx had worked it between his fingers to the consistency of clay, and then modelled these little flowers which he stuck on to a stem. It was so artistically done, and it was such a dainty little thing to do, that I saw at once that he was interesting and that he possessed that marvellous French taste.

Since then we have become very good friends, and he is teaching me to speak French. He plays beautifully, and was trained in the famous Brussels conservatory, of which Dupont is the head. Servais also got his musical education there. They both advise me to go there for a year, as Dupont is a very great master indeed, and Brussels is the very home and centre of art and taste of every description—a "little Paris"—but more earnest, more German. Gurickx went through the art-school in Brussels as well as the conservatory, so that he paints as well as plays, and he had quite a struggle with himself to decide to which art he should devote himself. His style is the grandiose and fiery. Rubinstein is his model, and he plays Liszt's Rhapsodies as I never heard any one else. He brings out all their power, brilliancy and careering wildness, and makes the greatest sensation of

them. Such tremendous sweeping chords! Liszt himself doesn't play the chords as well as Gurickx;—perhaps
because he does not care now to exert the strength.

But to return to Jena. After dinner Liszt said, "Now
we'll go to Paradise." So we put on our things, and
proceeded to walk along the river to a place called Paradise, on account of its loveliness. We passed the University, on one corner of which is a tablet with "W. von
Goethe" written against the wall of the room which
Goethe occupied. It seemed strange to me to be passing
the room of my beloved Goethe, with our equally
beloved Liszt!—This walk along the river was enchanting. The current was very rapid, and the willows were
all blowing in the breeze. There is an odd triangular-
shaped hill that rises on one side very boldly and abruptly,
called the Fox's Head. The way was under a double
row of tall trees, which met at the top and formed a
green arch over our heads. It was all breeze and freshness, and the sunlight struck picturesquely aslant the
hill-sides. I started to walk with Liszt, but he was so
surrounded that it was difficult to get near him, so I
walked instead with an interesting young artist named
O., who was at once extraordinarily ugly and extremely
clever.

After our walk we went to the concert, wnich was
lovely, and then at seven we were all invited to tea at
the house of a friend of Liszt's. He was a very tall
man, and he had a very tall and hospitable daughter,
nearly as big as himself, who received us very cordially.
The tea was all laid on tables in the garden, and the
sausages were cooking over a fire made on the grounds.

We sat down pell-mell, anywhere, I next to Liszt, who kept putting things on my plate. When supper was over he retreated to a little summer house with some of his friends, to smoke. We sauntered round the grass plat in front of it until Liszt called us to come in and sit by him, which we did until he was ready to go.

I've heard of a new music master lately. When my friend Miss B. was here, she told me that she had met a "Herr Director Deppe" in Berlin, after I left, and had told him all about me and my struggle to conquer the piano. He seemed very much interested and said, "O, if she had only come to me! *I* would have helped her," and from all I can hear I think he must be the man for me. He is interested in Sherwood, who used to talk to me about him last winter. Sherwood says he is wholly disinterested and devoted to art, and lives entirely in music, and that he is a noble-hearted man, and the "most musical person he ever met." Sherwood often wavers between him and Kullak, and Deppe would like to teach Sherwood if he could, simply out of interest for him.—Deppe has a pupil whom he has trained entirely himself, and whom he is going to bring out next winter. Sherwood says he never heard anything so beautiful as her playing. She is spending the summer near Deppe, and he hears her play the programme she is going to give in Berlin next winter, every day. Think what immense certainty that must give!

CHAPTER XXI.

WEIMAR, *August* 23, 1873.

Liszt has returned from his trip, and I have played
to him twice this week, and am to go again on Monday.   He praised me very much on Tuesday, and said
I played admirably.   I knew he was pleased, because
whenever he corrected me he would say, "*Nein, Kindchen*" in such a gentle way!   "*Kind*" is the German
for child, and "*Kindchen*" is a diminutive, and whenever he calls you that you can tell he has a leaning
toward you.

This week is the first time that I have been able to
play to him without being nervous, or that my fingers
have felt warm and natural.   It has been a fearful
ordeal, truly, to play there, for not only was Liszt himself present, but such a crowd of artists, all ready to
pick flaws in your playing, and to say, " She hasn't got
much talent."   I am so glad that I stayed until Liszt's
return, for now the rush is over, and he has much
more time for those of us who are left, and plays a
great deal more himself.   Yesterday he played us a
study of Paganini's, arranged by himself, and also his
Campanella.   I longed for M., as she is so fond of
the Campanella.   Liszt gave it with a velvety softness,
clearness, brilliancy and pearliness of touch that was
inimitable.   And oh, his grace!   *Nobody* can com-

pare with him! Everybody else sounds heavy beside him!

However, I have felt some comfort in knowing that it is not Liszt's genius alone that makes him such a player. He has gone through such technical studies as no one else has except Tausig, perhaps. He plays everything under the sun in the way of *Etuden*—has played them, I mean. On Tuesday I got him talking about the composers who were the fashion when he was a young fellow in Paris—Kalkbrenner, Herz, etc.—and I asked him if he could not play us something by Kalkbrenner. "O yes! I must have a few things of Kalkbrenner's in my head still," and then he played part of a concerto. Afterward he went on to speak of Herz, and said: "I'll play you a little study of Herz's that is infamously hard. It is a stupid little theme," and then he played the theme, "but *now* pay attention." Then he played the study itself. It was a most hazardous thing, where the hands kept crossing continually with great rapidity, and striking notes in the most difficult positions. It made us all laugh; and Liszt hit the notes every time, though it was disgustingly hard, and as he said himself, "he used to get all in a heat over it." He had evidently studied it so well that he could never forget it. He went on to speak of Moscheles and of his compositions. He said that when between thirty and forty years of age, Moscheles played superbly, but as he grew older he became too old-womanish and set in his ways—and then he took off Moscheles, and played his Etuden in his style. It was very funny. But it showed how

Liszt has studied *everything*, and the universality of his knowledge, for he knows Tausig's and Rubinstein's studies as well as Kalkbrenner and Herz. There cannot be many persons in the world who keep up with the whole range of musical literature as he does.

Liszt loved Tausig as his own child, and is always delighted when we play any of his music. His death was an awful blow to Liszt, for he used to say, " He will be the inheritor of my playing." I suppose he thought he would live again in him, for he always says, " Never did such talent come under my hands." I would give anything to have seen them together, for Tausig was a wonderfully clever and captivating man, and I can imagine he must have fascinated Liszt. They say he was the naughtiest boy that ever was heard of, and caused Liszt no end of trouble and vexation; but he always forgave him, and after the vexation was past Liszt would pat him on the head and say, *"Carlchen, entweder wirst du ein grosser Lump oder ein grosser Meister* (You'll turn out either a great blockhead or a great master)." That is Liszt all over. He is so indulgent that in consideration of talent he will forgive anything.

Tausig's father, who was himself a music-master, took him to Liszt when he was fourteen years old, hoping that Liszt would receive the little marvel as a pupil and protégé.

But Liszt would not even hear the boy play. " I have had," he declared positively, " enough of child prodigies. They never come to much." Tausig's father apparently acquiesced in the reply, but while he and

Liszt were drinking wine and smoking together, he managed to smuggle the child on to the piano-stool behind Liszt, and signed to him to begin to play. The little Tausig plunged into Chopin's A flat Polonaise with such fire and boldness that Liszt turned his eagle head, and after a few bars cried, "I take him!" I heard Liszt say once that he could not endure child prodigies. "I have no time," said he, "for these artists *die* WERDEN *sollen* (that *are* to be)!"

WEIMAR, *Septemeber* 9, 1873.

This week has been one of great excitement in Weimar, on account of the wedding of the son of the Grand Duke. All sorts of things have been going on, and the Emperor and Empress came on from Berlin. There have been a great many rehearsals at the theatre of different things that were played, and of course Liszt took a prominent part in the arrangement of the music. He directed the Ninth Symphony, and played twice himself with orchestral accompaniments. One of the pieces he played was Weber's Polonaise in E major, and the other was one of his own Rhapsodies Hongroises. Of these I was at the rehearsal. When he came out on the stage the applause was tremendous, and enough in itself to excite and electrify one. I was enchanted to have an opportunity to hear Liszt as a concert player. The director of the orchestra here is a beautiful pianist and composer himself, as well as a splendid conductor, but it was easy to see that he had to get all his wits together to follow Liszt, who gave full rein to his imagination, and let the *tempo* fluctuate as he felt inclined. As for Liszt, he scarcely *looked* at the keys, and it was astounding to see his hands go rushing up and down the piano and perform passages of the utmost rapidity and difficulty, while his head was turned all the while towards the orchestra, and he kept up a running fire of remarks with them continually. "You violins, strike in *sharp* here." " You trumpets, not too loud there," etc. He did everything with the most immense *aplomb*, and without seeming to pay any attention to his hands, which moved of themselves as if they were independent beings and had their own brain and everything! He never did the same thing twice alike. If it were a scale the first time, he would make it in double or broken thirds the second, and so on, constantly surprising you with some new turn. While you were admiring the long roll of the wave, a sudden spray would be dashed over you, and make you catch your breath! No, never was there such a player! The nervous intensity of his touch takes right hold of you. When he had finished everybody shouted and clapped their hands like mad, and the orchestra kept up such a *fanfare* of applause, that the din was quite overpowering. Liszt smiled and bowed, and walked off the stage indifferently, not giving himself the trouble to come back, and presently he quietly sat down in the parquet, and the rehearsal proceeded. The concert itself took place at the court, so that I did not hear it. Metzdorf was there, however, and he said that Liszt played fabulously, of course, but that he was not as inspired as he was in the morning, and did not make the same effect.

WEIMAR, *September* 15, 1873.

The other day an excursion was arranged to Sondershausen, a town about three hours' ride from Weimar in the cars. There was to be a concert there in honour of Liszt, and a whole programme of his music was to be performed. About half a dozen of the " Lisztianer "—as the Weimarese dub Liszt's pupils— agreed to go, I, of course, being one. Liszt himself, the Countess von X. and Count S. were to lead the party. The morning we started was one of those perfect autumnal days when it is a delight simply to *live*.

After breakfast I hurried off to the station, where I met the others, everybody being in the highest spirits. Liszt and his titled friends travelled in a first class carriage by themselves. The rest of us went second class, in the next carriage behind. We were very gay indeed, and the time did not seem long till we arrived at Sondershausen, where we exchanged our seats in the cars for seats in an omnibus, and drove to the principal hotel. There were not sufficient accommodations for us all, owing to the number of strangers who had come to the festival, so Mrs. S. and I went to a smaller hotel in a more distant part of the town to engage rooms, intending to return and dine with Liszt and the rest. Just as our noisy vehicle clattered up to the inn and some of the gentlemen jumped out to arrange matters, the solemn strains of a chorale were heard from a church close by, with its grand and rolling organ accompaniment. Somehow it made me feel sad to hear it, and a sense of the *transitoriness* of things came over me. It seemed like one of those voices from the other world that call to us now and then.

After we had engaged our rooms, we drove back to the hotel where Liszt was staying, and where we were to dine immediately. It was in the centre of the town, and directly opposite the palace, which rose boldly on a sort of eminence with great flights of stone steps sweeping down to the road on each side. It looked quite imposing. An avenue wound up the hill to the right of it. In the dining-room of the hotel a long table was spread and all the places were carefully set. My place was next Count S. and not far from Liszt. So I was very well seated. Everybody began talking at once the minute dinner was served, as they always do at table in Germany. Toward the close of it were the usual number of toasts in honour of Liszt, to which he responded in rather a bored sort of way. I don't wonder he gets tired of them, for it is always the same thing. He did not seem to be in his usual spirits, and had a fatigued air.

After dinner he said, "Now let us go and see Fräulein Fichtner." Fräulein Fichtner was the young lady who was going to play his concerto in A major at the concert that evening. She is a well-known pianist in Germany, and is both pretty and brilliant. We started in a procession, which is the way one always walks with Liszt. It reminds me of those snow-balls the boys roll up at home—the crowd gathers as it proceeds! When

we got to the house we entered an obscure corridor
and began to find our way up a dark and narrow stair-
case. Some one struck a wax match. "Good!" called
out Liszt, in his sonorous voice. *"Leuchten Sie voraus*
(Light us up)." When we got to the top we pulled
the bell and were let in by Fräulein Fichtner's mother.
Fräulein Fichtner herself looked no ways dismayed at
the number of her guests, though we had the air of
coming to storm the house. She gaily produced all
the chairs there were, and those who could not find a
seat had to stand! She was in Weimar for a few days
this summer. So we had all met her before, and I
had once heard her play some duets by Schumann with
Liszt, who enjoyed reading with " Pauline," as he calls
her. It is to her that Raff has dedicated his exquisite
"Maerchen (Fairy story)." She is a sparkling bru-
nette, with a face full of intelligence. They say she
writes charming little poems and is gifted in various
ways. Not to tire her for the concert we only stayed
about twenty minutes.

Going back, Liszt indulged in a little graceful *badi-
nage* apropos of the concerto. You know he has
written two concertos. The one in E flat is much
played, but this one in A very rarely. It is exceedingly
difficult and is one of the few of his compositions that
it interests Liszt to know that people play. " I should
write it otherwise if I wrote it now," he explained to
me as we were walking along. " Some passages are
very troublesome (*haecklig*) to execute. I was younger
and less experienced when I composed it," he added,
with one of those illuminating smiles " like the flash
of a dagger in the sun," as Lenz says.

When we reached the hotel everybody went in to take a siesta—that " Mittags-Schlaf " which is law in Germany. I did not wish to sleep and felt like exploring the old town. So Count S. and I started on a walk. Sondershausen is a dreamy, sleepy place, with so little life about it that you hardly realize there are any people there at all. It is pleasantly situated, and gentle hills and undulations of land are all about it, but it seems as if the town had been dead for a long time and this were its grave over which one was quietly walking. We took the road that wound past the castle. It was embowered in trees, and behind the castle were gardens and conservatories. The road descended on the other side, and we followed it till we came unexpectedly upon a little circular park. Such a deserted, widowed little park it seemed ! Not a soul did we encounter as we wandered through its paths. Bordering them were great quantities of berry-laden snow-berry bushes, of which I am very fond. The park had a sort of rank and unkempt aspect, as if it were abandoned to itself. The very stream that went through it flowed sluggishly along, and as if it hadn't any particular object in life.—I enjoyed it very much, and it was very restful to walk about it. One felt there the truth of R.'s favourite saying, " It doesn't make any difference. *Nothing* makes any difference."

Count S. rattled on, but I didn't hear more than half of what he said. He is a pleasure-loving man of the world, fond of music, but a perfect materialist, and untroubled by the *"souffle vers le beau"* which torments so many people. At the same time he is ap-

preciative and very amusing, and one has no chance
to indulge. in melancholy with *him*.   We sauntered about till late in the afernoon, and then returned
to the hotel for coffee before going to the concert,
which began at seven.   The concert hall was behind
the palace and seemed to form a part of it.   Liszt,
the Countess von X., and Count S. sat in a box, aris-
tocratic-fashion.   The rest of us were in the parquet.
I was amazed at the orchestra, which was very large
and played gloriously.   It seemed to me as fine as that
of the Gewandhaus in Leipsic, though I suppose it
cannot be.—"Why has no one ever mentioned this
orchestra to me?"   I asked of Kellermann, who sat
next, " and how is it one finds such an orchestra in
such a place?"   "Oh," said he, " this orchestra is very
celebrated, and the Prince of Sondershausen is a great
patron of music."   This is the way it is in Germany.
Every now and then one has these surprises.   You
never know when you are going to stumble upon a
jewel in the most out-of-the-way corner.

We were all greatly excited over Fräulein Fichtner's
playing, and it seemed very jolly to be behind the
scenes, as it were, and to have one of our own number performing.   We applauded tremendously when
she came out.   She was not nervous in the least, but
began with great *aplomb*, and played most beautifully.
The concerto made a generally dazzling and difficult
impression upon me, but did not "take hold" of me
particularly.   I do not know how Liszt was pleased
with her rendering of it, for I had no opportunity of
asking him.   She also played his Fourteenth Rhapsody

with orchestral accompaniment in most bold and
dashing style.   Fräulein Fichtner is more in the bra-
vura than in the sentimental line, and she has a certain breadth, grasp, and freshness.   The last piece on
the programme was Liszt's Choral Symphony, which
was magnificent.   The chorus came at the end of it,
as in the Ninth Symphony.   Mrs. S. said she was
familiar with it from having heard Thomas's orchestra play it in New York.—That orchestra, by the way,
from what I hear, seems to have developed into something remarkable.   It is a great thing for the musical
education of the country to have such an organization travelling every winter.   And what a revelation
is an orchestra the first time one hears it, even if it
be but a poor one!—Music come bodily down from
Heaven!   And here in their musical darkness, the
Americans in the provinces are having an orchestra of
the very highest excellence burst upon them in full
splendour.   What *could* be more American?   They
always have the best or none!

At nine o'clock in the evening the concert was
over, and we all returned to the hotel for supper.   We
were all desperately hungry after so much music and
enthusiasm.   Everybody wanted to be helped at
once, and the waiters were nearly distracted.   Count
S. sat next me and was very funny.   He kept
rapping the table like mad, but without any success.
Finally he exclaimed, "*Jetzt geh'* ich *auf Jagd*
(Now *I'm* going hunting)!" and sprang up from
his chair, rushed to the other end of the dining-
room, possessed himself of some dishes the waiters

were helping, and returned in triumph. I couldn't help laughing, and he made a great many jokes at the expense of the waiters and everybody else. I could not hear any of Liszt's conversation, which I regretted, but he seemed in a quiet mood. I do not think he is the same when he is with aristocrats. He must be among *artists* to unsheathe his sword. When he is with "swells," he is all grace and polish. He seems only to toy with his genius for their amusement, and he is never serious. At least this is as far as *my* observation of him goes on the few occasions I have seen him in the *beau monde.* The presence of the proud Countess von X. at Sondershausen kept him, as it were, at a distance from everybody else, and he was not overflowing with fun and gayety as he was at Jena. She, of course, did not go with us to see Fräulein Fichtner, which was fortunate. After supper one and all went to bed early, quite tired out with the day's excitement.

This haughty Countess, by the way, has always had a great fascination for me, because she looks like a woman who " has a history." I have often seen her at Liszt's matinees, and from what I hear of her, she is such a type of woman as I suppose only exists in Europe, and such as the heroines of foreign novels are modelled upon. She is a widow, and in appearance is about thirty-six or eight years old, of medium height, slight to thinness, but exceedingly graceful. She is always attired in black, and is utterly careless in dress, yet nothing can conceal her innate elegance of figure. Her face is pallid and her hair dark. She makes an impression of icy coldness and at the same

time of tropical heat. The pride of Lucifer‐to the
world in general—entire abandonment to the individual. I meet her often in the park, as she walks along
trailing her " sable garments like the night," and surrounded by her four beautiful boys—as Count S.
says, " each handsomer than the other."   They have
such romantic faces ! Dark eyes and dark curling hair.
The eldest is about fourteen and the youngest five.

   The little one is too lovely, with his brown curls
hanging on his shoulders ! I never shall forget the
supercilious manner in which the Countess took out
her eye-glass and looked me over as I passed her one
day in the park. Weimar being such a " *kleines Nest*
(little nest)," as Liszt calls it, every stranger is immediately remarked. She waited till I got close up, then
deliberately put up this glass and scrutinized me
from head to foot, then let it fall with a half-dis-
dainful, half-indifferent air, as if the scrutiny did not
reward the trouble.—I was so amused.   Her arrogance
piques all Weimar, and they never cease talking
about her. I can never help wishing to see her in a
fashionable toilet. If she is so *distinguée* in rather less
than ordinary dress, what *would* she be in a Parisian
costume? I mean as to grace, for she is not pretty.—
But as a psychological study, she is more interesting,
perhaps, as she is.   She always seems to me to be gradually going to wreck—a burnt-out volcano, with her
own ashes settling down upon her and covering her
up.   She is very highly educated, and is preparing her
eldest son for the university herself. What a subject
she would have been for a Balzac !

We stayed over the next day in Sondershausen, as there was to be another orchestral concert—this time with a miscellaneous programme. Fräulein Fichtner had already departed, but the first violinist played Mendelssohn's famous concerto for violin.—Not in Wilhelmj's masterly style, but extremely well. We took the train for Weimar about five P. M. Going back I was in the carriage with Liszt. He sat opposite me, and gradually began to talk. The conversation turned upon Weitzmann, my former harmony teacher, who, you remember, was so determined to make me learn. Liszt remarked upon the extent of his knowledge and said, " If I were not so old I should like to go to school again to Weitzmann." He was talking to Weitzmann one day, he said, and Weitzmann proposed to him that he should write a canon. " I sat down and worked over it a good while, but finally gave it up.—I know not why, but I never had any success in writing canons. Weitzmann then sat down, and in half an hour had produced two excellent ones." He gave this as an instance of Weitzmann's readiness.—A canon, you know, is a sort of musical puzzle. The right hand plays the theme. The left hand takes it up a little later and imitates the right. The two interweave, and the theme forms the melody and the accompaniment at the same time, according as it is played by the right or left hand—something on the principle of singing rounds. The difficulty consists in avoiding monotony with this continual iteration of the theme, which can be brought on at different intervals, inverted, etc., at will. It seems to be more a mathematical than a musical style of composition. I should suppose that *Bach* could fire off canons without end! He developed it in every imaginable form.—Liszt, however, is of rather a different school!

We got back to Weimar about eight in the evening, and this delicious excursion, like all others, *had to end.* But the quiet old town, with its musical name and its great orchestra, will long remain in my memory.

Adieu, Sondershausen!

CHAPTER XXII.

Farewell to Liszt! German Conservatories and their Methods. Berlin Again. Liszt and Joachim.

WEIMAR, *September* 24, 1873.

We had our last lesson from Liszt a few days ago, and he leaves Weimar next week. He was so hurried with engagements the last two times that he was not able to give us much attention. I played my Rubinstein concerto. He accompanied me himself on a second piano. We were there about six o'clock P. M. Liszt was out, but he had left word that if we came we were to wait. About seven he came in, and the lamps were lit. He was in an awful humour, and I never saw him so out of spirits. "How is it with our concerto?" said he to me, for he had told me the time before to send for the second piano accompaniment, and he would play it with me. I told him that unfortunately there existed no second piano part. "Then, child, you've fallen on your head, if you don't know that at least you must have a second copy of the concerto!" I told him I knew it by heart. "Oh!" said he, in a mollified tone. So he took my copy and played the orchestra part which is indicated above the piano part, and I played without notes. I felt inspired, for the piano I was at was a magnificent grand that Steinway presented to Liszt only the other day. Liszt was seated at another grand facing me, and the room was

(263)

dimly illuminated by one or two lamps. A few artists were sitting about in the shadow. It was at the twilight hour, " *l'heure du mystère*," as the poetic Gurickx used to say, and in short, the occasion was perfect, and couldn't happen so again. You see we always have our lessons in the afternoon, and it was a mere chance that it was so late this time. So I felt as if I were in an electric state. I had studied the piece so much that I felt perfectly sure of it, and then with Liszt's splendid accompaniment and his beautiful face to look over to—it was enough to bring out everything there was in one. If he had only been himself I should have had nothing more to desire, but he was in one of his bitter, sarcastic moods. However, I went rushing on to the end—like a torrent plunging down into darkness, I might say—for it was the end, too, of my lessons with Liszt!

In answer to your musical questions, I don't know that there is much to be told about conservatories of which you are not aware. The one in Stuttgardt is considered the best; and there the pupils are put through a regular graded method, beginning with learning to hold the hand, and with the simplest five finger exercises. There are certain things, studies, etc., which *all* the scholars have to learn. That was also the case in Tausig's conservatory. First we had to go through Cramer, then through the Gradus ad Parnassum, then through Moscheles, then Chopin, Henselt, Liszt and Rubinstein. I haven't got farther than Chopin, myself, but when I went to Kullak I studied Czerny's School for Virtuosen a whole year, which is the book he "swears by." I'm going on with them this winter. It takes years to pass through them all, but when you *have* finished them, you are an artist.

I think myself the "Schule des Virtuosen" is indispensable, much as I loathe it. First, there is nothing like it for giving you a technique. It consists of passages, generally about two lines in length, which Czerny has the face to request you to play from twenty to thirty times successively. You can imagine at that rate how long it takes you to play through one page! Tedious to the *last* degree! But it greatly equalizes and strengthens the fingers, and makes your execution smooth and elegant. It teaches you to take your time, or as the Germans call it, it gives you " *Ruhe* (repose)," the grand *sine qua non !* You learn to "play out" your passages (" *aus-spielen*," as Kullak is always saying) ; that is, you don't hurry or blur over the last notes, but play clearly and in strict time to the end of the passage. I saw Lebert, the head of the Stuttgardt conservatory, here this summer, and had several long conversations with him, and he told me he considered Bach the best study, and put the Well-Tempered Clavichord at the foundation of everything. The Stuttgardters study Bach every day, and I think it a capital plan myself. I have begun doing it, too. It was a great thing for me, that quarter of Bach that I took with Mr. Paine in Cambridge, and was one of your inspirations, when you "builded better than you knew."—I never *saw* a person with such an instinct to find out the right thing as you have ! If it hadn't been for that, I should never have

got so familiarized with Bach, or got into the way
of studying him for myself, as I have done a great
deal. It is as great for the fingers as it is "good for
the soul." Lenz, in his sketch of Chopin, says that
Chopin told him when he prepared for a concert he
never studied his own compositions at all, but shut
himself up and practiced Bach!

However, I suppose it comes to the same thing in
the end if one studies Bach, Czerny, or Gradus, only
you must *keep at* one of them all the while. The
grand thing is to have each of your five fingers go
"dum, dum," an equal number of times, which is the
principle of all three! Tausig was for Gradus, you
know, and practiced it himself every day. He used to
transpose the studies in different keys, and play just
the same in the left hand as in the right, and enhance
their difficulties in every way, but *I* always found
them hard enough as they were written! Bach
strengthens the fingers and makes them independent.
Czerny equalizes them and gives an easy and elegant execution, and Gradus is not only good for finger technique—it trains the arm and wrist also, and
gives a much more powerful execution.

I think that in all conservatories they have at least
six lessons a week, two solo, two in reading at sight,
and two in composition. Then there are often lectures held on musical subjects by some of the Professors, or by some one who is engaged for that purpose.
All large conservatories have an orchestra, composed
generally out of the scholars themselves, with a few
professionals hired to eke out deficiencies. With this

the best piano scholars play their concertos once a month, or once in six weeks. The number of public representations varies in every conservatory. In the Hoch Schule in Berlin they have two yearly in the Sing-Akademie. Kullak *professes* to have *one*, but he has so little interest in his scholars that he omits it when it suits his convenience. In Stuttgardt I believe they have four. I don't know much about the interior arrangements of Kullak's conservatory, because I only went to his own class. I lived too far away to attempt the theory and composition class. Liszt says that Kullak's ;pupils are always the best schooled of any, which rather surprised me, because there is a certain intimacy between him and Stuttgardt, and he always recommends scholars to the Stuttgardt conservatory.

The Stuttgardters do have immense technique, and I think they are better taught how to study. It strikes me as if Stuttgardt were the place to get the machine in working order, but I rather think that Kullak trains the head more. There is a young American here named Orth, who studied two years with Kullak, then he spent a year in Stuttgardt, and now he is going to return to Kullak. He says he thinks that not Lebert, but Pruckner, is the real backbone of the Stuttgardt conservatory, but that even with *him* one year is sufficient. Fräulein Gaul, on the contrary, with whom Lebert has taken the greatest possible pains, thinks him a magnificent master, and certainly he has developed her admirably. It is probably with him as with them all. If they take a fancy to you, they will do a great deal for you; if not, *nothing!* Liszt is no exception to this rule. I've seen him snub and entirely neglect young artists of the most remarkable talent and virtuosity, merely because they did not please him personally.

BERLIN, *October* 8, 1873.

Voilà! as Liszt always says. Here I am back again in old Berlin, and if I ever felt "like a cat in a strange garret," I do now. I left dear little Weimar two days ago, and parted from our adored Liszt a week ago to-day. He has gone to Rome. *Never* did I feel leaving anybody or any place so much, and Berlin seems to me like a great roaring wilderness. The distances are so *endless* here. You either have to kill yourself walking, or else spend a fortune in droschkies. The houses all seem to me as if they had grown. There is an immense number of new ones going up on all sides, and the noise, and the crowd, and the confusion are enough to set one distracted, after the idyllic life I've been leading. Ah, well! *Es war eben zu schön!* (It was *too* beautiful!)

Yesterday and to-day I've been looking about for a new boarding-place. I've had two invitations to dinner since my return, but everybody and everything seems so dull and stupid, prosaic and tedious to me, that I declined them both, and haven't given any of my friends my address until I have had a little time to let myself down gradually from the delights of Weimar.

Liszt was kindness itself when the time came to say good-bye, but I could scarcely get out a word, nor could I even thank him for all he had done for me. I did not wish to break down and make a scene, as I felt I should if I tried to say anything. So I fear he thought me rather ungrateful and matter-of-course, for he couldn't know that I was feeling an excess of emotion which kept me silent. I miss going to him inexpressibly, and although I heard my favourite Joachim last night, even *he* paled before Liszt. He is on the violin what Liszt is on the piano, and is the only artist worthy to be mentioned in the same breath with him. Like Liszt, he so vitalizes everything that I have to take him in all over again every time I hear him. I am always astonished, amazed and delighted afresh, and even as I listen I can hardly believe that the man *can* play so ! But Liszt, in addition to his marvellous playing, has this unique and imposing personality, whereas at first Joachim is not specially striking. Liszt's face is all a play of feature, a glow of fancy, a blaze of imagination, whereas Joachim is absorbed in his violin, and his face has only an expression of fine discrimination and of intense solicitude to produce his artistic effects. Liszt never looks at his instrument; Joachim never looks at anything else. Liszt is a complete actor who intends to carry away the public, who never forgets that he is before it, and who behaves accordingly. Joachim is totally oblivious of it. Liszt subdues the people to him by the very way he walks on to the stage. He gives his proud head a toss, throws an electric look out of his eagle eye, and seats himself with an air as much as to say, "Now I am going to do just what I please with you, and you are nothing but puppets subject to my will." He said to us in the class one day, "When you come out on the stage, look as if you didn't care a rap for the audience, and as if you knew more than any of them. That's the way I used to do.—Didn't that provoke the critics though!" he added, with an ineffable look of malicious mischief. So you see his principle, and that was precisely the way he did at the rehearsal in the theatre at Weimar that I wrote to you about. Joachim, on the contrary, is the quiet gentleman-artist. He advances in the most unpretentious way, but as he adjusts his violin he looks his audience over with the calm air of a musical monarch, as much as to say, "I repose wholly on my art, and I've no need of any 'ways or manners.'" In reality I admire Joachim's principle the most, but there is something indescribably fascinating and subduing about Liszt's willfulness. You feel at once that he is a great genius, and that you *are* nothing but his puppet, and somehow you take a base delight in the humiliation! The two men are intensely interesting, each in his own way, but they are extremes.

[Beside his playing and his compositions, what Liszt has done for music and for musicians, and why, therefore, he stands so pre-eminently the greatest and the best beloved master in the musical world, may appear to the general reader in the following extract taken from a translation in *Dwight's Journal*, Oct. 23, 1880, of "Franz Liszt, a Musical Character Portrait" by La Mara, in the

Gartenlaube : "We must count it among the exceptional merits of Liszt, that he has paved the way to
recognition for innumerable aspirants, as he always
shows an open heart and open hands to all artistic
strivings. He was the first and most active furtherer of
the immense Bayreuth enterprise, and the chief founder
of the Musical Societies or Unions that flourish throughout Germany. And for how many noble and philan-
thropic objects has he not exerted his artistic resources!
If, during his earlier virtuoso career, he made his genius
serve the advantage of others far more than his own—
saving out of the millions that he earned only a modest
sum for himself, while he alone contributed many thousands for the completion of Cologne Cathederal, for the
Beethoven monument at Bonn, and for the victims of
the Hamburg conflagration—so since the close of his
career as a pianist his public artistic activity has been
exclusively consecrated to the benefit of others, to artistic
undertakings, or to charitable objects. Since the end of
1847, not a penny has come into his own pocket either
through piano-playing and conducting, or through teaching. All this, which has yielded such rich capital and
interest to others, has cost only sacrifice of time and
money to himself."]—ED.

CHAPTER XXIII.

Kullak as a Teacher. The Four Great Virtuosi, Clara Schumann, Rubinstein, Von Bülow, and Tausig.

I've been in a sort of mental apathy since I got back—the result, I suppose, of so much artistic excitement all summer. Of course I am practicing very hard, and I am taking private lessons of Kullak again. I played him my Rubinstein concerto two weeks ago and told him I wanted to play it in a concert. He says I need more power in it in many places, and by practicing it every day I hope I shall at last work up to it, as I've conquered the technical difficulties in it. There were two pages in it I thought I never *could* master. It is the same with all concertos. They are fearfully difficult things to play, and far more difficult, *I* think, than solos are, because the effort is so sustained. They are to me the most interesting things to listen to of all, and I can't imagine how you can think that piano and orchestra are " not made to go together." However, I never myself appreciated concertos until I came to Germany.

Kullak is the most awfully discouraging teacher that can be imagined. When you play to him, it is like looking at your skin through a magnifying glass. All your faults seem to start out and glare at you. I don't think, though, that I ever fairly do myself justice

when I play to him, because he has a sort of benumb-
ing effect on me, and I feel to him something the way
that Owen did to old Peter in Hawthorne's story of
" The Artist of the Beautiful." I can't help acknowl-
edging the truth of his observations even when I am
wincing under them, and I yet feel at the same time
that he does not wholly get at the soul of the thing.
Kullak is *so* pedantic! He *never* overlooks a technical imperfection, and he ties you down to the technique so that you never can give rein to your imagination. He sits at the other piano, and just as you are
rushing off he will strike in himself and say, " Don't
hurry, Fräulein," or something ¡like that, and then
you begin to think about holding back your fingers and
playing every note even, etc. Now I never expect to get
that perfection of technique that all these artists have
who have been training throughout their childhood
while their hand was forming. Kullak's own technique
is magnificent, but now that I've graduated, as it were,
he ought to let me play my own way, and not expect me
to play as *he* does, and then I could produce my own
effects. That is just the difference between him and
Liszt. Liszt's grand principle is, to leave you your
freedom, and when you play to him, you feel like a
Pegasus caracoling about in the air. When you play
to Kullak, you feel as if your wings were suddenly
clipped, and as if you were put into harness to draw
an express wagon! However, I don't think it would
be well to go to Liszt without having been through
such a training first, for you want to know what you
are about when you study with *him*. You must have

18

a good solid *basis* upon which to raise his airy super-
structures. Kullak I regard as the basis.

You ask me in your letter to write you a comparison—
a summing up—between Clara Schumann, Bülow, Tausig and Rubinstein, but I don't find it very easy to do, as
they are all so different. Clara Schumann is entirely a
classic player. Beethoven's sonatas, and Bach, too, she
plays splendidly; but she doesn't seem to me to have
any *finesse,* or much poetry in her playing. There's
nothing subtle in her conception. She has a great deal
of fire, and her whole style is grand, finished, perfectly
rounded off, solid and satisfactory—what the Germans
call *gediegen.* She is a *healthy* artist to listen to, but
there is nothing of the analytic, no Balzac or Hawthorne
about her. Beethoven's Variations in C minor are, perhaps, the best performance I ever heard from her, and
they are immensely difficult, too; I thought she did
them better than Bülow, in spite of Bülow's being such a
great Beethovenite. I think she repeats the same pieces
a good deal, possibly because she finds the modern fashion of playing everything without notes very trying.
I've even heard that she cries over the necessity of doing
it; and certainly it is a foolish thing to make a point of,
with so very great an artist as Clara Schumann.—If
people could *only* be allowed to have their own individuality!

Bülow's playing is more many-sided, and is chiefly distinguished by its great vigor; there is no end to his
nervous energy, and the more he plays, the more the
interest increases. He is my favourite of the four. But
he plays Chopin just as well as he does Beethoven. and

Schumann, too. Altogether he is a superlative pianist, though by no means unerring in his performance. I've heard him get dreadfully mixed up. I think he trusts *too* much to his memory, and that he does not prepare sufficiently. He plays everything by heart, and such programmes! He always hits the nail plump on the head, and such a grasp as he has! His chords take firm hold of you. For instance, in the beginning of the two last movements of the Moonlight Sonata, you should hear him run up that arpeggio in the right hand so lightly and pianissimo, every note so delicately articulated, and then *crash-smash* on those two chords on the top! And when he plays Bach's gavottes, gigues, etc., in the English Suites, a laughing, roguish look comes over his face, and he puts the most indescribable drollery and originality into them. You see that "he sees the point" so well, and that makes *you* see it, too. Yes, it is good fun to hear Bülow do these things.—Perhaps the best summing up of his peculiar greatness would be to say that he impresses you as using the instrument only to express ideas. With him you forget all about the piano, and are absorbed only in the thought or the passion of the piece.

Rubinstein you've heard. Most people put him next to Liszt. Your finding him cold surprised me, for if there is a thing he is celebrated here for, it is the fire and passion of his playing, and for his imagination and spontaneity. I think that Tausig, Bülow, and Clara Schumann, all three, have it all cut and dried beforehand, how they are going to play a piece, but Rubinstein creates at the instant. He plays without *plan*. Probably the afternoon you heard him he did not feel in the mood, and so was not at his best. As a composer he far out-ranks the other three.

Tausig resembled Liszt more in that subtlety which Liszt has, and consequently he was a better Chopin player than anybody else except Liszt. I never shall forget his playing of Chopin's great Ballade in G minor the very first time I heard him in concert. It is a divine composition, and his rendering of it was not only all warmth and fervour; it was also so wonderfully poetic that it fairly cast a spell upon the audience, and a minute or two went by before they could begin to applaud. It was like a dream of beauty suspended in the air before you—floating there—and you didn't want to disturb it. Tausig had an intense love for Chopin, and always wished he could have known him. I think that he had more virtuosity, and yet more delicacy of feeling, than either Rubinstein or Bülow. His finish, perfection, and above all his touch, were above anything. But, except in Chopin, he was cold, at least in the concert room. In the conservatory he seemed to be a very passionate player ; but, somehow, in public that was not the case. Unfortunately, I had studied so little at that time, that I don't feel as if I were competent to judge him. He was Liszt's favourite, and Liszt said, "He will be the inheritor of my playing ;" but I doubt if this would have been, for the winter before Tausig died, Kullak remarked to me that his playing became more and more "dry" every year, probably on account of his morbid aversion to "Spectakel," as he called it; whereas Liszt gives the reins to the emotions always.

When I was in Weimar I heard a great deal about Tausig's *escapades* when he was studying there as a boy. They say he was awfully wild and reckless at that time, and Liszt paid his debts over and over again. Sometimes in aristocratic parties, when Liszt did not feel like playing himself, he would tell Tausig to play, and perhaps Tausig would not feel like it, either. He had the most enormous strength in his fingers, though his hands were small, and he would go to the piano and pretend he was going to play, and strike the first chords with such a crash that three or four strings would snap almost immediately, and then, of course, the piano was used up for the evening!

Tausig's father once procured him a splendid grand piano from Leipsic, and shortly after, Tausig whittled off the corners of all the keys, so as to make them more difficult to strike, and his father had to pay a large sum to have them repaired. Another time he was presented with a set of chess-men, and the next day some one on visiting him observed the pieces all lying about the floor. "Why, Tausig, what has happened to your chess-men?" "Oh, I wanted to see if they were easily broken, so I knocked up the board." He seemed to be possessed with a spirit of destruction. Gottschal told me that one time when Tausig was "hard up" for money, he sold the score of Liszt's Faust for five thalers to a servant, along with a great pile of his own notes. The servant disposed of them to some waste-paper man, and Gottschal, accidentally hearing of it, went to the man and purchased them. Then he went to Liszt to tell him that he had the score. As it happened the publisher had written for it that very day and Liszt was turning the house upside down, looking for it everywhere.

At that time he was living in an immense house on a hill here, that they call the Altenburg. Liszt occupied the first floor, a princely friend the second, and the [top story was one grand ball-room in which were generally nine grand pianos standing. They used to give the most magnificent entertainments, and Liszt spent thirty thousand thalers a year. He lived like a prince in those days—very different from his present simplicity. Well, he was in an awful state of mind because his score was nowhere to be found. "A whole year's labor lost!" he cried, and he was in such a rage, that when Gottschal asked him for the third time what he was looking for, he turned and stamped his foot at him and said, "You confounded fellow, can't you leave me in peace, and not torment me with your stupid questions?" Gottschal knew perfectly well what was wanting, but he wished to have a little fun out of the matter. At last he took pity on Liszt, and said, "Herr Doctor, *I* know what you've lost. It is the score to your Faust." "Oh," said Liszt, changing his tone immediately, "do you know anything of it?" "Of course I do," said Gottschal, and proceeded to unfold Master Tausig's performance, and how he had rescued the precious music. Liszt was transported with joy that it was found, and called up-stairs, "Carolina, Carolina, we're saved! Gottschal has rescued us;" and then Gottschal said that Liszt embraced him in his transport, and could not say or do enough to make up for his having been so rude to him. Well,

you would have supposed that it was now all up with
Master Tausig; but not at all. A few days afterward was Tausig's birthday, and Carolina took Gottschal aside, and begged him to drop the subject of
the note stealing, for Liszt doted so on his Carl that
he wished to forget it. Sure enough, Liszt kissed
Carl and congratulated him on his birthday, and con-
soled himself with his same old observation, "You'll
either turn out a great blockhead, my little Carl, or a
great master."

Tausig had a great ambition to be a composer, and
in his early youth he published a number of compositions. Later on he became intensely critical of his
own work, and finally bought up all the copies he
could lay hands on and burnt them! This is entirely
characteristic of his sense of perfection, which was
extreme, and may serve as an example to young composers who are ambitious of saying something in
music, when very often they have nothing to say!
Indeed, I am often amazed at the temerity with which
men will rush into print, quite oblivious of the fact
that it requires enormous talent to produce even a
short piece of music that is worth anything. Only a
genius can do it.

Tausig, in my opinion, *did* possess exceptional
genius in composition, though he left but few works
behind him to attest it. Prominent among these are
his unique arrangements of three of Strauss's Waltzes.
He had a passion for philosophy, and was deeply read
in Kant and Hegel. These "arrangements" betray his
metaphysical and tentative turn, and could only have

been the product of the highest mental force and culture. Calling the waltz itself the warp of the composition, then through its simple threads we find darting backwards and forwards a subtle, complicated and tragic mind, an exquisitely refined and delicate sentiment, and a piquante, aerial fancy, until finally is wrought a brilliant and bewildering transcription—transfiguration rather—of endless fascination and tantalizing beauty, which no one but a virtuoso can play and no one but a connoisseur can comprehend. In a peculiar manner his music leaves a *stamp* upon the heart, and to those who can appreciate it, Tausig, as a composer, is a deep and irreparable loss.—If he had not original ideas of his own, he certainly possessed the power of putting an entirely new face on those of others.

WITH DEPPE.

(281)

CHAPTER XXIV.

Gives up Kullak for Deppe. Deppe's Method in Touch and in Scale-Playing. Fräulein Steiniger. Pedal Study.

BERLIN, *December* 11, 1873.

Since I last wrote you I have taken a very important step, which is *this*: After taking three or four lessons of Kullak I HAVE GIVEN HIM UP! and am now studying under a new master. His name is Herr Capelmeister Deppe. I suppose you will all think me crazed, but I think I know what I am about. He seems to me a very remarkable man, and is to me the most satisfactory teacher I've had yet. Of course I don't count in the unapproachable Liszt when I say that, for Liszt is no "*professeur du piano*," as he himself used scornfully to remark.

I made Herr Deppe's acquaintance quite by chance, at a musical party given for Anna Mehlig by an American gentleman living here. I had often heard of him, and was very anxious to know him, but somehow had never compassed it. He is a conductor, to begin with, and I have often seen him conduct orchestral concerts. In fact, that was what he first came to Berlin for, a few years ago—to conduct Stern's orchestral concerts during the latter's absence in Italy. Deppe is an accomplished conductor, and I have never heard Beethoven's second Overture to Leonora sound as I have under his bâton.

But it was Sherwood who first called my attention
to him as a teacher. He rushed into my room one
day, and said, " Oh, I've just heard the most beautiful
playing that ever I heard in my life !" I asked him
who it was that had taken him so by storm, and he
said it was a young English girl named Fannie Warburg, and that she was a pupil of Deppe's. "Well,
what is it about her that is so remarkable," said I.
" Oh, *everything!*—execution, expression, style, touch
—all are *perfect!* I never heard anything to equal
her, and I feel as if I never wanted to touch the piano
again."

This was such strong language for Sherwood, who
is generally very critical and anything but enthusiastic, that my interest was immediately excited. He went
on to tell me that Deppe had been training this young
English girl, now only eighteen years of age, with the
greatest care, for six years, and that he had such an
interest in her that he did not confine himself to giving
her lessons only, but set himself to form her whole
musical taste by taking her to the best concerts and
to hear the great operas, calling her attention to every
peculiarity of structure in a composition, and giving
her all sorts of hints which only a man of profound
musical culture *could* give. Sherwood said, moreover,
that in summer he made her go to Pyrmont, which is a
watering place near Hanover, where he goes himself
every year, and that there he heard her play *every day*
Mozart's concertos and all sorts of things. I thought
to myself at the time that the man who would take so
much trouble for a pupil as that, would have been

just the one for me, for it was easy to see that Deppe was teaching more for the love of Art than for love of money—a rare thing in these materialistic days! Afterward, you know, Miss B. spoke to me about him in Weimar, and I wrote you what she said.

Well, as I was saying, I went to this musical party given to Anna Mehlig, where there were a number of musicians and critics. I was listening to Mehlig play, when suddenly Sherwood, who was also present, stole up to me and said, " Come into the next room and be introduced to Deppe." At these magic words I started, and immediately did as I was bid. I found Deppe in one corner looking about him in an absent sort of way. He was a man of medium height, with a great big brain, keen blue eyes and delicate little mouth, and he had a most cheery and sunny expression. He shook hands, and then we sat down and got into a most animated conversation—all about music. I told him how interested I was by all I had heard of him—how I had returned to Kullak for a last trial—how tired I was of his eternal pedagogism, and how I should like to study with *him*.

He asked me what my chief difficulty was, whereupon I answered "the technique, of course." He smiled, and said "that was the smallest difficulty, and that anybody could master execution if they knew how to attack it, unless there was some want of proper development of the hand." I said I had studied very hard, but that I hadn't mastered it, and that there was always some hard place in every piece which I couldn't get the better of. He said he was sure he could rem-

edy the deficiency, and that if I would show him my
hand without a glove, he could tell directly what I was
capable of. I wouldn't pull it off, however, because I
was afraid he might find some radical defect or weakness in it, but I was so charmed with the way he made
light of the technique, and with the absolute certainty he seemed to have that I could overcome it,
that I promised him that I would go and play to him
the following Wednesday.

Accordingly on the following Wednesday I presented
myself. I had expected to stay about half an hour,
but I ended by staying *three solid hours,* and we talked
as fast as we could all the while, too! So you may
imagine we had a good deal to say. He lives in two
little rooms on the Königgrätzer Strasse, only four
doors from the W.'s, where I boarded for so long.
Now if I had only known I was close to such a teacher!
We must often have passed each other in the street,
and where *was* my good angel that he did not touch
my arm and say, "There's the man for you?"—Frightful to think how near one may be to one's best happiness, or even salvation, and not know it!

Deppe's front room was pretty much filled up with
a grand piano, which, as well as the chairs and most
other articles of furniture, was covered with music.
I glanced over the pieces a little, and there was nearly
every set of Etudes under the sun, it seemed to me, as
well as concertos and pieces by all the great composers, fingered and marked with pencil in the most
minute way. It was enough simply to turn the leaves,
to see what a study he must have made of everything

he gave his scholars. His inner room had double doors to it to prevent the sound from penetrating. I rapped at the outside one, and presently I heard a great turning and rattling of keys, and then they opened, and Deppe was before me. He put out his hand in the most cordial and friendly way, and greeted me with the most winning smile in the world. I took off my things and began to play to him. He listened quietly, and without interrupting me. When I had finished he told me that my difficulties were principally mechanical ones—that I had conception and style, but that my execution was uneven and hurried, my wrist stiff, the third and fourth fingers* very weak, the tone not full and round enough, that I did not know how to use the pedal, and finally, that I was too nervous and flurried.

"If possible, you must get over this agitation," said he. "*Hören Sie Sich spielen* (Listen to your own playing). You have talent enough to get over all your difficulties if you will be patient, and do just as I tell you." "I will do anything," I said. "Very good. But I warn you that you will have to give up all playing for the present except what I give you to study, and *those* things you must play very slowly."

This was a pleasant prospect, as I was just preparing to give a concert in Berlin, under Kullak's auspices, and had already got my programme half learned! But I had "invoked the demon," and I felt bound to give the required pledge.—So here I am, after four years abroad with the "greatest masters," going back

---

*In German, the fourth and fifth fingers.

to first principles, and beginning with five-finger exercises! I had never been given any particular rule for holding my hand, further than the general one of curving the fingers and lifting them very high. Deppe objects to this extreme lifting of the fingers. He says it makes a *knick* in the muscle, and you get all the strength simply from the finger, whereas, when you lift the finger moderately high, the muscle from the whole arm comes to bear upon it. The tone, too, is entirely different. Lifting the finger so very high, and striking with force, stiffens the wrist, and produces a slight jar in the hand which cuts off the singing quality of the tone, like closing the mouth suddenly in singing. It produces the effect of a blow upon the key, and the tone is more a sharp, quick tone; whereas, by letting the finger just fall—it is fuller, less loud, but more penetrating. I suppose the hammer falls back more slowly from the string, and that makes the tone *sing* longer.

Don't you remember my saying that Liszt had such an extraordinary way of playing a melody? That it did not seem to be so loud and cut-out as most artists make it, and yet it was so penetrating? Well, dear, *there* was the secret of it! "*Spielen Sie mit dem Gewicht* (Play with *weight*)," Deppe will say. "Don't strike, but let the fingers *fall*. At first the tone will be nearly inaudible, but with practice it will gain every day in power."—After Deppe had directed my attention to it, I remembered that I had never seen Liszt lift up his fingers so fearfully high as the other schools, and especially the Stuttgardt one, make such a point of doing.*   That is where Mehlig misses it, and is what makes her playing so sharp and cornered at times. When you lift the fingers so high you cannot bind the tones so perfectly together.   There is always a break. Deppe makes me listen to every tone, and carry it over to the next one, and not let any one finger get an undue prominence over the other—a thing that is immensely difficult to do—so I have given up all pieces for the present, and just devote myself to playing these little exercises right.

Deppe not only insists upon the fingers being as curved as possible, so that you play exactly on the tips of them, but he turns the hand very much out, so as to make the knuckles of the third and fourth fingers higher than those of the first and second, and as he does *not* permit you to throw out the elbow in doing this, the *turn must be made from the wrist.* The *thumb* must also be slightly curved, and quite free from the hand.   Many persons impede their execution by not keeping the thumb independent enough of the rest of the hand.   The moment it contracts, the hand is enfeebled.   The object of turning the hand outward is to favour the third and fourth fingers, and give them a higher fall when they are lifted.   This strengthens them very much.   It also looks much prettier when the outer edge of the hand is high, and one of Deppe's grand mottoes is, " When it *looks* pretty then it is right."

After Deppe had put me through five-finger exercises on the foregoing principles, and taught me to lift

*See p. 220.
19

each finger and let it fall with a perfectly loose wrist, (a most deceitful point, by-the way, for it took me a long while to distinguish when I was stiffening the wrist involuntarily and when I wasn't,) he proceeded to the scale. He always begins with the one in E major as the most useful to practice. His principle in playing the scale is *not* to turn the thumb under ! but to turn a little on each finger end, pressing it firmly down on the key, and screwing it round, as it were, on a pivot, till the next finger is brought over its own key. In this way he prepares for the thumb, which is kept free from the hand and slightly curved.—He told me to play the scale of E major slowly with the right hand, which I did. He curved his hand round mine, and told me as long as I played right, his hand would not interfere with mine. I played up one octave, and then I wished to go on by placing my first finger on F sharp. To do that I naturally turned my hand outward, so as to make the step from my thumb on E to F sharp with the first, but it came bang up against Deppe's hand like a sort of blockade. "Go on," said Deppe. " I can't, when you keep your hand right in the way," said I. " My hand isn't in the way," said he, " but *your* hand is out of position."

So I started again. This time I reflected, and when I got my third finger on D sharp, I kept my hand slanting from left to right, but I prepared for the turning under of the thumb, and for getting my first finger on F sharp, by turning my wrist sharply out. That brought my thumb down on the note and prepared me instantly for the next step. In fact, my wrist car-

ried my finger right on to the sharp without any change
in the position of the hand, thus giving the most perfect legato in the world, and I continued the whole
scale in the same manner.   Just try it once, and you'll
see how ingenious it is—only one must be careful not
to throw out the elbow in turning out the wrist.   As
in the ascending scale one has to turn the thumb under twice in every octave, Deppe's way of playing
avoids twice throwing the hand out of position as one
does by the old way of playing straight along, and the
smoothness and rapidity of the scale must be much
greater.   The direction of the hand in running passages is always a little oblique.

Don't you remember my telling you that Liszt has
an inconceivable lightness, swiftness and smoothness
of execution?   When Deppe was explaining this to
me, I suddenly remembered that when he was playing
scales or passages, his fingers seemed to lie across the
keys in a slanting sort of way, and to execute these
rapid passages almost without any perceptible motion.
Well, dear, *there* it was again!   As Liszt is a great ex-
perimentalist, he probably does all these things by instinct, and without reasoning it out, but that is why
nobody's else playing sounds like his.   Some of his
scholars had most dazzling techniques, and I used to
rack my brains to find out how it was, that no matter
how perfectly any body else played, the minute Liszt
sat down and played the same thing, the previous playing seemed rough in comparison.   I'm sure Deppe is
the only master in the world who has thought that
out; though, as he says himself, it is the egg of Co-
lumbus—"when you know it!"

Deppe always begins the scale in the middle of the piano, and plays up three octaves with the right, and down three octaves with the left hand.   He says that all the difficulty is in going up, and that coming back is perfectly easy, as all you have to do is to let the fingers run!   He always makes me play each hand separately at first, and very slowly, and then both hands together in contrary direction, gradually quickening the tempo.   After that in thirds. sixths, octaves, etc.

BERLIN, *December* 25, 1873.

As you may imagine, this is anything but a " Merry Christmas" for me, for I am simply the most completely *bouleversée* mortal in this world!   Here I was a month ago preparing to give a concert of my own. Then I have the good or bad luck to make Herr Deppe's acquaintance, and to find out how I "ought" to have been studying for the last four years.   I give up Kullak and my concert plan, thinking I'll study with Deppe and come out under his auspices.   After two lessons with him, comes your letter with the news of this awful national panic in it.—*Could* anything be worse for a person who has really *conscientiously* tried to attain her object?   I'm like the professor who gave some lectures to prove a certain theory, and when he got to the fourteenth, he decided it was false, and devoted the remaining ones to pulling it all down!

However, after practicing the scale on Deppe's principles, I find that they open the road to an ease, rapidity, sureness and elegance of execution which, with my stiff hand, I've not been able to see even in the dim distance before! One of his grand hobbies is *tone*, and he never lets me play a note without listening to it in the closest manner, and making it sound what he calls "*bewüsst* (conscious)."—No more mechanical "straying of the hands over the keys (as the novelists always say of their heroines) thinking of all sorts of things the while," but instead, a close pinning down of the whole attention to hear whether one finger predominates over the other, and to note the effect produced. I was perfectly amazed to see how many little ugly habits I had to correct of which I had not been the least aware. It seems as though my ears had been opened for the first time! Such concentration is very exhausting, and after two or three hours' practice I feel as if I should drop off the chair.

I forgot to say before, that Deppe enjoins sitting very low—that is—not higher than a common chair. He says one may have "the soul of an angel," and yet if you sit high, the tone will not sound poetic. Moreover, in a low seat the fingers have to work a great deal more, because you can't assist them by bringing the weight of your arm to bear. "Your elbow must be *lead* and your wrist a *feather*." Of course the seat must be modified to suit the person. I prefer a low seat myself, and have even had my piano-chair cut off two inches.

Before definitely deciding to give up Kullak and come to *him*, Deppe insisted that I should hear one of his scholars play. Fannie Warburg is in England on

a visit, so I could not hear *her,* but he has another
young lady pupil of whom he is very proud, named
Fräulein Steiniger.   This young lady had been originally a pupil of Kullak's, and I had heard her play
once in his conservatory.   She was a girl of a good
deal of talent, but not a genius.   Deppe said that
when she came to him she had all my defects, only
worse.   She has been studying with him in the most
tremendous manner for fifteen months, and he wanted
me to see what he had made of her in that time.   She
was going to play in a concert in Lübeck, and he was
to rehearse her pieces with her on Saturday for the
last time.   He begged me to come then, and accordingly I went.

I was very much struck by her playing, which was
remarkable, not so much for sentiment or poetry, of
which she had little, but for the *mastery* she had over
the instrument, and for the perfection with which she
did everything.   There was a clarity and limpidity
about her trills and runs which surprised and delighted.
Her left hand was as able as the right, and had a way
of taking up a variation like nothing at all and running along with it through the most complicated passages, which almost made you laugh with pleasure!
There was a wonderful vitality, elasticity and *snap* to
her chords which impressed me very much, and a unity
of effect about her whole performance of any composition which I don't remember to have heard from the
pupils of other masters.   The position of the hand
was exquisite, and all difficulties seemed to melt away
like snow or to be surmounted with the greatest ease.

I saw at a glance that Deppe is a magnificent teacher, and I believe that he has originated a school of his own.

Fräulein Steiniger played a charming Quintette by Hummel, a beautiful Suite by Raff, a Prelude and Fugue by Bach, and two Studies, and all, as it seemed to me, exactly as they *ought* to be played. After she had finished, we had a long talk about Kullak. She said she staid with him year after year, doing her very best, and never arriving at anything. At last, as he did nothing for her, she resolved to strike out for herself, and went to Deppe, who was at that time conducting Stern's orchestral concerts, and asked him if he would not allow her to play in one of them. Deppe received her with his characteristic kindness and cordiality, but told her that before he could promise he must first hear her in private, and he set a time for the purpose.

She had prepared Beethoven's great E flat Concerto, which everybody plays here. It is as difficult for Deppe to listen to that concerto as it is for Liszt to hear Chopin's B flat minor Scherzo. "We poor conductors!" he will exclaim, "will the artists *always* keep bringing us Beethoven's E flat Concerto? Why not, for once, the B flat, or a Mozart concerto? *Then* we should say '*Ja, mit Vergnügen* (Yes, with pleasure).' *Aber Jeder will grossartig spielen heutzutage* (But everybody wants to play on a grand scale now-a-days). The mighty rushing torrent is the fashion, but who can do the wimpling, dimpling streamlet! Nobody has any fingers for the *kleine Passagen* (little fine passages). *Sie haben,* Alle, *keine Finger (None* of them have any fingers)." He then winds up by saying *he* is the only man in Germany who knows how to give them "fingers." "*Ich weiss worauf es ankommt (I* know what it depends on) !"

Nevertheless, he listened patiently for the thousandth time to the E flat concerto, as Steiniger played it. He then quietly called her attention to the fact that *she* had "no fingers," and she was in perfect despair. He saw that she was energetic and willing to work, and he at once took her in hand and began to drill her. She withdrew entirely from society and devoted herself to practicing, following his directions implicitly. She is now a beautiful artist, and he chalks out every step of her career. I don't doubt she will play in the Gewandhaus in Leipsic eventually, which is the height of every artist's ambition, and stamps you as "finished." Then you are recognized all over the world. Deppe does not mean to let her play here till she has first played in many little places and succeeded. As he said to me the other day, " When you wish to spring over tall mountains, you must first jump over little mounds *(kleine Graben.)*" He counsels me to take a lesson of this young lady every day for a time, so as to get over the technical part quickly.

As for Deppe's young protégée, Fannie Warburg, whom he has formed completely, everybody says that she is wonderful. Fräulein Steiniger says that when you hear her play you feel almost as if it were something holy, it is so perfect and so extraordinarily spirit-

ual. She is only eighteen. Deppe showed me the list
of compositions that she has already played in concerts
elsewhere, and I was astonished at the variety and
compass of it. Every great composer was represented.

Among other refinements of his teaching, Deppe
asked me if I had ever made any pedal studies. I said
" No—nobody had ever said anything to me about the
pedal particularly, except to avoid the use of it in
runs, and I supposed it was a matter of taste." He
picked out that simple little study of Cramer in D
major in the first book—you know it well—and asked
me to play it. I had played that study to Tausig, and
he found no fault with my use of the pedal; so I sat
down thinking I could do it right. But I soon found
I was mistaken, and that Deppe had very different
ideas on the subject. He sat down and played it
phrase by phrase, pausing between each measure, to let
it "sing." I soon saw that it is possible to get as
great a virtuosity with the pedal as with anything else,
and that one must make as careful a study of it.
You remember I wrote to you that one secret of
Liszt's effects was his use of the pedal,* and how he
has a way of disembodying a piece from the piano
and seeming to make it float in the air? He makes a
spiritual form of it so perfectly visible to your inward
eye, that it seems as if you could almost hear it breathe !
Deppe seems to have almost the same idea, though he
has never heard Liszt play. " The Pedal," said he, "is
the *lungs* of the piano." He played a few bars of a
sonata, and in his whole method of binding the notes

---

*See p. 224.

together and managing the pedal, I recognized Liszt. The thing floated!—Unless Deppe wishes the chord to be very brilliant, he takes the pedal *after* the chord instead of simultaneously with it.   This gives it a very ideal sound.—You may not believe it, but it is *true,* that though Deppe is no pianist himself, and has the funniest little red paws in the world, that don't look as if they could do anything, he's got that same touch and quality of tone that Liszt has—that indescribable *something* that, when he plays a few chords, merely, makes the tears rush to your eyes.   It is too heavenly for anything.

CHAPTER XXV.

Chord-Playing. Deppe no " Mere Pedagogue." Sherwood.
Mozart's Concertos. Practicing Slowly.
The Opera Ball.

BERLIN, *January* 2, 1874.

When I had got the principle of the scale pretty well
into my head, what should Deppe rummage out but
Czerny's " *Schule der Geläufigkeit* (School of Velocity)," which I hadn't looked at since the days of my
childhood and fondly flattered myself I had done with
forever. (We none of us know what stands before
us!) After having studied Cramer, Gradus and
Chopin, you may imagine it was rather a come down
to have to take to the School of Velocity again! And
to study it *very* slowly and with one hand only!!
That was adding insult to injury. Deppe knows what
he is about, though. He began picking out passages
here and there all through the book, and making me
play them, stretching from the thumb and turning on
the fingers as often as possible. After I have mastered
the passages I am to learn a whole study, first with
each hand alone, and then with both together!

Deppe next proceeded to teach me how to strike
chords. I had to learn to raise my hands high over
the key-board, and let them fall without any resistance
on the chord, and *then sink with the wrist,* and take
up the hand exactly over the notes, keeping the hand

(299)

extended. There is quite a little knack in letting the
hand fall so, but when you have once got it, the chord
sounds much richer and fuller.—And so on, *ad infinitum.* Deppe had thought out the best way of doing
everything on the piano—the scale, the chord, the
trill, octaves, broken octaves, broken thirds, broken
sixths, arpeggios, chromatics, accent, rhythm—all!
He says that the principle of the scale and of the
chord are directly opposite. "In playing the scale
you must gather your hand into a nut-shell, as it
were, and play on the finger tips. In taking the chord,
on the contrary, you must spread the hands as if you
were going to ask a blessing." This is particularly
the case with a wide interval. He told me if I ever
heard Rubinstein play again to observe how he strikes
his chords. "Nothing cramped about *him!* He
spreads his hands as if he were going to take in the
universe, and takes them up with the greatest freedom
and *abandon!*" Deppe has the greatest admiration
for Rubinstein's *tone,* which he says is unequaled, but
he places Tausig above him as an artist. He said
Tausig used to come to his room and play to him, and
he took off Tausig's little half bow and way of seating
himself at the piano and beginning at once, without
prelude or wasting of words, very funnily! He would
scarcely take time to say "*Guten Abend* (Good Evening)." Deppe thinks Tausig played some things
matchlessly, but that in others he was dry and soul-
less. Clara Schumann, he says, is the most "musical'
of all the great artists—and you remember how immensely struck I was with Natalie Janotha, who is
her pupil, and plays just like her.

From my telling you so much about technicalities, you must not think Deppe only a pedagogue. He is in reality the soul of music, and all these things are only "means to an end." As he says himself, "I always hear the music the people *don't* play." No pianist ever entirely suited him, and this it was that set him to examining the instrument in order to see what was the matter with it. He made friends with the great virtuosi, and studied their ways of playing, and the result of all his observation is that "Piano playing is the only thing where there is something to be done." He declares that there is so much musical talent going to waste in the world that it is "lying all about the streets," and he has a most ingenious way of accounting for the fact that there are so many great pianists in spite of their not knowing *his* method:— "Gifted people," he says, "play by the grace of God; but *everybody* could master the technique on *my* system !!"

To show you that it is not alone my judgment of Deppe—four of Kullak's best pupils, including Sherwood! left him for Deppe, after I did. They got so uneasy from what I told them, that they went to see Deppe, and as soon as they heard Fräulein Steiniger play, they had to admit that she had got hold of some secrets of which they knew nothing. Sherwood, you know, is a positive genius, yet he is beginning all over again, too. In short, we are all unanimous, while Deppe, on his side, is much gratified at having some American pupils.—He flatters himself that we will introduce all his cherished ideas into our "new and progressive country."

Ah, if I had only studied with Deppe before I went to Weimar! When I was there I didn't play half as often to Liszt as I might have done, kind and encouraging as he always was to me, for I always felt I wasn't *worthy* to be *his* pupil! But if I had known Deppe four years ago, what might I not have been now? After I took my first lesson of Deppe this thought made me perfectly wretched. I felt so dreadfully that I cried and cried. When I woke up in the morning I began to cry again. I was so afflicted that at last my landlady, who is very kind and sympathetic, asked me what ailed me. I told her I felt so dreadfully to think I had met the person I ought to have met four years ago, at the last minute, so.—" On the contrary, you ought to rejoice that you have met him *at all*," said she. " Many persons go through life without ever meeting the person they wish to, or they don't know him when they do."—Sensible woman, Frau von H. !—After that I stopped fretting, and tried to believe that there *is* " a divinity that shapes our ends, roughhew them how we may."

BERLIN, *February* 12, 1874.

I am now taking three lessons a week from Fräulein Steiniger and one lesson of Deppe himself, and he says I am almost through the technical preparation, though I still practice only with one hand, and *very* slowly all the time. Fräulein Steiniger says that she also practiced slowly all the time for six months, as I am now doing. In fact, she completely forgot how to play *fast,* and one day when Deppe finally said to her in the lesson, "Now play fast for once," she could not do it, and had to learn it all over again. Of course she very soon got her hand in again, and now she has the most beautiful execution, and can play *anything* perfectly.

Deppe wants me to play a Mozart concerto for two pianos with Fräulein Steiniger, the first thing I play in public. Did you know that Mozart wrote *twenty* concertos for the piano, and that nine of them are masterpieces? Yet nobody plays them. Why? Because they are too hard, Deppe says, and Lebert, the head of the Stuttgardt conservatory, told me the same thing at Weimar. I remember that the musical critic of the *Atlantic Monthly* remarked that "we should regard Mozart's passages and cadenzas as child's play now-a-days." *Child's play,* indeed! That critic, whoever it is, "had better go to school again," as C. always says!

Deppe is remarkable in Mozart, and has studied him more than anybody else, I fancy. Indeed, to turn over his concertos, and see how he has *fingered* them alone, is enough to make you dizzy. He is always saying, "You must hear Fannie Warburg play a Mozart concerto. *She* can do it!" and, indeed, I am most anxious to hear her.

It is ludicrous to hear Deppe talk about the artists that everybody else thinks so great. Having been a director of an orchestra for years, he has constantly directed their concerts, and he weighs them in a relentless balance! The other day he gave me Mendels-

sohn's Concerto in G minor, and just at the end of the
first movement is a fearful break-neck passage for
both hands. "There!" cried Deppe, "that's a good
healthy place. *Nehmen Sie* DAS *für Ihr tägliches Gebet*
(Take *that* for your daily prayer). When you can play
it eight times in succession without missing a note,
I'll be satisfied. That is one of the places that when
the pianists come to, they get their foot hard on to the
pedal and hold on to it—*Herr Gott!* how they hold
on to it—and so *lie* themselves through." He said he
never heard anyone do it right except those to whom
he had taught it. Steiniger played it for me the other
day and it so astonished my ears that I felt like
saying, "*Herr Gott!*" too. It was as if some one had
snatched up a handful of hail and dashed it all over
me. Br-r-r-zip! how it did go!—Like a bundle of
rockets touched off one after the other. And yet this
concerto is one of those things that everybody thrums,
and is one of the regular pieces you must have in
your repertoire. Deppe was quite shocked to find I had
never learned it.

My lesson usually lasts three hours! Nothing Deppe
hates like being hurried over a lesson. He likes to
have plenty of time to express all his ideas and tell
you a good many anecdotes in between! I usually
take my lessons from seven till ten in the evening.
Then he puts on his coat and saunters along with me
on his way to his "Kneipe," or beer-garden, for he is
far too sociable to go to bed without having taken a
friendly glass of beer with some one. Every block or
so he will stand stock still and impress some musical

point upon my mind, and will often harangue me for five or ten minutes before moving on. It seems to be impossible to him to walk and *talk* at the same time! In this way you may imagine it takes me a good while to get home.

On Tuesday there is to be a grand ball at the opera house which the Emperor and the whole court grace with their presence, and lead off the first Polonaise. There are two of these grand public balls every winter. The tickets are sold, and it is the sole occasion where the public can have the felicity of gazing upon royalty in close proximity. I have never been, though all my German friends have been dinning it into my ears for the last four years that I ought to go and see it, for the decorations are magnificent. This year there is to be but one, as the Emperor is not very well, and I expect it will be as much as one's life is worth to get in and get out again, such is the rush!

The German officers waltz perfectly, and with great spirit and elegance. Dancing is a part of their military training and they are obliged to learn it. But they are not very comfortable partners, for one rubs one's face against their epaulets unless they are just the right height, and you've no rest for your left hand. They take only two turns round the room and then stop a moment or two to fan you and rest—then they take two more. The consequence is, one never gets fairly going before one has to stop. At first I used to think the effect of so many people whirling round in the same direction dizzying and monotonous. But when I became accustomed to it, the continual revers-

20

ing of the Americans who come to Berlin struck me
as angular, in contrast to the graceful German cir-
cling. It is not "the thing" here for the girls to look
flushed and disordered—skirts torn, and hair out of
crimp—as our belles do at the end of an evening.
They retire from the ball-room with their dresses in
faultless condition, so that going to parties in Germany
must cost the *pater familias* considerably less than
with us! The floor is never so crowded with dancers
at one time, and as they are going in the same direction,
they don't run into each other as our couples do.
On the other hand, they don't have such a "good
time" out of it as do our girls, with their long five
and ten minute turns to those delicious waltzes!
Strange, that though Germany is the native home of
the waltz, and the Vienna waltzes surpass all others, the
Schottisch or Rhinelaender should be their favourite
dance. They dance it very gracefully and rythmically.

BERLIN, *March* 1, 1874.

I went the other evening to the Opera ball I wrote
you of in my last. The whole opera house, stage and
all, was floored over, and magnificently decorated with
evergreens, mirrors, fountains, and flowers. The
tickets are sold for some charitable purpose. Only
nice people can get in, because the whole thing is
systematically arranged, and nobody can give their
tickets to anybody else. I got mine through Mr. Bancroft, and I went with two other ladies and a gentleman.

We went very early, so as to get a box to sit in, and *never* shall I forget the first effect of the ball-room! That immense polished floor stretching out like one vast mirror or sheet of ice, the fountains flashing at the sides, the walls wreathed with green, a big orchestra sitting in the balcony at each end, and about a hundred pairs of magnificently dressed ladies and gentlemen descending the stairs into the rooms and promenading about. Light, diamonds, colour, everywhere. Oh, it was perfectly fairy-like! The floor was built over the tops of the chairs in the parquette, and the entrance was through the royal box, which is just in the centre of the opera house, facing the stage. This box is like a large recess, of course, and not like the ordinary boxes. There was an entrance on each side, coming in from the corridor, and a flight of broad steps, carpeted, had been improvised, which led from it down to the floor. It looked perfectly dazzling to see the pairs come in from both sides at once and descend the steps, and the ladies' dresses were displayed to perfection. Such toilets I never saw. The women were covered with lace, feathers, and diamonds. The simpler dresses were of tarletane (mine included!) but as they were quite fresh they gave a very dressy air. We had a splendid box, first rank, and the second from the proscenium boxes on the left, in which sat the royal family. In the box between us and the latter sat the wife of the French ambassador with the Countess von Seidlewitz and her sister, and behind them was a formidable array of magnificent-looking officers in full uniform, their breasts flashing with stars and orders and silver chains.

The Countess von Seidlewitz is a famous court beauty and is lady of honour to the Princess Carl (sister of the Empress). She sat just next to me, as only the partition of the box was between us, and she was the most beautiful woman I saw—perfectly imperial, in fact—white and magnificent as a lily. Her features were perfectly regular, and she had a proudly-cut mouth, and such dazzling little teeth! Then, her arms, neck, and shape were exquisite. She wore the severest kind of dress, and one that only such beauty could have borne. It was a white silk, with an immense train, of course, and without overskirt—simply caught up in a great puff behind. The waist was made with a small basque, but very low, and with very short sleeves. Round the neck was a white bugle fringe, and there were two or three rows of this fringe in front, graduating to the waist, smaller and smaller, and going round the basque. All the front breadth of the skirt was laid in folds of satin, in groups of three, and on the edge of every third row was the fringe again, graduating wider and wider toward the bottom. In her hair she wore a wreath of white verbenas or (snow-balls) and green leaves. Her sole ornament was a magnificent diamond locket and ear-rings of some curious design, the locket depending from a very fine gold chain, which challenged all observers to notice the faultlessness of her neck. One sly bit of coquetry was visible in two natural flowers, lilies-of-the-valley, with their leaves, which she had stuck in her corsage so that they should rest against her neck and show that they were not whiter than her skin.—You

see there were no folds anywhere, as there was no overskirt, but the whole dress hung in long lines and
showed the contour of the figure. Nothing but these
fringes (which gleamed and waved with every motion)
relieved it—not even a bit of black velvet anywhere,
for the lace round the neck was drawn through with
a white silk thread. There was another lady in the
same box whose dress was very beautiful, too, though
she herself was not. It was a green silk with green
tulle overdress puffed, and with ears of silver wheat
scattered over it. The tunic was of silver crape, the
bottom cut in scallops and trimmed with silver wheat.
A wisp of wheat was knotted round her neck for a
necklace, and a perfect sheaf of it in her hair. It was
an exquisite dress.

At ten o'clock everybody had arrived—about two
thousand people. The orchestra struck up the Polonaise, and the court descended from the box to make
the tour of the floor (*i. e.*, only the members of the
royal family with their ladies of honour). The Emperor was not very well, so he remained in his box,
but the Empress led off with the Duke of Edinburgh,
who happened to be here. She was dressed in laven-
der satin, covered with the most superb white lace.
Her hair was done in braids on the top of her head,
very high, and upon it was fastened a double coronet
of diamonds, stuck on in stars, etc., which flashed like
so many small suns. Round her neck depended from
a black velvet band, strings of diamonds of great size
and magnificence. It really almost made you start
when your eye caught them unexpectedly! The Em-

press is a very elegant-looking woman, and is every inch a queen.   She moved with stately step, bowing and bowing graciously from side to side to the crowd which parted and bent before her, and was followed by the Crown Prince and Princess, the Princess Carl, the Princess Friedrich Carl (a beauty) and her daughters, and I don't know who all, with their ladies of honour.   When the Countess von Seidlewitz came along, with her fringes waving and gleaming in front of her, she shone out from all the rest, and, in fact, from the whole two thousand guests, like the planet Venus among the other stars.—Stunning!

The orchestra banged away its loudest, and it was quite exciting.   The three balconies were crowded with people, and all the boxes.   The box of the diplomatic corps was just opposite us, and our gay little Mrs. F. sat in it dressed in white satin.   Some of my friends came and stood under my box and tried to get me to come down, but I would not, for I knew I should lose my place if I did, and, indeed, I would not want to dance there unless my dress were something superlative. You see, all the swells sat in their boxes and gazed right down on the dancers, who had a circular place roped off for them.   De Rilvas, the Spanish minister, looked so fine, however, with his broad blue ribbon across his breast and his gold cross depending from his neck, that I should have liked very well to have made the tour of the room with him.

CHAPTER XXVI.

A Set of Beethoven Variations. Fannie Warburg. Deppe's
Inventions. His Room. His Afternoon
Coffee. Pyrmont.

BERLIN, *April* 30, 1874.

I wish you were here now so that I could play you
a set of little variations by Beethoven called, "I've
only got a little hut." They are *bewitching*, and I
think I can now play them so as to express (as Deppe
says) "that he had indeed nothing but his little hut, but
was quite happy in it." In the last variation he dances
a waltz in his little hut! I have learned a great deal
from these tiny variations, taught in Deppe's inimitable fashion. When I first took them to him I began
playing the second of the variations—which is rather
plaintive and seems to indicate that the proprietor of
the little hut had a misgiving that there *might* be a
better abode somewhere on the earth—with a great
deal of "expression," as I thought. I soon found out
I was overdoing it, however, and that it is not always
so easy to define where good expression stops and bad
style begins. "Why do you make those notes stick out
so?" asked Deppe, as I was giving vent to my "soul-
longings," (as P. says). "Learn to paint in *grossen
Flaechen* (great surfaces)." He made me play it
again perfectly legato, and with no one note "sticking
out" more than another. I saw at once that he was

(311)

right about it, and that the effect was much better, while it took nothing from the real sentiment of the piece. It was one of those cases where a simple statement was all that was necessary. Anything more detracted from rather than added to it.

I have at last heard Fannie Warburg in a Mozart concerto, for she has got back from England. How she did play it! To say that the passages "pearled," would be saying nothing at all. Why, the piano just *warbled* them out like a nightingale! The last movement had the infectious gayety that Mozart's things often have, with a magnificent cadenza by himself. She rendered it so perfectly, and with such näive light-heartedness, that none of us could resist it, and we all finally burst into a laugh! There was a little orchestra accompanying, which Deppe had got together and was directing. When she got to the cadenza, he laid down his bâton, and retired to lean against the door and enjoy it. She did it in the most masterly manner, and O, it was *so* difficult! I thought of the Boston critic, who considered Mozart's compositions "child's play." They *are* child's play—that is, they are *nothing at all* if they are not faultlessly played, and every fault *shows*, which is the reason so few attempt them. Your hand must be "in order," as Deppe says, to do it.

Fannie Warburg is a sweet little eighteen-year-old maiden. A shy little bud of a girl without any vanity or self-consciousness. She has a lovely hand for the piano, and the way she uses it is perfectly exquisite. It is small and plump, but strong, with firm little fingers. Every muscle is developed, and indeed it could not be otherwise, after such a six years' training. One of Deppe's rules is that when you raise the finger the knuckle must not stick out. The finger must "sit firm *(fest-sitzen)* in the joint." Fannie Warburg's fingers *"sitzen"* so *"fest"* that when she plays she positively has a little row of dimples where her knuckles ought to be. It looks too pretty for anything—just like a baby's hand. She does not seem to have the slightest ambition, however, and I doubt whether she will ever do anything with her music after she leaves Deppe. Her mother was from Hamburg, and had taken lessons of Deppe there when they were both quite young. She thought him such a remarkable teacher that she declared her daughter should have no other master. So when Fannie was twelve years old she brought her to him, and he has been giving her lessons ever since—something like Samuel's mother bringing him to the Temple, wasn't it?—and indeed when I go into Deppe's shabby little room I always feel as if I were in a little Temple of Music! I like to see the furniture all bestrewn with it, and Deppe himself seated at his table surrounded with piles of manuscript, pen in hand, going over and arranging them, bringing order out of chaos. Other orchestra leaders are always writing and begging him to lend them his copies of Oratorios, etc.

Deppe has all sorts of practical little ideas peculiar to himself. For instance, he has invented a candlestick to stand on a grand piano. In shape it is curved, like those things for candles attached to upright pianos, but

with a weighted foot to hold it firm. It is a capital
invention, for you put one each side of the music-rack,
and then you can turn it so as to throw the light on your
music, just as you can turn those on the upright pianos.
It is on the same principle, only with the addition of the
foot. It is much more convenient than a lamp, because
it doesn't rattle, and you can throw the light on the
page so much better.—Then he always insists on our
having our pieces bound separately, in a cover of stout
blue paper, such as copy books are bound in. He entirely
disapproves of binding music in books. "Who will lug
a great heavy book along?" he will ask, "and besides,
they don't lie open well."

The other day Deppe told me he wanted me to come
and hear Fräulein Steiniger take her lesson, as she had
some interesting pieces to play. I found her already
there when I arrived. Deppe was in an uncommonly
good humour, and kept making little jokes. She played
a string of things, and finally ended off with Liszt's
arrangement of the Spinning Song from Wagner's Flying Dutchman. Deppe is dreadfully fussy about this
piece, and made some such subtle and telling points
regarding the *conception* of the composition, that they
were worthy of Liszt himself. I mean to learn it, and
when I come home I will play it to you as Deppe taught
it to Steiniger, and you will see how fascinating it is. I
know you'll be carried away with it.

Toward the end of the lesson it was growing rather late,
and time also for Deppe's coffee, which beverage you know
the Germans always drink late in the afternoon, accompanied with cakes. He had just laid down his violin, as

he and Fräulein Steiniger had played a sonata together,
and had seated himself at the piano to show her about
some passage or other. Deeply absorbed, he was har-
anguing her as hard as he could, when the maid of all
work suddenly entered with the coffee on a tray, and
was apparently about to set it down on the piano in
close proximity to the violin. *"Herr Gott, nicht auf die
Violin!* (Good gracious, not on the violin)!" exclaimed
Deppe, springing frantically up and rescuing the beloved
instrument. "Where then?" said the girl. "Oh, anywhere, only not on the violin." She set it down on a
chair and vanished. There were only three chairs in the
room, and the sofa was covered with music. Fräulein
Steiniger occupied one chair, I the second, and the coffee
the third. Deppe glanced around in momentary bewild-
erment, and then sat himself plump down on the floor,
took his coffee, stretched out his legs, and began stirring
it imperturbably. "But Herr Deppe!" remonstrated
Steiniger. "Well," said he, with his light-hearted laugh,
"what else can I do when I have no chair?" There was
no carpet on the floor, which was an ordinary painted
one, and he looked funny enough, sitting there, but he
enjoyed his coffee just as well!—After he had finished
drinking it, the shades of night were falling, and it
occurred to him it would be well to illuminate his
apartment. He is the happy possessor of five minute
lamps and candlesticks, no two of which are the same
height. The lamps are two in number, and are about
as big as the smallest sized fluid lamp that we used in old
times to go to bed by. The three candlesticks are of
china, and adorned with designs in decalcomania—

probably the handiwork of grateful pupils, for in Germany
there is no present like a "*Hand-Arbeit* (something
done by the hand of the giver)." It is the correct thing
to give a gentleman. When Fräulein Steiniger and I
only are present, Deppe usually considers the two lamps
sufficient. But if others are there and he is going to
have some music in the evening he will produce the
three minute candlesticks, with an end of candle in each,
light them, and dispose them in various parts of the
room. When, however, as on great occasions, the five
lamps and candlesticks are supplemented by two *more*
candles on the piano in the curved candlesticks of
Deppe's own invention, the blaze of light is something
tremendous to our unaccustomed eyes! Nothing short
of the Tuileries or the "Weisser Saal" at the palace here
could equal it!

BERLIN, *May* 31, 1874.

This season with Deppe has been of such immense
importance to me, that I don't know *what* sum of money
I would take in exchange for it. By practicing in his
method the tone has an entirely different sound, being
round, soft and yet penetrating, while the execution of
passages is infinitely facilitated and perfected. In fact,
it seems to me that in time one could attain anything by
it, but time it *will* have. One has to study for months
very slowly and with very simple things, to get into the
way of playing so, and to be able to think about each
finger as you use it—to "*feel* the note and make it conscious." Deppe won't let me finish anything at present,

so I can't tell how far along I am myself. His principle is, never to learn a piece completely the first time you attack it, but to master it three-quarters, and then let it lie as you would fruit that you have put on a shelf to ripen;—afterward, take it up again and finish it. The principle *may* be a good one, but it prevents my ever having anything to play for people, and consequently I have ceased playing in company entirely. In fact, I find it impossible, and I don't see how Sherwood manages it. *He* has a whole repertoire, and sits down and plays piece after piece deliciously. But then he is a perfect genius, and will make a sensation when he comes out. He has that natural repose and imperturbability that are everything to an artist, but which, unfortunately, so few of us possess. His compositions, too, are exquisite, and so poetical! Mrs. Wrisley,* of Boston, and Fräulein Estleben, of Sweden, who left Kullak when I did, are also gifted creatures, whereas I think I am only a steady old poke-along, who *won't* give up! Sherwood, however, is head and shoulders above all of us.

[The following extract, taken from the report in the *Musical Review* of Mr. Sherwood's address before the Music Teachers' National Association in Buffalo, in June, 1880, would seem to show that whether this distinguished young virtuoso, now by far the leading American concert-pianist, gained his ideas on the study of touch and tone from Herr Deppe or not, he certainly endorses them in both his playing and his teaching:—"It makes a great deal of difference whether a piano be struck with a stick, with mechanical fingers, or with fingers that are full of life and magnetism. I have examined Rubinstein's

---

* Now Mrs. Sherwood.

hand and arm, and found that they are not only full of
life and magnetism, but that they are extremely elastic,
and the fingers are so soft that the bones are scarcely felt.
Can practice produce these qualities? I believe so, and I
make it a point both with my pupils and myself to practice slow motions. It is much easier to strike quickly
than slowly, but practice in the slow movement will
develop both muscular and nervous power. And the
tone obtained by this motion is much better than that
obtained by striking. The mechanical practice in vogue
at Leipsic and other European conservatories often fails
because the subject of æsthetics and tone beauties are
neglected." See pp. 288, 302-3, 334.]—ED.

My lessons with Deppe are a genuine musical excitement to me, always. In every one is something so
new and unexpected—something that I never dreamed
of before—that I am lost in astonishment and admiration. The weeks fly by like days before I know it.
Deppe gives me the most beautiful music, and never
wastes time over things which will be of no use to me
afterward. Every piece has an *aim*, and is lovely,
also, to play to people. Now, in Tausig's and Kullak's conservatories I wasted quantities of time over
things which are beautiful enough, and do to play to
one's self, but which are not in the least effective to
play to other people either in the parlour or in the concert-room—as Bach's Toccata in C, for example. Such
things take a good while to learn, and are of no practical advantage afterward. But Deppe has an organ-
ized *plan* in everything he does.

In my study with Kullak when I had any special

difficulties, he only said, "Practice always, Fräulein. *Time* will do it for you some day. Hold your hand any way that is easiest for you. You can do it in *this* way—or in *this* way"—showing me different positions of the hand in playing the troublesome passage—"or you can play it with the *back* of the hand if that will help you any!" But Deppe, instead of saying, "Oh, you'll get this after years of practice," shows me how to conquer the difficulty *now*. He takes a piece, and while he plays it with the most wonderful *fineness* of conception, he cold-bloodedly dissects the mechanical elements of it, separates them, and tells you how to use your hand so as to grasp them one after the other. In short, he makes the technique and the conception *identical,* as of course they ought to be, but I never had any other master who trained his pupils to attempt it.

Deppe also hears me play, I think, in the true way, and as Liszt used to do : that is, he never interrupts me in a piece, but lets me go through it from beginning to end, and *then* he picks out the places he has noted, and corrects or suggests. These suggestions are always something which are not simply for that piece alone, but which add to your whole artistic experience—a *principle,* so to speak. So, without meaning any disparagement to the splendid masters to whom I owe all my previous musical culture, I cannot help feeling that I have at last got into the hands not of a mere piano virtuoso, however great, but, rather, of a profound musical *savant*—a man who has been a violinist, as well as a director, and who, without being a player himself, has made such a study of the piano, that probably all pianists except Liszt might learn something from him. You may all think me "enthusiastic," or even *wild*, as much as you like ; but whether or not I ever conquer my own block of a hand—which has every defect a hand *can* have !—when I come home and begin teaching you all on Deppe's method, you'll succumb to the genius and beauty of it just as completely as I have. You will *then* all admit I was RIGHT !

July 22.—I have finally made up my mind to go to Pyrmont when Deppe does, and spend several weeks, keeping right on with my lessons, and perhaps, giving a little concert there. I have always had a curiosity to visit one of the German watering places, as I'm told they are extremely pleasant.

PYRMONT, *August* 1, 1874.

Here I am in Pyrmont, and there's no knowing where I shall turn up next ! Fräulein Steiniger got here before me, but Deppe has not yet arrived from Brussels, whither he has gone to be present at the yearly exhibition of the Conservatoire there. He has been appointed one of the judges on piano-playing. Pyrmont is a lovely little place. It is in a valley surrounded by hills, heavily wooded, and has a beautiful park, as all German towns have, no matter how small. The avenues of trees surpass anything I ever saw. The soil has something peculiar about it, and is particularly adapted to trees. They grow to an immense height, and their stems look so strong, and their foliage is so tremendously luxuriant, that it seems as if they were ready to burst for very life !

Fräulein Steiniger went with me to look up some rooms. Every family in Pyrmont takes lodgers, so that it is not difficult to find good accommodations. The women are renowned for being good housekeepers and their rooms are charmingly fitted up, but the prices are very high, as they live the whole year on what they make in summer. People come here to drink the waters of the springs, and to take the baths, which are said to be very invigorating. My rooms are near the principal *"Allée"* or Avenue, leading from the Springs. About half way down is a platform where the orchestra sit and play three times a day—at seven in the morning (which is the hour before breakfast, when it is the thing to take a glass or two of the water, and promenade a little), at four in the afternoon, when everybody takes their coffee in the open air, and at seven in the evening. As I don't drink the waters I do not rise early, and am usually awakened by the strains of the orchestra. There is a little piazza outside my window where I take my breakfast and supper. For dinner I go to "table-d'hôte" at a hotel near.—It is a great relief to get out of Berlin and see something green once more. I find the weather very cool, however, and one needs warm clothing here.

There are the loveliest walks all about Pyrmont that you can imagine, and beautiful wood-paths are cut along the sides of the hills. My favourite one is round the cone of a small hill to the right of the town. The path completely girdles it, and you can start and walk round the hill, returning to the point you set out from. It is like

21

MUSIC-STUDY IN GERMANY.

a leafy gallery, and before and behind you is always this curving vista. Whenever I take the walk it reminds me of—

> "Curved is the line of beauty,
> Straight is the line of duty;
> Follow the last and thou shalt see
> The other ever following thee."

It is the first time I ever succeeded in combining the curved and the straight line at the same time—because, of course, it is my *duty* to take exercise!

CHAPTER XXVII.

The Brussels Conservatoire. Steiniger. Excursion to Kleinberg. Giving a Concert. Fräulein Timm.

PYRMONT, *August* 15, 1874.

Deppe has got back from Brussels, and, as you may
imagine, he had much to tell about his flight into the
world, particularly as he had also been to London.
He had a delightful time with the professors of the
Brussels Conservatoire, who were all extremely polite
to him, and he heard some talented young pupils.
There was one girl about seventeen, whom he said
he would give a good deal to have as *his* pupil,
so gifted is she, though her playing did not suit him
in many respects. He said he could have made some
severe criticisms, but he refrained—partly because he
felt the uselessness of it, partly because he says "it *is*
extraordinary how amiable one gets when *young ladies*
are in question !" He was very enthusiastic over the
violin classes. "What a bow the youngsters do draw !"
he exclaimed. Dupont, the great piano teacher inBrus-
sels, must be a man of considerable *"esprit,"* judging
from the two of his compositions that I am familiar
with—the "Toccata" and the "Staccato." I used to hear
a good deal about him from his pupil Gurickx, whom
I met in Weimar. Certainly Gurickx played magnificently, and with a *brio* I have rarely heard equalled.
He is like an electric battery. Quite another school,

however, from Deppe's—the severe, the chaste and the classic! Extreme *purity of style* is Deppe's characteristic, and not the passionate or the emotional. For instance, he has scarcely given me any Chopin, but keeps me among the classics, as he says on that side my musical culture has been deficient. He says that Chopin has been "so played to death that he ought to be put aside for twenty years!"—But if Chopin were really sympathetic to him he could never say *that!* The truth is, the modern "problematische Natur" has no charms for a transparent and simple temperament like his.

Steiniger has been playing most beautifully lately. She has given two concerts of her own here, and has played at another. Then she rehearsed with orchestra Mozart's B flat major concerto—the most difficult concerto in the world, and oh, *so* exquisite! Though I had long wished to do so, I never had heard it before, and as I listened I felt as if I never could leave Deppe until I could play *that!* I wish you could have heard it. It is sown with difficulties—enough to make your hair stand on end! Steiniger played it with an ease and perfection truly astonishing. The notes seemed fairly to run out of her fingers for fun. The last movement was Mozart all over, just as merry as a cricket!—I doubt whether anybody can play this concerto adequately who has not studied with Deppe. The beauty of his method is that the greatest difficulties become play to you.

I love to see Deppe direct the orchestra when Steiniger plays a concerto of Mozart. His clear blue eyes

dance in his head and look so sunny, and he stands so
light on his feet that it seems as if he would dance off
himself on the tips of his toes, with his bâton in his
hand! He is the incarnation of Mozart, just as Liszt
and Joachim are of Beethoven, and Tausig was of
Chopin. He has a marvellously delicate musical organization, and an instinct how things ought to be played
which amounts to second sight. Fräulein Steiniger
said to him one day: "Herr Deppe, I don't know why
it is, but I can't make the opening bars of this piece
sound right. It doesn't produce the impression it
ought." "I know why," said Deppe. "It is because
you don't strike the chord of G minor before you begin,"
—and so it was. When she struck the chord of G
minor, it was the right preparation, and brought you
immediately into the mood for what followed. It
fixed the key.

Aside from music, Deppe, like all artists, has the
most childlike nature, and I think Mozart is so
peculiarly sympathetic to him because he has such a
simple and sunny temperament himself. We made
a beautiful excursion the other day in carriages, through
the hills, to a little village far distant, where we drank
coffee in the open air. Deppe, who knows every foot
of the ground about Pyrmont, which he has frequented
from his youth up, kept calling our attention to all
the points of the scenery over and over again with the
greatest delight, quite forgetting that he repeated the
same thing fifty times. "That little village over there
is called Kleinberg. It has a school and a church, and
the pastor's name is Koehler," he would say to me

first.   Then he would repeat it to every one in our
carriage.   Then he would stand up and call it over to
the carriage behind us.   Then when he had got out
he said it to the assembled crowd, and as I walked on
in advance with Fräulein Estleben, the last thing I
heard floating over the hill-top was, "The pastor's
name is Koehler,"—so I knew he was still instructing
some one in the fact.   "I wonder how often Deppe
has repeated that?" I said to Fräulein Estleben. "At
least fifty times," said she, laughing.   "I'm going back
to him and ask him once more what the name of the
pastor is."   So I went back, and said, "By the way,
Herr Deppe, what did you say the name of the pastor
of that village is?"   "*Koehler*," said dear old Deppe,
with great distinctness and with such simple good faith
that I felt reproached at having quizzed him, though
the others could scarcely keep their countenances, as
they knew what I was after.

I have been preparing for some time to give a concert
of Chamber Music in the salon of the hotel here, and expect it to take place a week from to-day.   My head feels
quite *lame* from so much practicing, the consequence, I
suppose, of so much listening.   I am to play a Quintette, Op. 87, in E major, by Hummel, for piano and
strings, and a Beethoven Sonata, Op. 12, in E flat, for
violin and piano, and the other instruments will play a
Quartette by Haydn in between.   It is a beautiful little
programme, I think—every piece perfect of its kind.
If I succeed in this concert as I hope, I shall probably
listen to Deppe's implorings and remain under his
guidance another season.   Deppe believes that one

must go through successive steps of preparation before
one is fitted to attack the great concert works. I've
found out (what he took good care not to tell me in
the beginning!) that his "course" is three years!!
and you can't hurry either him or his method. Your
fingers have got to grow into it.—I do not at all
regret, with you, not having hitherto played in concert; on the contrary, I think it providential that I
did not. You see, you and I started out with wholly
impracticable and ridiculous ideas. We thought that
things could be done quickly. Well, they *can't* be
done quickly and be worth anything. One must
keep an end in view for years and gradually work up
to it. The length of time spent in preparation has to
be the same, whether you begin as a child (which is
the best, and indeed the only proper way), or whether
you begin after you have grown up. It is a ten years'
labour, take it how you will.

PYRMONT, *August* 15, 1874.

My concert came off yesterday evening, and Deppe
says it was a complete success. I did not play any
solos, after all, though I had prepared some beautiful
ones, for Deppe said the programme would be too
long, and he was not quite sure of my courage.
"You'd be frightened, if you were a *Herr Gott!*" said
he; but, contrary to my usual habit, I wasn't frightened in the least, and I think I did as well as such a
shaky, trembly concern as I, could have expected, par-

ticularly as my hands are two little fiends who *won't*
play if they don't feel like it, do what I will to make
them !—My programme was *à la* Joachim (!')—only
three pieces of Chamber Music :—

1. Quintette, Op. 87, E major,   -   - Hummel.

2. Quartette, G major,   -   -   -   -   Haydn.

3. Sonata for piano and violin, } - - - Beethoven.
    Op. 12, E flat.

Deppe arranged the whole thing most practically.
We had a large *salle* in the Hotel Bremen which was
admirably proportioned, and a new grand piano from
Berlin.   Deppe had only so many chairs placed as he
had given out invitations, and the consequence was
that every chair was filled, and there were no rows of
empty seats.   My "public" was very musical and
critical, and there were so many good judges there
that I wonder I wasn't nervous; but a sort of inspiration came to me at the moment.

The musicians who accompanied me were exceedingly good ones for such a place as Pyrmont, and my
strictly *classic* selections were received with great
favour by the audience !   That quintette of Hummel's
is a most charming composition—so flowing and elegant—and one can display a good deal of virtuosity in
the last part of it.   I played first and last, and the
quartette in between was performed by the stringed
instruments alone.   After I had finished the quintette, Deppe, who was at the extreme end of the hall,
sent me word that I was "doing famously, and that
he was delighted," and this encouraged me so that my

sonata went beautifully, too.   When it was over, ever
so many people came up and congratulated me, and
Fräulein Timm, Deppe's head teacher in Hamburg,
even complimented me on my "extraordinary facility
of execution."   I couldn't help laughing at that, with
my stubborn hand which never will do anything, and
which only the most intense study has schooled—but
in truth I was quite surprised myself at the plausible
way in which it went over all difficulties!   Quite a
number of Deppe's scholars were present, all of them
critics and several of them beautiful pianists.   Two
nice American girls, sisters, from the West, came on
from Berlin on purpose for my concert.   They helped
me dress, and presented me with an exquisite bouquet.
One of them is taking lessons of Deppe, and the other
has a great talent for drawing, and has been two
years studying in Berlin.   She says she has only made
a "beginning" now, and that she wishes to study
"indefinitely" yet.—So it is in Art!   I think her
heads are excellent already.

After the concert was over, Deppe gave me a little
champagne supper, together with Fräuleins Timm,
Steiniger, and these two young ladies.   When he
poured out the wine he said he was going to propose
a toast to two ladies; one of them, of course, was
myself, "and the other," said he, "is in America,
namely, the friend of Fräulein Fay, whom I judge to
be a woman of genius, so truly and rightly does she
feel about art (I've translated H's letters to him),
and so nobly has she sympathized with and stood by
Fräulein Fay.—To Mrs. A., whose acquaintance I long

to make!"—You may be sure I drank to *that* toast
with enthusiasm. Ah, it was a pleasant evening,
after so many years of fruitless toil! The fat
and jolly old landlord came himself to put me
into the carriage and to say that everybody in the
audience had expressed their pleasure and gratifica-
tion at my performance. I rather regret now that I
did not play my solos, but perhaps it is just as well to
leave them until another time. I have "sprung over
one little mound"—to use Deppe's simile—and got an
idea of the impetus that will be necessary to "carry
me over the mountain."

PYRMONT, *September* 4, 1874.

After the unwonted exaltation of the success of
my little concert, I have been suffering a cor-
responding reaction, partly because Fräulein Timm,
Deppe's Hamburg assistant, with whom I am now
studying, began her instructions, as teachers always
do, by chucking me into a deeper slough of despond
than usual. Consequently, I haven't been very bright,
though I am gradually coming up to the surface
again, for I'm pretty hard to drown!

Fräulein Timm belongs to the single sisterhood,
but is one of the fresh and placid kind, and as neat as
wax. She's got a great big brain and a remarkable gift
for teaching, for which she has a *passion*. I quite
adore her when she gets on her spectacles, for then
she looks the personification of Sagacity! She has

been associated with Deppe for years in teaching, and "keeps all his sayings and ponders them in her heart." Indeed, she knows his ideas almost better than he does himself, and carries on the whole circle of pupils that he left in Hamburg when he came to Berlin. Every now and then he runs down to see how they are getting on, gives them all lessons, reviews what they have done, and brings Fräulein Timm all the new pieces he has discovered and fingered. She also comes occasionally to Berlin to see him, takes a lesson every day, fills herself with as many new ideas as possible, and then returns to her post. Together, they form a very strong pair, and I think it a capital illustration of your theory that men ought to associate women with them in their work, and that "men should *create*, and women *perfect*."

Deppe makes Fräulein Timm and Fräulein Steiniger his partners and associates in his ideas, and the consequence is they add all their ingenuity to impart them to others. This spares him much of the tedious technical work, and leaves him free for the higher spheres of art, as they take the beginners and prepare them for him. *He* has made *them* magnificent teachers, and they employ their gifts to further *him*. I don't doubt that through them his method will be perpetuated, and even if he should die it would not be lost to the world. On the other hand, he has given them something to live for.—Curious that the *practicalness* of this association with women doesn't strike the masculine mind oftener!

So I am going down to Hamburg to study for a

time with this Fräulein Timm, as I think she will
develop my hand quicker than Deppe, even.   Deppe
has always urged me to it, but I never would do it,
as I did not know her personally, and did not wish to
leave him.   Now that I have tried her, however, I find
he was right, as he *always* is!   At present she is
throwing her whole weight upon my wrist, which I
hope will get limber under it! She has an obstinacy
and a perseverance in sticking at you that drive
you almost wild, but make you learn " lots " in
the end.   I think my grand trouble all these years has
been a stiff wrist and a heavy arm.   I have borne
down too heavily on wrist and arm, whereas the whole
weight and power must be just in the tips of the
fingers, and the wrist and arm must be quite light
and free, the hand turning upon the wrist as if it
were a pivot.

Pyrmont is an exquisite little place, and I regret to
leave it.   At first I almost perished with loneliness,
but now that I have a few acquaintances here I am
enjoying it.   It is a fashionable watering place, but
chiefly visited by ladies.   There are about a hundred
women to one man !   The first week I was here I
lived at a Herr S.'s, but finding it too expensive I
looked up another lodging and am now living with a
jolly old maid.   I like living with old maids.   I think
they are much neater than married women, and they
make you more comfortable.   As the season is now
over, this one's house is quite empty, and it is exquisitely kept.   I took two rooms in the third story,
small but very cozy, and with a lovely view of the
hills.

We have just had the loveliest illumination I ever saw. It was one Sunday evening—"Golden Sunday" they call it here, though why they *should* call it so, I know not. I accepted the information, however, without inquiry into first causes, and went out in the evening to promenade in the Allée with the rest. The Allée is not all on a level, but descends gradually from the springs to a fountain which is at the opposite end. Rows and rows of Japanese lanterns were festooned across the trees. As you walked down the path, you saw the festoons one below the other. The fountain was illuminated with gas jets behind the water. You could not see the water till you got close up, and at a distance only the rows of gas jets were apparent. As you neared it, however, the watery veil seemed flung over them, like the foamy tulle over a bride. It was very fascinating to look at, and I kept receding a few paces and then returning. As I receded, the watery veil would disappear, and as I approached it would again take form. It reminded me of some people's characters, of which you see the bright points from the first, and think you know them so well, but when you draw closer, even in the moments of greatest intimacy, you always feel a veil between you and them—a thin, impalpable something which you cannot annihilate, even though you may see *through* it.

We walked up and down the Allée a long time listening to the orchestra, which was playing. The magnificent great trees looked more beautiful than ever, with their lower boughs lit up by the lanterns, and their upper ones disappearing mysteriously into shadow.   At last the tapers in the lanterns burned out one after another, the avenue was wrapped in gloom, and we finished this poetic evening in the usual prosaic manner by returning home and going to bed!

CHAPTER XXVIII.

Music in Hamburg. Studying Chamber Music. Absence
of Religion in Germany. South Americans.
Deppe once more. A Concert
Début. Postscript.

HAMBURG, *February* 1, 1875.

Hamburg is a lovely city, though I *am* having such a
dreadfully dreary and stupid time here—partly because
my boarding-place is so intensely disagreeable, and
partly because I made up my mind when I came to
make no acquaintances and to do nothing but study.
I have stuck to my resolution, though I'm not sure it
is not a mistake, for there is a most elegant and luxurious society in this ancestral town of ours.*
Life is solid and material here, however, and music is
at a low ebb. The Philharmonic concerts are wretched,
and nobody goes to even the few piano concerts there
are. That little Laura Kahrer, now Frau Rappoldi, that
I heard in Weimar at Liszt's, has been wanting to come
here with her husband, who is an eminent violinist, but
she has not dared to do it, because all the musicians
tell her she would not make her expenses. She played
at the Philharmonic, too, but since then they won't
have any more piano playing at the Philharmonic.

---

*The writer's grandmother was the daughter of a leading Hamburg mer-
chant who fled with his family to America when Napoleon entered it.

(335)

Nobody cares for it, unless Bülow or Rubinstein or
Clara Schumann are the performers. I thought Frau
Rappoldi played magnificently, but I was the only person who *did* think so. She made a dead failure here.
Everybody was down on her. As to the criticism, it was
about like this : "Frau Rappoldi played quite prettily and in a lady-like manner, but she had no tone,
etc." Poor thing! The next day when Schubert
went to see her she wept bitterly, and well she might.
Schubert is one of the directors of the Philharmonic,
and it was through him she got the chance of playing.
He, too, felt awfully cut up at her want of success.
"That is what one gets," said he to me, "by recom-
mending people. If they don't succeed, *you* get all
the blame for it." He felt he had burnt his fingers!
I think the whole secret of Frau Rappoldi's want of
success was that she did not *look* pretty. She was so
dowdily dressed, and her hair looked like a Feejee
Islander's. People laughed at her before she began.
Too true!—that "dress makes the woman."*

Deppe's darling Fannie Warburg'gave a concert here
last month, and she, also, got a pretty poor criticism,
and for the same reason,viz. : people haven't the musical
sense to appreciate her—at least in my opinion. The
action of her hands on the piano is grace itself, and
the elasticity of her wrist is wonderful. Her touch
completely realizes Deppe's ideal of "letting the notes
fall from the finger-tips like drops of water," and she
executes better with the left hand, if that be possible,
than with the right! At any rate, there is *no* differ-

*Frau Rappoldi is now a celebrity.

ence.   It is the most heavenly enjoyment to hear her,
and you feel as if you would like to have her go on
forever.   And yet, I don't believe she will make a great
career.   She has not fire enough to make the public appreciate the immensity of her performance.   No rush—
no *abandon!*   She has no *presence* either, but is a
timid, meek, childlike little maiden—docility itself, but
a *made* player, as it were, not a spontaneous one.   Such
is life !   To me, her playing is the purest music—*"die
reine Musik"*—and the bigger the hall the more that
tone of hers rolls out and fills it !

HAMBURG, *March* 1, 1875.

I wish I could write up Deppe's system for publication, but it is a very difficult thing to give any adequate idea of.   Fräulein Timm tells me it is only
comparatively recently that he has perfected it himself to its present point (though he has long had the
conception of it), and that accounts for its not being
known.   He was completely buried in Hamburg,
where there is no scope for art.   I believe his ambition
is to found a School of this exquisitely pure and perfect and almost idealized piano-playing, which may
serve as a counterpoise to the warmer and more sen-
suous prevailing one—*sculpture* as contrasted with
painting!
I have been chiefly studying *Kammer-Musik* (Chamber Music) this winter—that is, trios, quartettes, etc.
Fräulein Timm is giving me such a training as I never
had before.   She has the most astonishing talent for

teaching, and has reduced it to a science. I don't play anything up to tempo under her—always slow, slow, *slow*. She really dissects every tone, and shows me when and why it doesn't sound well. My whole attention is now bent upon *tone*. Ah, M., *that's* the thing in playing!—To bring out the *soul* there is in the key simply by touching it, as the great masters do.—It is the pianist's highest art, though amid the dazzle of piano pyrotechnics the public often forget it.

I am just finishing Beethoven's third Trio, Op. 1. The last movement is the loveliest thing! It makes me think of a wood in spring filled with birds. One minute you hear a lot of gossiping little sparrows twittering and chippering, and then comes some rare wild bird with a sort of cadence, and then come other and whistle and call. It is bewitching, and the most perfect imitation of nature imaginable; gay—*so* gay! as only Beethoven can be when he begins to play. Everything is on the wing. It is, of course, exceedingly difficult, because, like all this pure, classic music, to make any effect it has to be executed with the utmost perfection. I am so infatuated with it that when I get through practicing it, I feel as if I were tipsy!

These Beethoven trios are a perfect mine in themselves. Each one seems to be entirely different from all the rest. There are twelve in all, and Deppe wants me to learn them all. Think what a piece of work! This enormous amount of literature that you must have to form a repertoire—the trios, quartettes, quintettes, concertos, etc., it is that makes it so long before one is a finished artist. And then you must consider

the hours and hours that go to waste on *studies,* just
to get your hand into a condition to play these masterpieces. Oh, the arduousness of it is incalculable! I
often ask myself, "What demon has tempted me here?"
as I sit and drudge at the piano. I play all day, take
a walk with L. in the afternoon, and at night tumble
into bed and sleep like a log—that is, when my hardest
of beds and shivering room will *let* me sleep. That is
my life, day after day. I only see the people of the
house at meals.

I am the only lady in this family. All the other
boarders are very young men, almost boys, who are
here to learn German or commerce. There are three
South Americans, one Portugese, one Brazilian, one
Russian and one Frenchman. I hear Spanish and
French all the while, but no English, and with the
German it is very confusing.—I feel very sorry for all
these young fellows, their lives are so bare and disagreeable, and so wholly devoid of any influence that can
make them better or happier. As for our landlady, it
would take a Balzac to do justice to such a combination.
She is a good housekeeper. The cooking is excellent,
and my room (when warm) is pleasant. Indeed, the
Hamburg standard of housekeeping is much higher
than in Berlin. Things are *much* daintier. But her
power of making you physically and mentally uncomfortable in other ways is unsurpassed. Were it not
that my stay is indefinite, and that I have already
moved once, I would not remain here. As it is, I prefer putting up with it to the trouble and expense of
changing; beside which, I have found that when once

you have left your own home-circle, you have to bear, as a rule, with at least one intensely disagreeable person in every house.

My opinion of human nature has not risen since I came abroad, and I think that this winter has quite cured me of my natural tendency to skepticism.—I now realize too well what people's characters, both men and women, may become without religion either in themselves or in those about them.   I suppose there *is* religion in Germany, but *I* have seen very little of it, either in Protestants or Catholics, and the results I consider simply dreadful!   You see, there is *no* adequate motive to check the indulgence of *any* impulse —I have come to the conclusion that jealousy is the national vice of the Germans.   Everybody is jealous of everybody else, no matter how absurdly or causelessly.   Old women are jealous of young ones, and even sisters in the same family are jealous of each other to a degree that I couldn't have believed, had I not seen it.

HAMBURG, *Easter Sunday*, 1875.

With regard to playing in concert, I find myself doubting whether on general principles it is best to get one's whole musical training under one master only, as Fannie Warburg, for instance, has done; for my experience teaches me that though nearly all masters can give you something, none can give you everything.   If, with my present light, I could begin my study over again, I should first stay three years with Deppe, in order to endow the spirit of music that I hope is within me, with the outward form and perfection of an artist. Next, I should study a year with Kullak, to give my playing a brilliant *concert dress,* and finally, I would spend two seasons with Liszt, in order to add the last ineffable graces—(for never, *never* should an artist complete a musical course without going to LISZT, while he is on this earth!) —The trouble is, however, that one master always feels hurt if you leave him for another! No one can bear the imputation that he *can't* "give you everything."

But in truth I am getting very impatient to be at home where I can study by myself, and take as much time as I think necessary to work up my pieces. Deppe and Fräulein Timm are like Kullak in one thing. They never will give me time enough, but hurry me on so from one thing to another, that it is impossible for me to prepare a programme. So I have given up my plan of a concert in Berlin this spring. They have one set of ideas and I another, and I see I shall never be able to play in public until I abandon masters and start out on my own course. Two people never think exactly alike. Masters can put you on the road, but they can't make you go. You must do that for yourself. As Dr. V. says, "If you want to do a thing you have got to *keep* doing it. You mustn't stop—certainly not!" Concert-playing, like everything else, is *routine,* and has got to be learned by little and little, and perhaps, with many half-failures. But if the "great public" will only tolerate one as a pupil long enough, eventually, one

22

must succeed. At any rate, IT is probably the best and
the only "master" for me now!

On Wednesday I return for awhile to Berlin, to the
American boarding-house, No. 15 Tauben Strasse,
whither you can all direct as formerly. This winter has
been rather a contrast to last. Then I lived entirely
among North Americans, whereas here I am almost
exclusively with South Americans. There are any r um-
ber of these latter in Hamburg, and you have no idea
how fascinating many of them are—so handsome and so
bright. They all have a talent for music and dancing.
Their music is entirely of a light character, but they
have *rhythm* and grace in a remarkable degree.
When I hear them play I always think of George
Sands's description in her novel *"Malgré-tout"* of
the artist Abel—the hero of the book, and a great
violinist. She says, *" Il racla un air sur son violon
avec entrain."*—That is just what these South Americans do—*" racler!"* They all play the piano just as
with us the negro plays the fiddle, without instruction,
apparently, and simply because "it is their nature to."
I saw at once where Gottschalk got his " Banjo" and
" Bananier," and the peculiar style of his compositions
generally, and since I've met so many South Americans I can readily imagine why he spent so much of
his time in South America. I long to go there myself.
I think it must be a fascinating place for an artist.

One of the South Americans here at the house is a
boy of fifteen, named Juan di Livramento, or, I should
say, Juan Moreiro Aranjo di Livramento! (They all
have about a dozen names in the grandiloquent style

of the Spaniards.) This boy is a curious youngster. He is tall and lithe, with the most magnificent dark eyes I ever saw or conceived, thick silky black hair, all in a tumble about his head, a delicate and very expressive face, and a clear olive complexion—a perfect type of a Spaniard. He seems born to dance the Bolero, like Belinda, in Mrs. Edwards's novel. It is the prettiest thing to see him do it—and in fact he does it on all occasions without any reference to propriety, being an utterly lawless individual. He frequently gets up from the dinner-table, throws his napkin over his shoulders, snaps his thumbs, and begins a dance in the corner of the room, between the courses. It has got to be such an every-day thing that nobody looks surprised or pays any attention to him. We dine late, and as there are a good many boarders, it takes some time always to change the plates. Juan, who is like so much mercury, never can sit still during these intervals. When asked to ring the bell for the servant, he will spring up like a shot, give it a violent pull, and then take advantage of being up to dance in the corner, or at least to cut a few antics, fling his leg over the back of his chair, and come down astride of it. This is his usual mode of resuming his seat.

On the days when he doesn't dance, he keeps up a continual talking. He will rattle on in Spanish till Herr S. gets desperate, and tries to reduce him to order. It is a rule that German must be spoken at table, but Juan thinks it sufficient if he applies the rule only so far as not to speak Spanish, his native language. He goes to school where, of course, he learns

English and French, and he is always trying to get off some remarks in these languages. He speaks all wrong, but that does not cause him the least embarrassment.—On Sundays especially is Juan perfectly irrepressible, for then Frau S. goes to dine and spend the evening with her parents, and Herr S. is left to maintain order. He is an indulgent old man, and very fond of Juan, so that the latter has not the least fear of him, and I nearly die trying to keep my face straight when they have one of their scenes.

"You shall NOT speak Spanish at the table," said poor old S. the other day, in a rage. Spanish is jargon to him, and Juan had been talking it for some time at the top of his voice across Herr S., to his friend Candido, who sat opposite. Juan knew very well that that meant he must speak German, but instead of that he began in foreign languages, and said to Herr S., in English, "Do you spoke Russish (Do you speak Russian)?"

Herr S., to whom English is as unintelligible as Spanish, naturally making no reply to this brilliant remark, Juan continued—"'Spring is Coming,' Poem by James K. Blake," and then he began to recite with much gesticulation—

> "Spring is coming, spring is coming,
> Birds are singing, insects humming;
> Flowers are peeping from their sleeping,
> Streams escape from winter's keeping, etc."

I won't pretend to say what the rest of it was, as his pronunciation was utterly unintelligible. Herr S. rolled up his eyes and made no further protest, for he

found he only got " out of the frying-pan into the fire,"
Juan having a historical anecdote called " The Dead
Watch," which he occasionally substitutes for the
poem.

After dinner he generally has an affectionate turn,
and goes round the table shaking hands with those
still seated, or putting his arm around their necks, and
then he seems like some gentle wild animal which
comes and rubs its head up against you, and it is
impossible to help loving him. As soon, however, as
T. or anybody thrums a waltz on the piano, he
instantly throws himself into the attitude to dance.
He is so very light on his feet that you don't hear
him, and often I am surprised on looking up, without
thinking, to see Juan poised on one toe like a ballet
dancer, and his great eyes shining soft on me like two
suns. It is most peculiar. There are *no* eyes like the
Spanish eyes. Not only have they so much *fire*, but
when their owners are in a sentimental mood, they can
throw a languor and a sort of droop into them that is
irresistible. This is the way Juan does, and though he
is too young to be sentimental, he *looks* as if he were.
One minute he is all ablaze, and the next perfectly
melting.—The other day Frau S. took him to task
for his extreme animation.—"*Junge*," (German for
"Boy"),"you mustn't scream so all over the house. You
really are a nuisance." Juan was offended at this, and
began to defend himself. "Why do you scold me," he
said. "I'm always in good humour. I never sulk or
find fault with anything. *Ja, immer vergnügt* (Yes,
always in a good humour), and ready to amuse every-

body, and I never get angry." Frau S. admitted
that was true, but at the same time suggested it would
be well for him to remember we were not all deaf.
Juan withdrew in dudgeon.—Well, I suppose you are
tired of hearing about him, but these South Americans
are a type by themselves, and I felt as if I must touch
off one of them for the benefit of the family.

BERLIN, *April* 18, 1875.

Since my return I have been enjoying extremely
what I suppose I must consider my last lessons with
Deppe. After studying with Fräulein Timm I know
much better what he is driving at. The technique
seems to be unfolding to me like a ribbon. So all her
maulings were to some purpose! Yesterday I played
him a sonata of Beethoven's and he said, "God grant
that you may still be left to me some time longer!
Now you are really beginning to be my scholar."—And
indeed, having studied his technique so long with Fräuleins Timm and Steiniger, it does seem hard that I
have to leave him! How I wish I could stay on indefinitely and give myself up to his purely *musical* side
and get the benefit of all his deep and beautiful ideas.
There never *was* such a teacher! If I could only come
up to his standard I should be perfectly happy. Lucky
girl—that Steiniger! Think of it! She has *nine* concertos that she could get up for concert any minute.
That's the crushing kind of repertoire he gives his pupils—so exhaustive and complete in every department. He knows the whole piano literature, and is

continually fishing up some new or old pearl or other
to surprise one with.

I find Deppe is getting to be much more recognized
in Berlin this year than he was before. He has just
been directing a new opera here which has created
quite a sensation, and he is continually engaged in
some great work. Fortunate that I found him out
when I did! for he takes fewer pupils than ever. He
says he can't teach people who are not sympathetic to
him. The other day he presented a beautiful overture
of his own composition to the Duke of Mecklenburg,
who accepted it in person and sent Deppe an exquisite
pin in token of recognition. When simple little Deppe
gets *that* stuck in his scarf, he will be a terrific swell!

Now for a piece of news! I was paying my French
teacher, Mademoiselle D., a call one evening last week,
and I played for her and for a friend of hers who is
very musical, and who gives lessons herself. She at
once said very decidedly that I " ought to be heard in
concert." Her brother is the director of the Philharmonic Society in a place called Frankfurt-an-der-
Oder—a little city not far from here. What should
she do but write to her brother about me, and what
should *he* do but immediately write up for me to come
down and play in a Philharmonic concert there the first
week in May. As I have been so anxious to play in a
concert before leaving Germany, and yet have seen no
way to do it, I am going, of course, and am most grateful to his sister for thinking of it. But it is always
the Unexpected that helps you out!

BERLIN, *May* 13, 1875.

Well, dear, my little début was a decided success, and I had one encore, beside being heartily applauded after every piece. I went on to Frankfurt on Monday morning, and when I got there Herr Oertling, the Philharmonic Director, was at the station to meet me with a droschkie. We drove to the Deutches Haus, an excellent hotel, where I was shown into a large and comfortable room. Here I rested until dinner time, and after dinner, about five o'clock, Herr Oertling came back. He took me to the house of a musical friend of his who was to lend me his grand piano, and there we tried our sonata. As soon as Oertling touched his violin I saw that he was a superior artist, and that immediately inspired me. His playing carried me right along, and I think I played well. At all events, he seemed entirely satisfied, and said, " We could have played that sonata without rehearsing it." After we finished the sonata, I played for about an hour, all sorts of things. There were quite a number of people present to judge of my powers. Herr W., the owner of the piano, was a remarkable judge of music, and made some excellent criticisms and suggestions. We stayed there to supper, but I went back to the hotel early and went to bed about half-past nine, where I slept like a log till eight the next morning.

After breakfast Oertling came to take me to try the pianos of a celebrated manufacturer of uprights. I played there three or four hours. The maker's name was Gruss, and his pianos were the best uprights I had ever seen; nearly as powerful as a grand, and with a superb tone and action. On the wall was a testimonial from Henselt, framed. It seems Henselt goes to Frankfurt every year to visit a Russian lady there, who is the grandee of the place and a great patroness of artists. In the afternoon, Oertling came for me to go and rehearse in the hall. Everything went beautifully, and I returned to the hotel in good spirits. By the time I was dressed for the concert, which was to begin at seven, Oertling appeared again, in evening costume, and presented me with a bouquet. We drove to the hall through a pouring rain. It was crowded, notwithstanding, for he had had the assurance to print that the concert was "to be brilliant through the performance of an American Virtuosin, named Miss Amy Fay. This young lady has studied with the greatest masters, and has had the most perfect success everywhere in her concert tours!" Did you ever!—You can imagine how I felt on reading it and seeing that I was expected to perform as if I had been on the stage all my life! Oertling had arranged the programme judiciously. Our sonata came *first,* so that I plunged right in and didn't have to wait and tremble! Then came two pieces by the orchestra; next, my three solos in a row, and a symphony of Haydn closed the programme. The sonata went off very smoothly. In my first solo I occasionally missed a note, but my second was without slip, and my third—Chopin's Study in Sixths—was encored, though I took the tempo too fast. How-

ever, the Frau Excellency von X. said she had frequently heard it from Henselt, but that I played it
"just as well as he did." That's absurd, of course,
though not bad considered as a *compliment!* They
all said, "What a pity Henselt wasn't here !" I said to
myself, "What a blessing Henselt wasn't !"—though I
would give much to see him, as he is the greatest piano
virtuoso in the world after Liszt.

After the concert Oertling and some of the musicians accompanied me to the hotel, where I was obliged
to sit at table and have my health drunk in champagne till two o'clock in the morning ! for you know
when the Germans once begin that sort of thing
there's no end to it. They drank to my health, and
then they drank to my future performance in the first
Philharmonic next season, and then they drank to our
frequent reunion, etc., etc. When they had finished
I had to respond. So I toasted the Herr Director and
I toasted the piano-maker, and I toasted the orchestra,
and what not. At last I was released and could go to
my room. The next morning I left for Berlin, which
I reached in time for dinner, and as soon as I appeared
at table the boarders saluted me with a burst of applause !—I found it a very pleasant *finale.*

I translate for you the criticism from the *Frankfurter Zeitung und Allgemeiner Anzeiger* for May 11.
Herr Oertling sent it to me yesterday :

"The Philharmonic concert which took place last
Friday evening, must be considered as an excellent rec-
ommendation of the active members of that association to the public. For not only did the playing of

the pianist, Fräulein Amy Fay, give great pleasure to all those who love and understand music, but there was also no fault to be found with the interpretations of the orchestra. * * * With regard to the performance of Fräulein Fay, we were equally charmed by her clear and certain touch and by her conception of the various solo pieces she played. The concert opened with the Sonata in E flat major for violin and piano by Beethoven. The whole effect of the work was a very sympathetic and satisfactory one, and showed a thoughtful interpretation on the part of the artist. The beauty of her conception was especially evident in the Raff "Capriccio," and in Hiller's "Zur Guitarre," given as an encore upon her recall by the audience, and we can but congratulate the teacher of the young lady, Herr Ludwig Deppe, of Berlin, upon such a scholar."

[Two weeks after the concert, the relative to whom most of the foregoing letters were written, joined the writer at Berlin, and the correspondence came to an end. In the following September, after an absence of six years, my sister returned home.—My sister hopes that no American girl who reads this book will be influenced by it rashly to attempt what she herself undertook, viz.: to be trained in Europe from an amateur into an artist. Its pages have afforded glimpses, only, of the trials and difficulties with which a girl may meet when studying art alone in a foreign land, but they should not therefore be underrated. Piano teaching has developed immensely in America since the date of the first of the foregoing letters, and not only such celebrities as Dr. William Mason, Mr. Wm. H. Sherwood, and Mrs. Rivé King, but various other brilliant or exquisite pianists in this country are as able to train pupils for the technical demands of the concert-room as any masters that are to be found abroad. American teachers best understand the American temperament, and therefore are by far the best for American pupils until they have got beyond the pupil stage.—Not manual skill, but musical insight and conception, wider and deeper musical comprehension, and " concert style " are what the young artist should now go to seek in that marvellous and only real home of music—GERMANY.]—ED.

INDEX

INDEX

INDEX 355

INDEX   355

INDEX

INDEX

INDEX

Fichtner, 254, 255, 257,
258-59, 261
Franco-Prussian War, 79,
90, 96-100, 105-7,
112-14, 115-16, 124-
28
Frankfort, 131, 133, 348-51
*Frankfurter Zeitung und
Allgemeiner An-
zeiger*, 350-1
Frederick the Great, 75

Gaul, 211, 228, 267
Gewandhaus Orchestra, 63,
90, 118, 257
Glück, 166
Goethe, 51, 53, 147-49, 151-
52, 154, 187-88, 246
Goldsmith, 151
Gottschalk, Louis Moreau,
42, 47, 176, 277-79
"Bananier," 342
"La Morte," 42
"The Banjo," 342
Gounod
Faust, 51
Gradus Ad Parnassum
(Clementi), 116,
264, 266, 299
Grantzow, 171-73
Graun
"Tod Jesu," 59
Gruss, 349
Gurickx, 244, 245, 246, 264,
323

Hamburg, 154, 330-32, 335-
46
Handel and Haydn Festi-
val (Boston), 169
Harvard University, 187
Haupt, 60
Hawthorne, 274
Haydn
*Jahreszeiten (The Sea-
sons)*, 55, 57
String Quartet, 111, 326
*String Quartet in G
Major*, 328
Symphony, 183, 349
Hegel, 279
Heidelberg, 140-44
Henselt, 221, 229, 349, 350
Herz, 249, 250
Hiller
"*Zur Guitarre*," 351
Hugo, Victor, 171
Hummel, 154
*Quintette, Op. 87 in E
Major*, 295, 326,
328
Hund, Alicia, 117

Janotha, Natalie, 300
Jena, 244, 246, 259
Jews, 33, 122
Joachim, 20, 25, 26, 27, 42,
107, 111, 121-22, 161-
62, 179, 198, 227,
269, 270, 325, 328